IMAGES
of America

AROUND WOODBURY

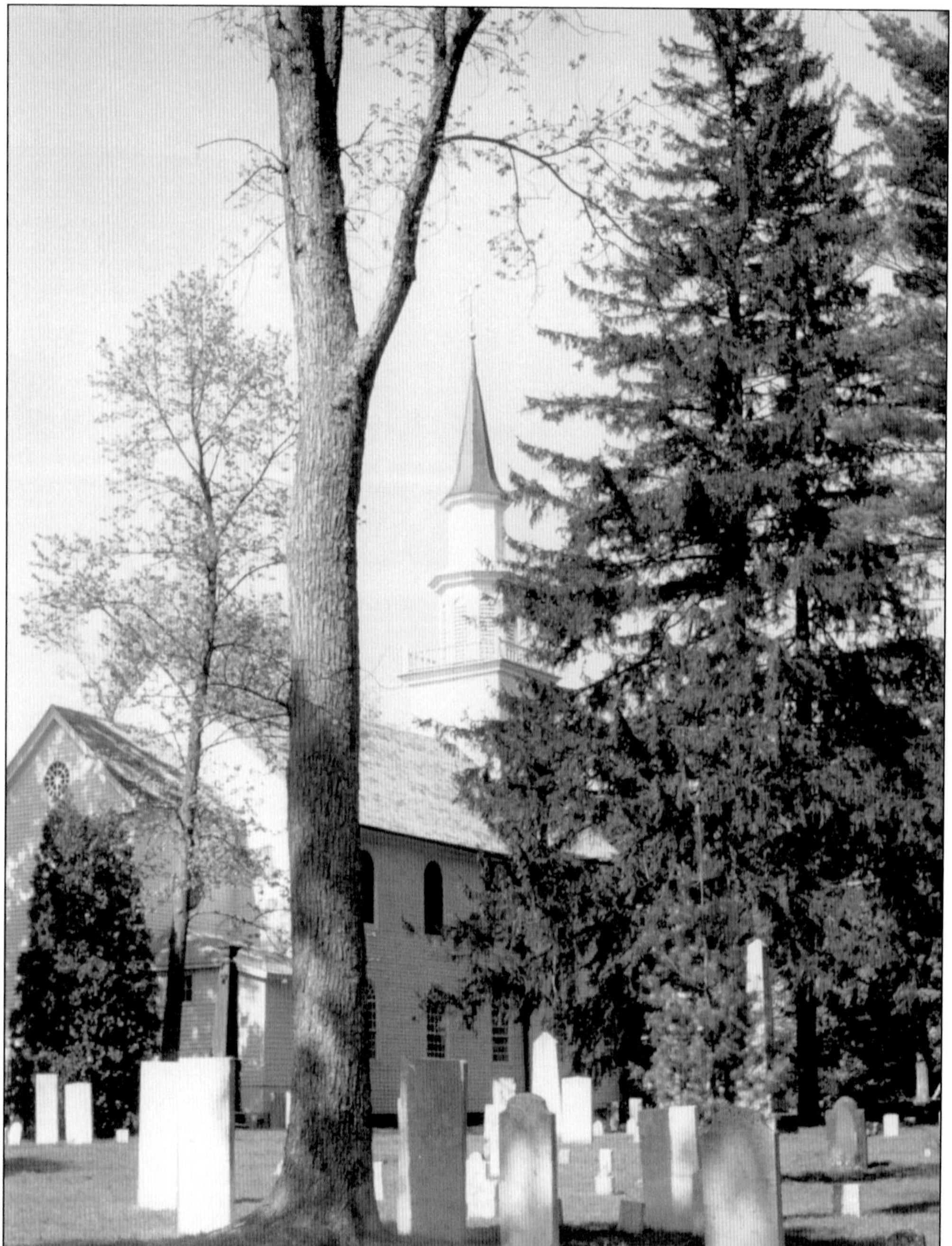

This photograph of St. Paul's Church in Woodbury was taken from the Old South Cemetery by Alexandra Darrow.

IMAGES
of America

AROUND WOODBURY

Frederick W. Chesson

ARCADIA PUBLISHING

ISBN 978-0-7385-0460-5

Published by Arcadia Publishing
Charleston, South Carolina

Printed in the United States of America

Library of Congress Catalog Card Number: 00104074

For all general information contact Arcadia Publishing at:
Telephone 843-853-2070
Fax 843-853-0044
E-mail sales@arcadiapublishing.com
For customer service and orders:
Toll-Free 1-888-313-2665

Visit us on the Internet at www.arcadiapublishing.com

In grateful memory of my own Woodbury connections:
Frederick Scovill Cooke, 1872–1935
Ellen A. Benham Cooke, 1878–1971
Louise Judson Cooke, 1904–1988

On the cover: Time stands still on a hot summer's day in 1895. For these five Woodbury boys, what could be finer than a refreshing drink of cold springwater, filling the Gordon Tannery trough on upper Main Street? The boys have been tentatively identified as Dave Barlow, Winfred Dawson, George Scott, and the Comber brothers.

Contents

ACKNOWLEDGMENTS

I am greatly pleased to recognize the following friends and organizations for assistance in the creation of this work.
To Aldis "Bud" Morgan, for initiating and sustaining this project.
To Bob Cowles and Mert Hornbecker, for their most generous contributions of archival materials and photographic services.
To Esther Townsend and Tom Lautenschlager, for use of family and area photographs.
To Michael Pinevich, for use of the *White Pine* booklet, with its *c.* 1915-era photographs.
To the Woodbury, Southbury, and Bethlehem Historical Societies and the Woodbury Library, for generous pictorial and historical assistance.
To Vin Daury, Ed Manzi, Carleton Quint, and George Sturgis, for valuable historical insights.
Also, another tip of the hat to Charles Rufus Harte (1870–1956), whose photographs of the Greater Woodbury area, taken during his trolley building days with the Connecticut Company, have opened windows on a now vanished world.

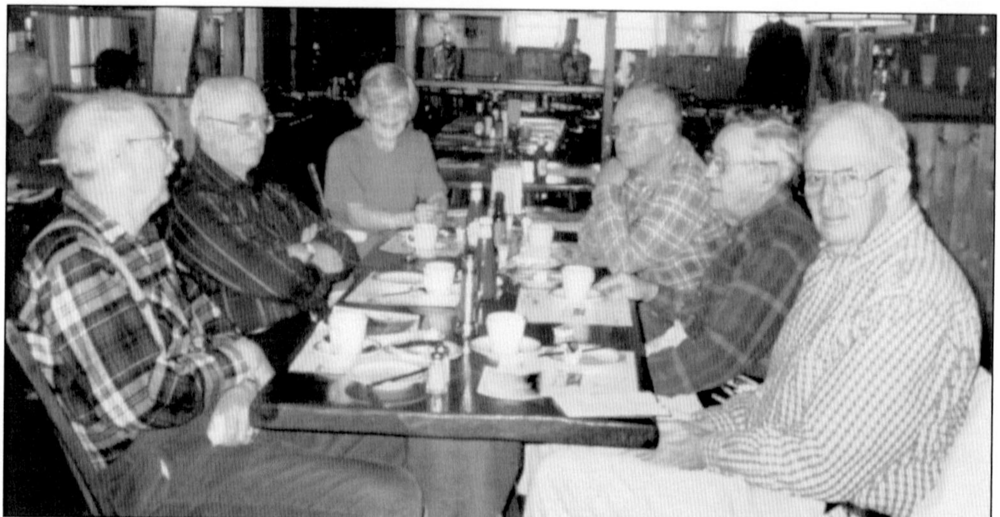

The Charcoal Chef Historical Subcommittee meets in executive session, from left to right, Vin Daury, Bud Morgan, Esther Townsend, Bob Cowles, Carleton Quint, and George Sturgis.

KEY TO PHOTOGRAPH CREDITS

BHS: Bethlehem Historical Society
C-H: Joint collections of Robert Cowles and Merton Hornbecker
CRH: Charles Rufus Harte photographic archive
ETT: Esther Terrill Townsend
FWC: Frederick W. Chesson family collections
SHS: Southbury Historical Society
TL: Thomas Lautenschlager collections
WP: *White Pine* promotional booklet of 1915

FOREWORD

(Adapted from Bud Morgan's feature in Voices, *August 25, 1999.)*

One of the elements defining *family* is a collection of photographs. More often though, it is an accumulation. We all have, somewhere among the mass and muddle comprising our worldly goods, pictures of all and any size, shape, condition, and vintage.

Depending on how extensive family archives may be, prints may range from the earliest reverse-image daguerreotype, through Victorian sepia-tone, Brownie Kodak drugstore-processed shots, down to Kodachrome slides, curled Polaroids, and even digitally enhanced and stored images.

The older the image, the more formally it is apt to be posed. Prior to the Eastman company's dollar Brownie *c.* 1900, one went to a studio and followed the photographer's precise instructions for a "proper sitting." During the Civil War, early photojournalists followed the troops, often photographing the stunned survivors and the extremely quiet heaps of the slain. Surviving even today are many tiny prints, called *cartes de visite* after the very obligatory calling cards of the Victorian era. Their fading amber images depict a largely anonymous sea of faces, uniforms, and staring expressions of total war.

By 1990, it was estimated that Americans were snapping more than 15 billion photographs annually, enough for several views of every individual on the globe. With the rise of throwaway and digital cameras, the present year will doubtless see the figure increase spectacularly. Every family event, parade, outing, or special occasion now evokes a flood of sparkling color images, the ubiquitous Internet adding to the deluge with every E-mail image of Cousin Lois and Tom with kids at Wild Whoopie Water World.

But the trouble is that photography has become so casual that once we have our films developed, we glance and comment briefly at our largely competent results. Then it is off into a sticky-page album, or more likely an already overstuffed box or table drawer. There the photographs repose indefinitely, or until the next house-move clean out of our ultra-mobile generation, gathering dust and fading into 21st century anonymity. Digital images even have their own unique problems of accidental or purposeful erasure.

So, when was the last time a batch of color photographs from Walgreen's was ensconced in "Ye Olde Familye Albume" or at least marked with a hastily scrawled identification as to date and content?

We know the guilty result: What *was* that place? Who *are* those strange people, anyway? Are you *sure* that's Uncle Carl and Aunt Min?

Is it all going to end up like those poor CDVs and studio poses—fluttering around the local flea market like drab, dispirited sparrows? Surely, it is high time to set aside an hour or so for the sake of present family genealogy and to assist our future descendants . . . and compilers of "This Old Town"-style books. . . .

INTRODUCTION

This is not a pictorial history of Greater Woodbury but rather a historical picture collection gathered from various sources, as indicated in the acknowledgments. William Cothren's three-volume tome is perhaps the best overall source for serious historical study of ancient Woodbury. The regional libraries all have additional resources, including valuable oral histories from local residents, many of whom are regrettably now gone.

Woodbury, parent colony of more than a half-dozen offspring, arose from a 1665 theological schism among the residents of Stratford, itself the product of dissension within Puritan ranks. In 1672, the dissenters were allowed to go north and establish a plantation at Pomperaug. Various purchases were made over a number of years from the local Pootatuck Indians, and the town was named by a patent of 1681.

As other parts of the extensive grant and purchases were settled, the new residents began to clamor for their own parishes. In May 1731, a new Ecclesiastical Society was formed and named Southbury; Roxbury followed the next year. In 1739, the residents of the Northern Purchase agitated for their own church and finally obtained corporate identity as Bethlehem in 1787. Judeah settlers built their own church in 1742 and became Washington in 1779, honoring the Father of Their Country. Southbury had its own secession when South Britain separated in 1766.

Within Woodbury, a 20-year debate broke out over a new society, culminating in the Strict Congregational Society and its North Church, built in 1818.

Thus, a combination of orthodoxy and dissent, of theocracy and democracy, conservation and innovation, all somehow merged to form a both dynamic and stable Yankee society in and around Woodbury.

—Frederick W. Chesson
June 2000

One

All Around the Towns

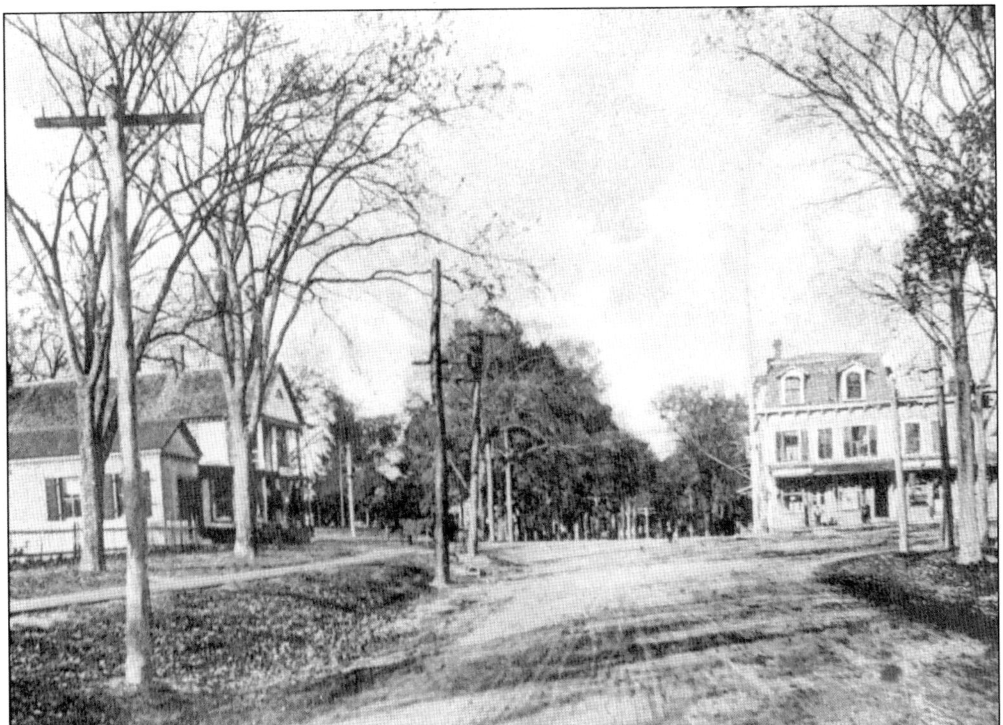

This is a view of Woodbury's Main Street in the early 1900s. At the time, the town's population was less than 2,000 and the 19th century was still preserved in architecture and the semirural way of life. (C-H.)

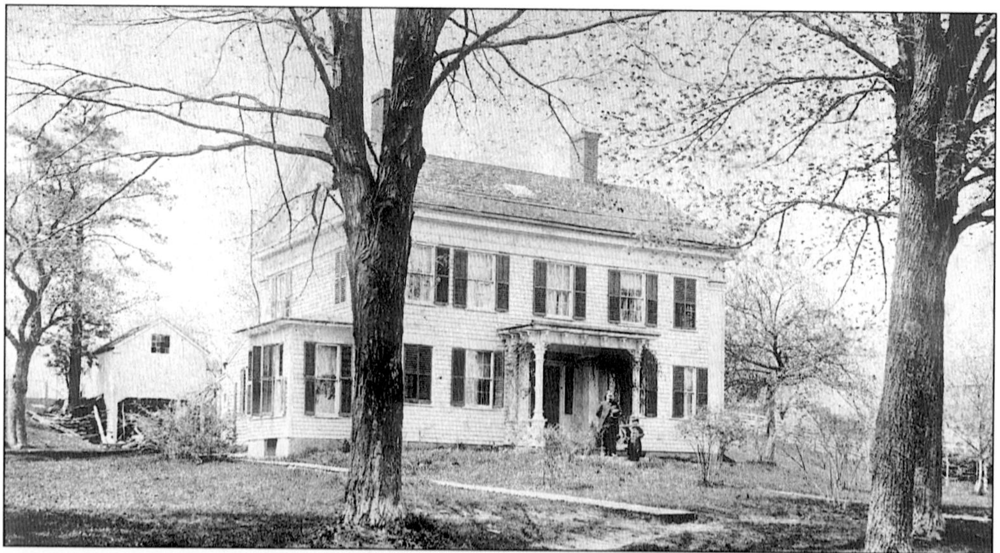

The Cable House at 35 Main Street North is typical of homes in Old Woodbury. It was the residence of the Cables, an early and prominent Woodbury family.(C-H.)

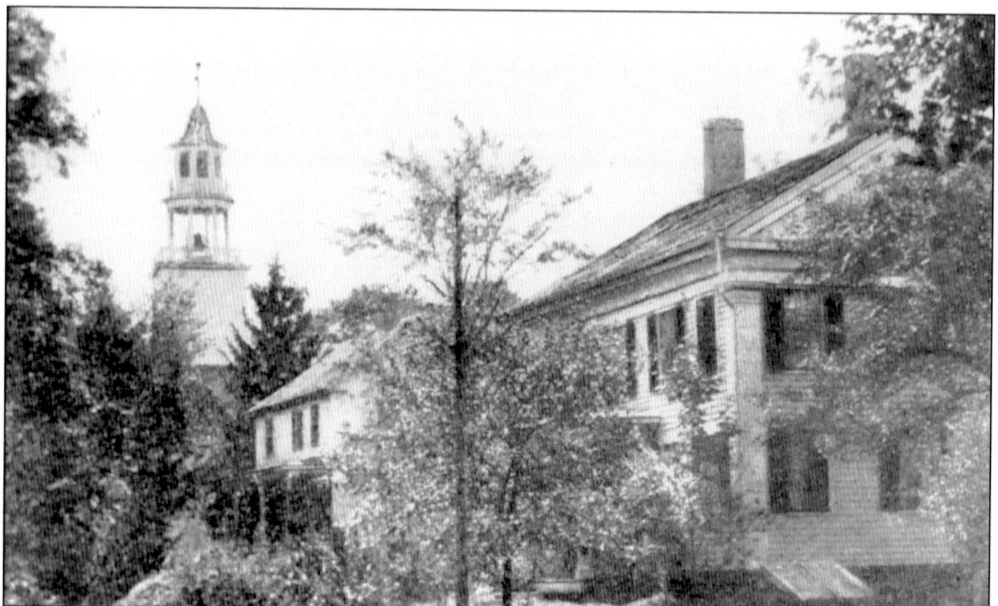

This view of the Cable House includes other buildings in the neighborhood. (C-H.)

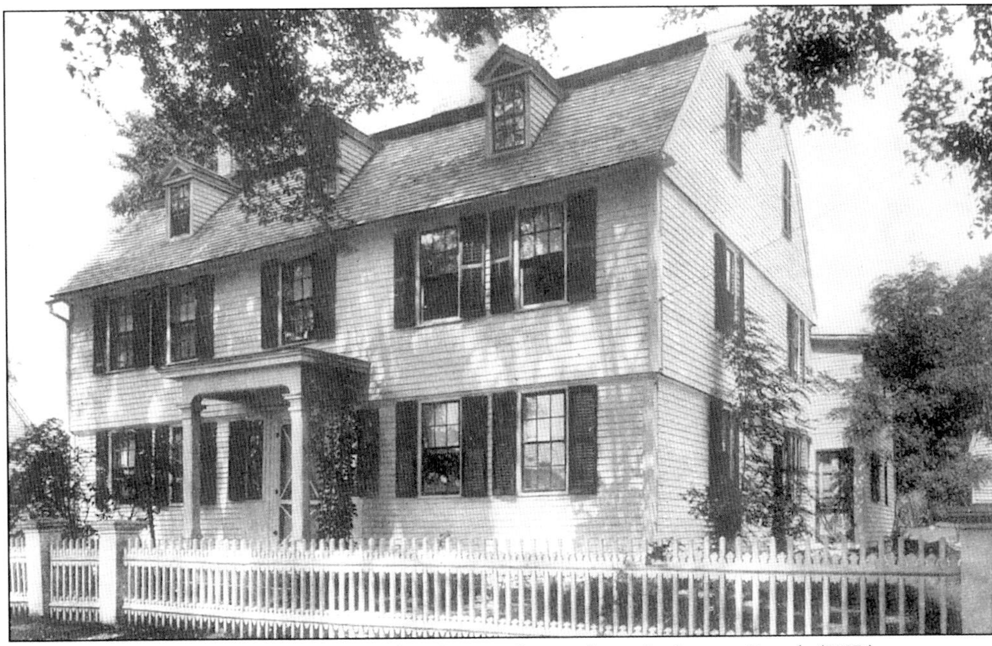

This is the fine home of merchant Jabez Bacon, located on the Lower Road. (W.P.)

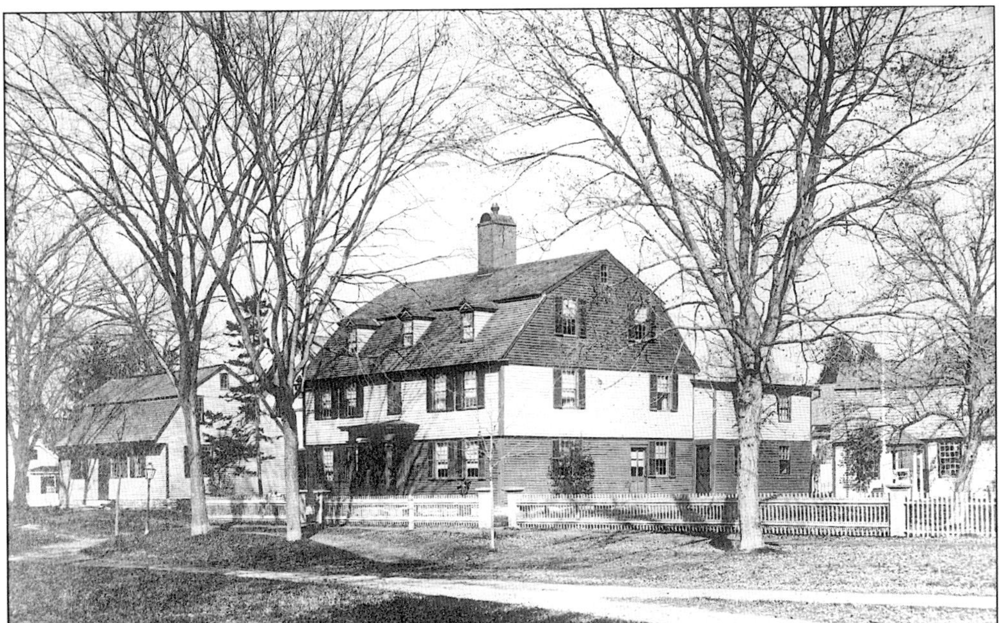

As his name implies, the resident of the house, Jabez Bacon, made a fortune dealing in meat products, mainly pork, during the Revolutionary War era. (C-H.)

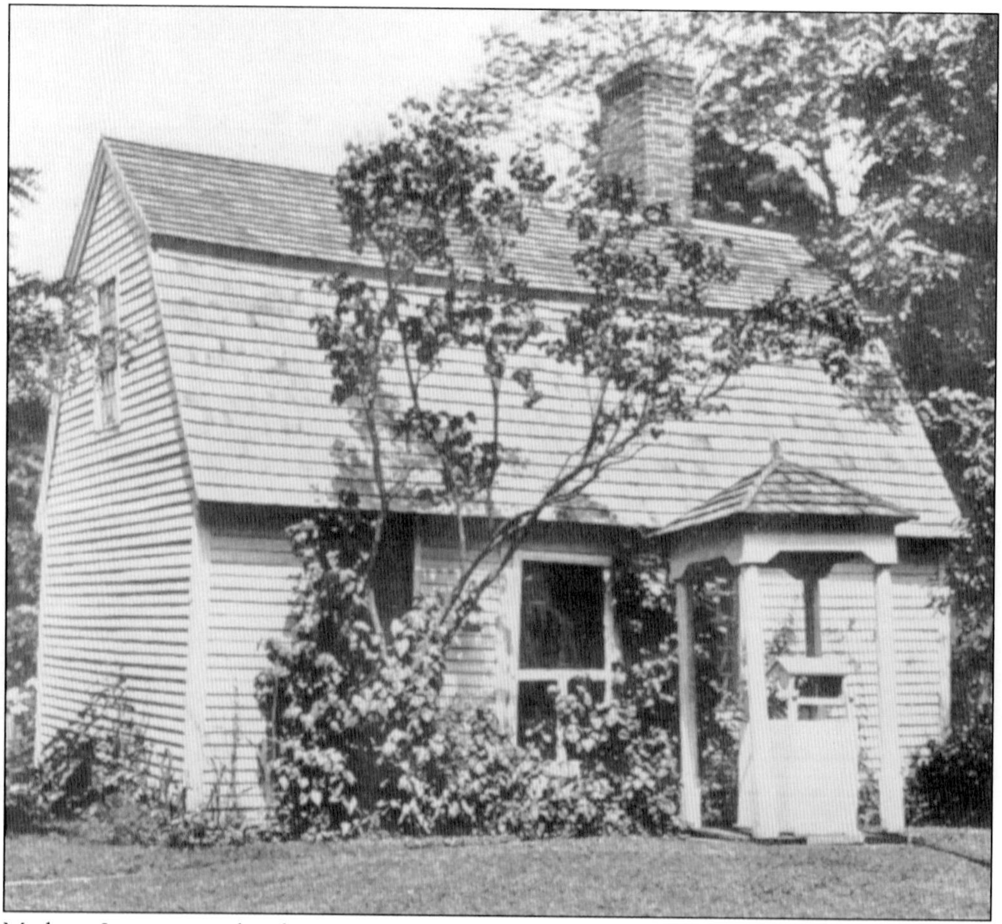

Mathew Lyons was the first Irishman in Woodbury. Fleeing the Great Potato Famine, he made for America, entrusting his passage money to the ship's captain. Upon arrival in New York City, he found that he had been "taken for a ride" and was penniless. Jabez Bacon, came to Lyons's "rescue," taking him home as a bondsman and placing him in the so-called "slave house," which is shown. After. a time as an indentured servant, Lyons was traded to a Litchfield farmer for a pair of oxen. Fleeing this virtual slavery, Lyons joined Ethan Allen's Green Mountain Boys, fighting at Ticonderoga. After Independence, Lyons became a representative of Vermont. He later moved west to the Connecticut Reserve in Ohio and also became its House of Representatives member. Finally, he moved down to Arkansas, where he was again elected to Congress; however, he died before he could take his seat. The slave house back in Woodbury served as a kitchen for the mansion and later became a tearoom, as shown in this c. 1915 photograph. (WP.)

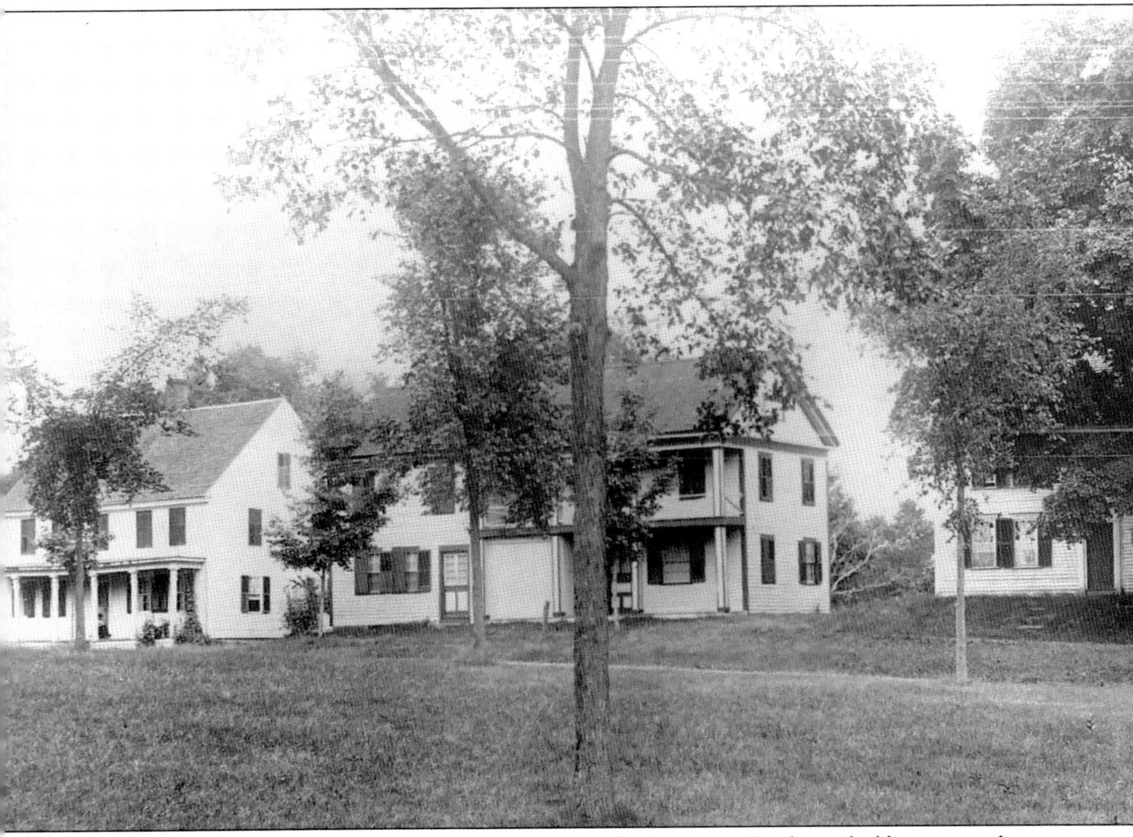

In 1739, Bethlehem became its own Ecclesiastical Society. Nearly a half century later, Bethlehem was incorporated as a town. This is a photograph of the town center. (BHS.)

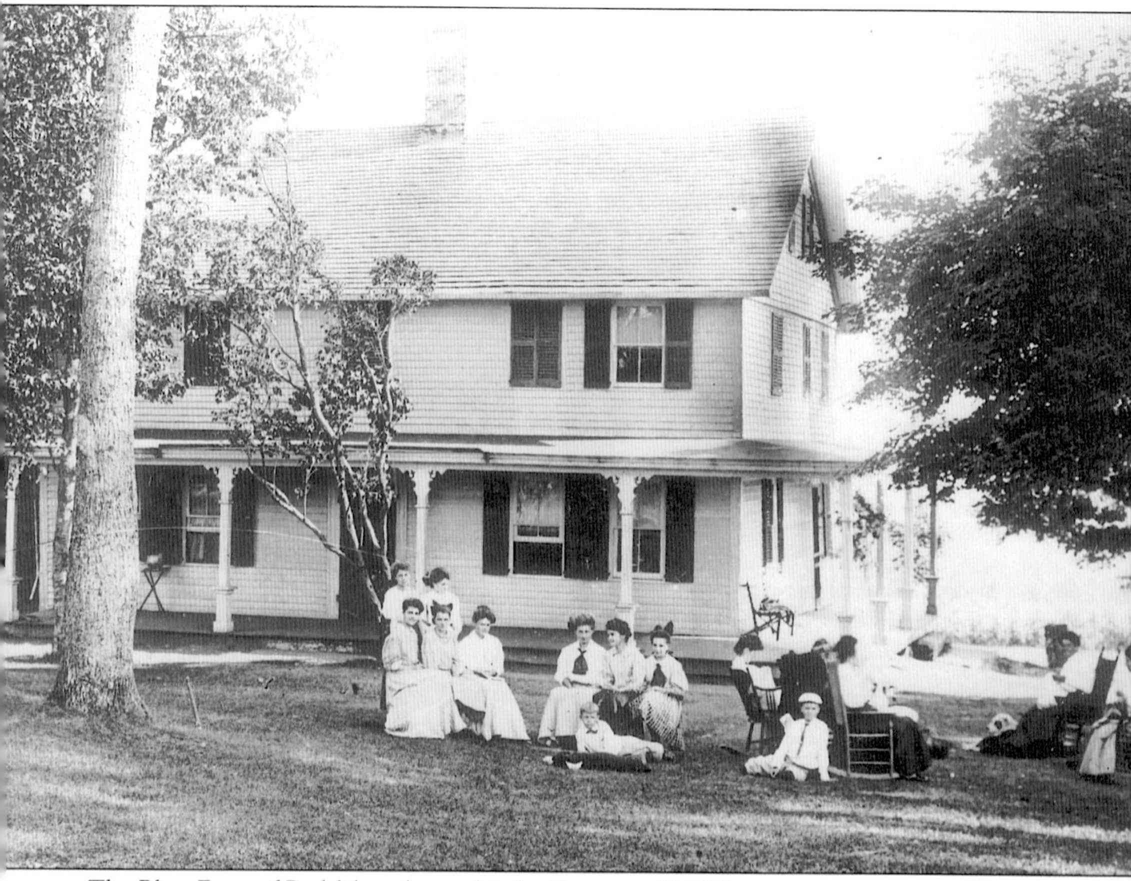

The Bloss Farm of Bethlehem hosts this family group. (BHS.)

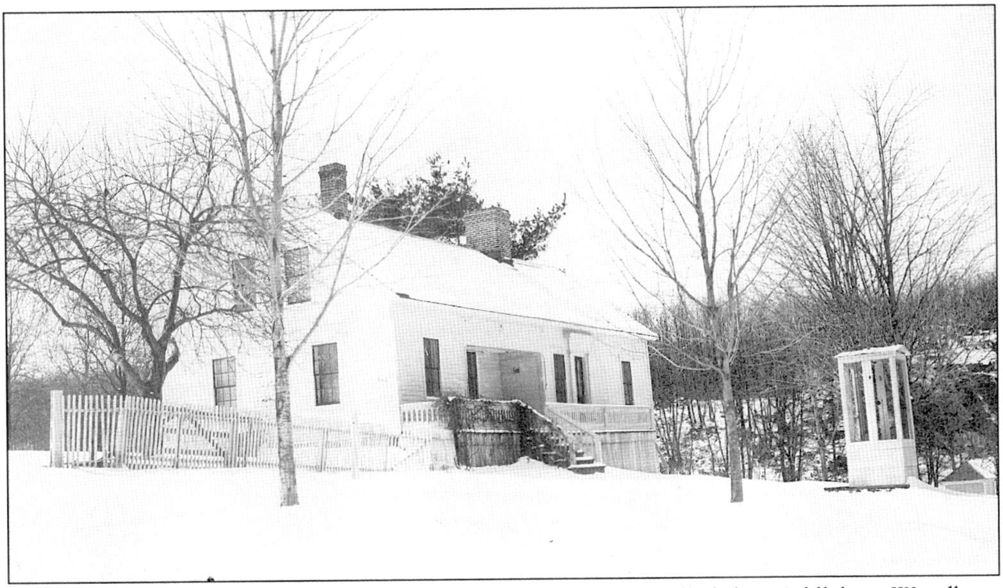

This modest farmhouse belonged to the Stevens family. It straddled the Middlebury-Woodbury Line. The photograph was taken on March 5, 1912, by Charles R. Harte, who was inspecting the nearby trolley line. Over the years, area homes ranged from rough cabins to substantial farm dwellings to the mansions of the wealthy and sometimes famous. Land values rose appreciably as working farms were sold for housing developments. (CRH.)

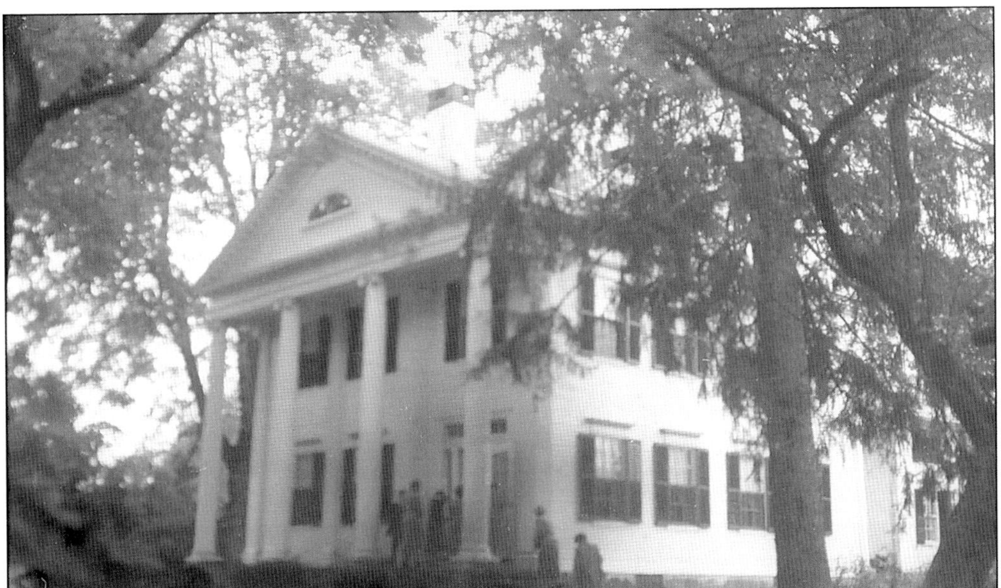

In sharp contrast to the above farmhouse is the elegant Mitchell House, also known as the Pillar House. Its owner was Mitchell S. Mitchell, and its location was on Mansion House Road in Southbury. This photograph was taken in 1954 by Harte's now ancient folding Kodak camera. (CRH.)

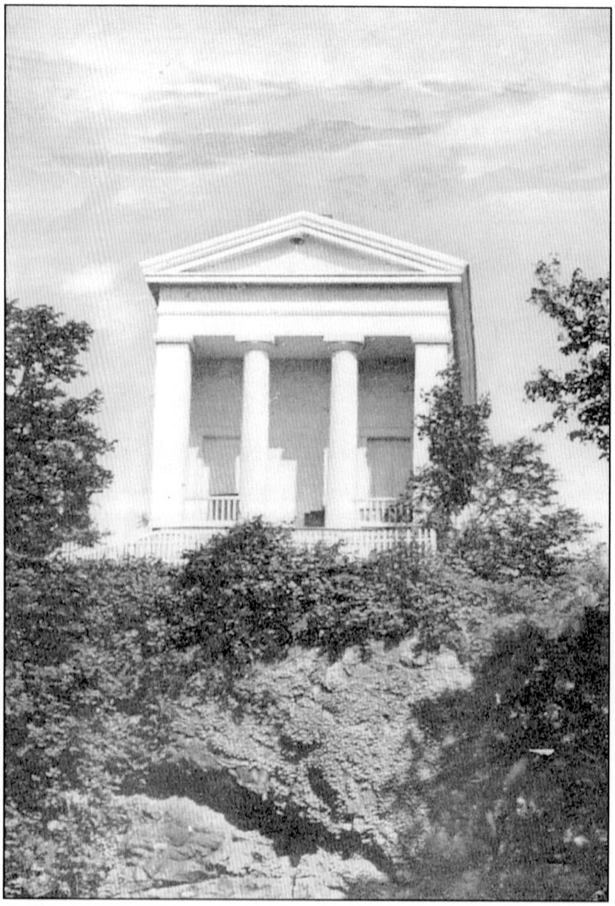

Erected upon a sheer drop overlooking Main Street in 1839, King Solomon's Lodge No. 7 is the area's most distinguished Masonic Temple. (FWC.)

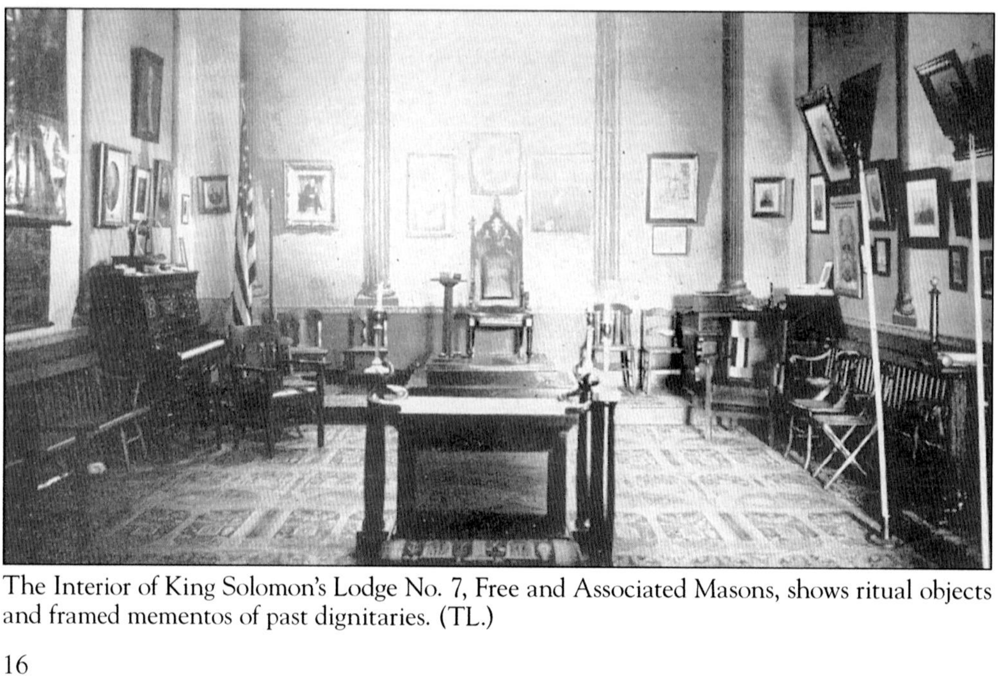

The Interior of King Solomon's Lodge No. 7, Free and Associated Masons, shows ritual objects and framed mementos of past dignitaries. (TL.)

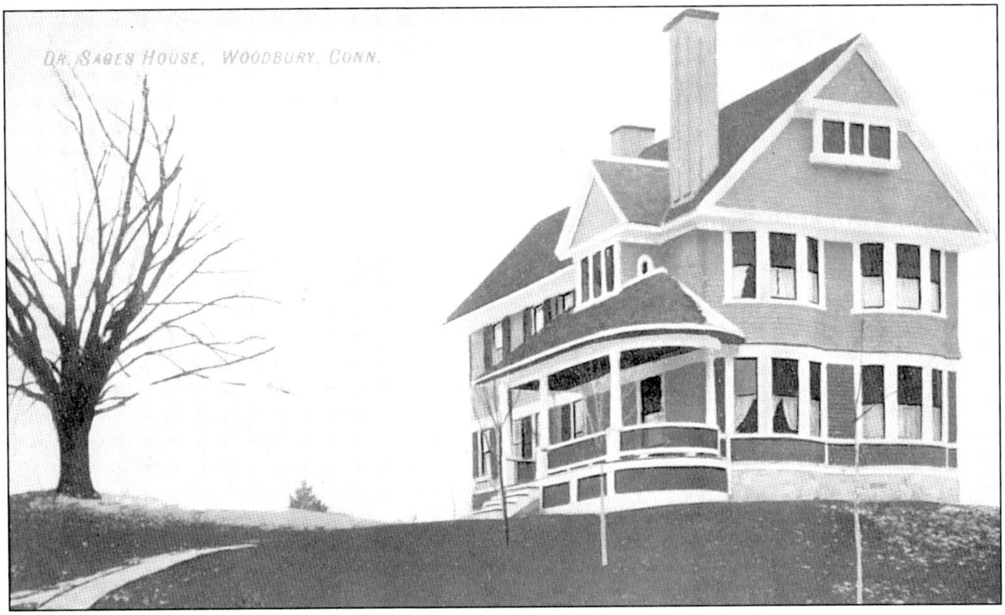

Dr. Sage's fine Victorian home was another Woodbury landmark. (TL.)

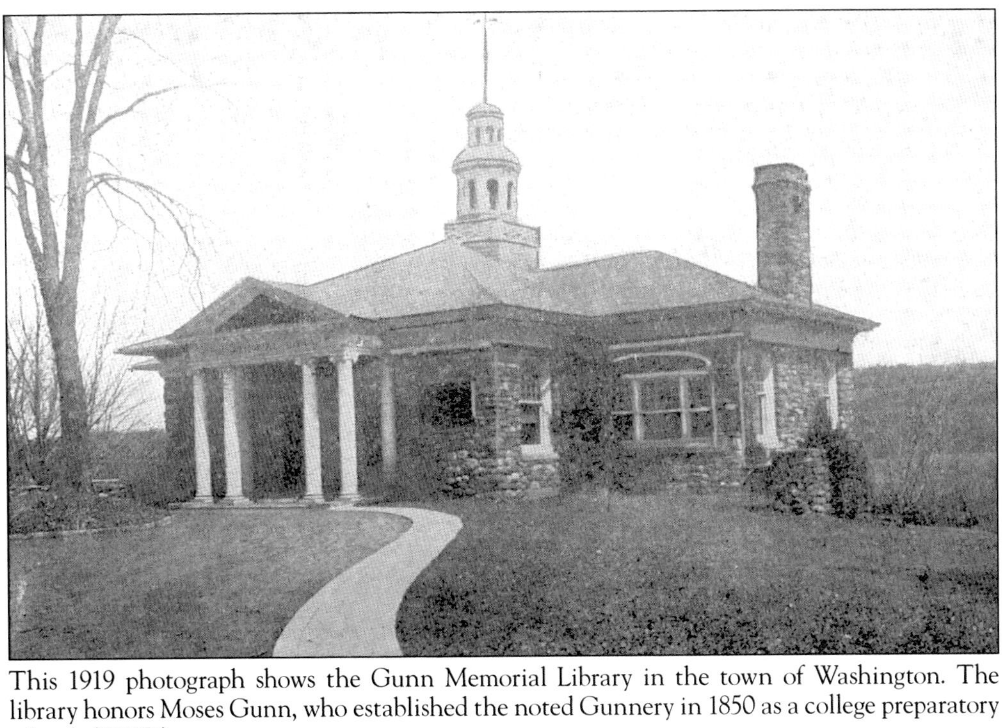

This 1919 photograph shows the Gunn Memorial Library in the town of Washington. The library honors Moses Gunn, who established the noted Gunnery in 1850 as a college preparatory school. (FWC.)

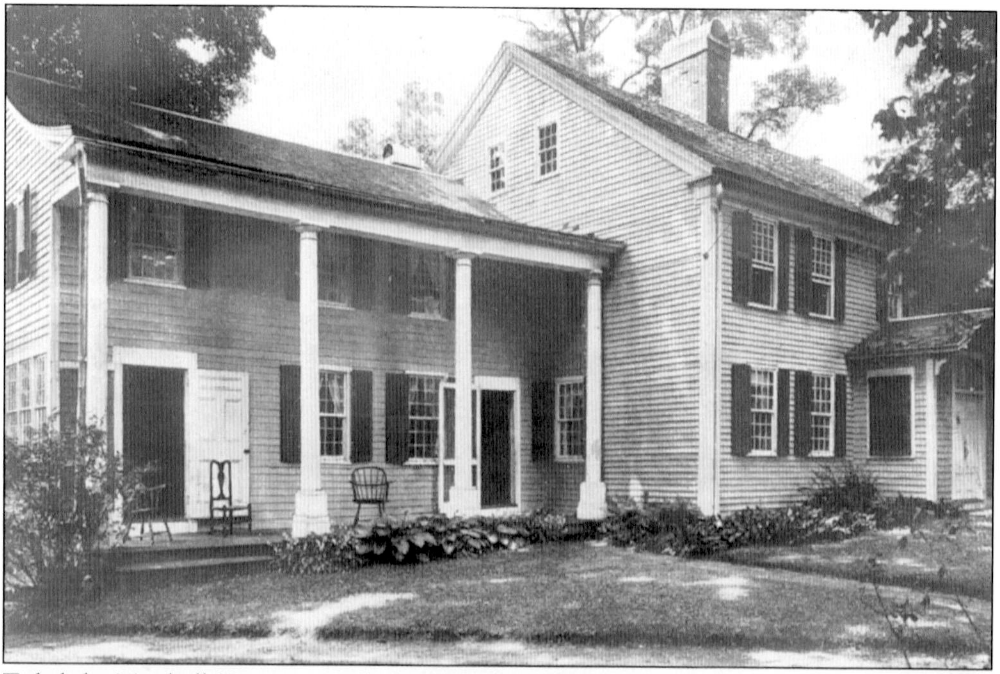

Titled the Marshall House in 1915, this Woodbury home has a core that dates as far back as the early 17th century. (WP.)

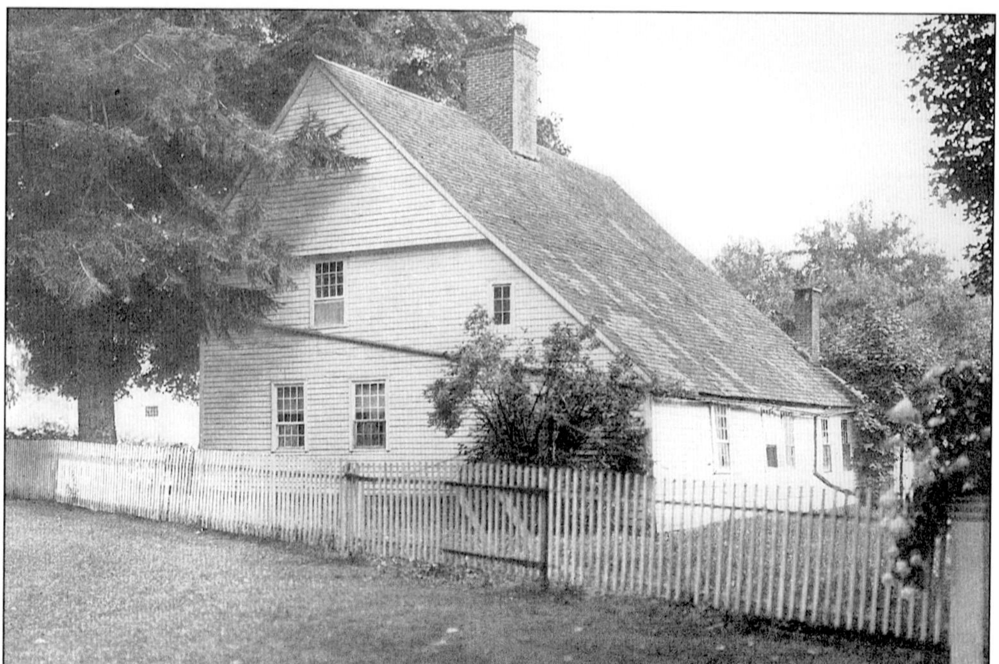

This view shows Woodbury's famous Hurd House *c.* 1915, prior to removal of its "modern addition." The house is located on Lower Road. (WP.)

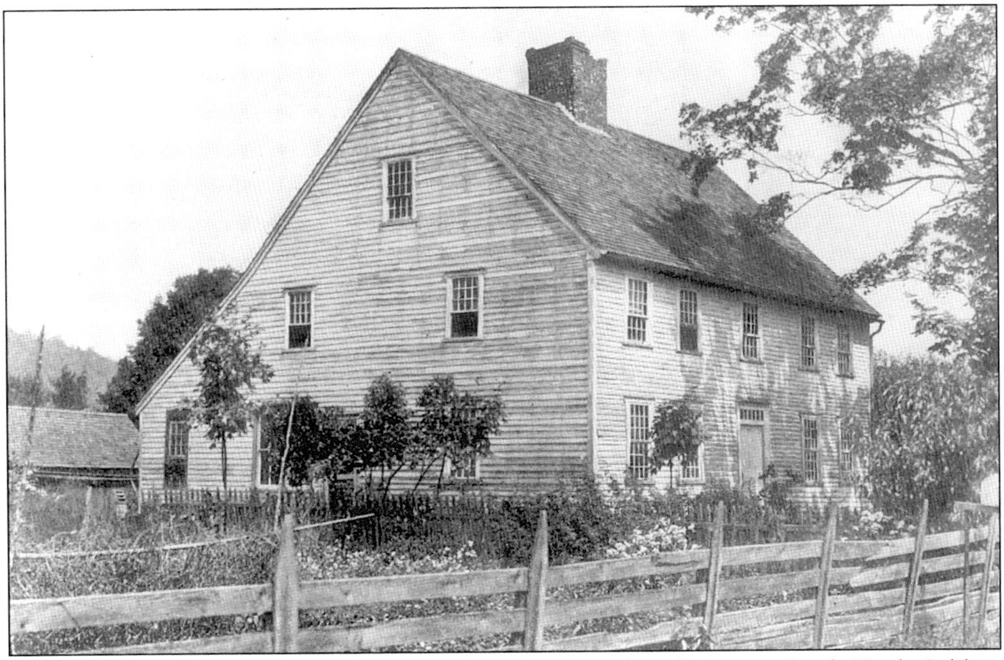

This classic saltbox house is located on the Southbury Road on the way to Sandy Hook. Saltbox style homes—compact, economic frame dwellings with large central chimneys—dominated Colonial New England for many years. Both the Glebe and Hurd Houses in Woodbury were of this style. (WP.)

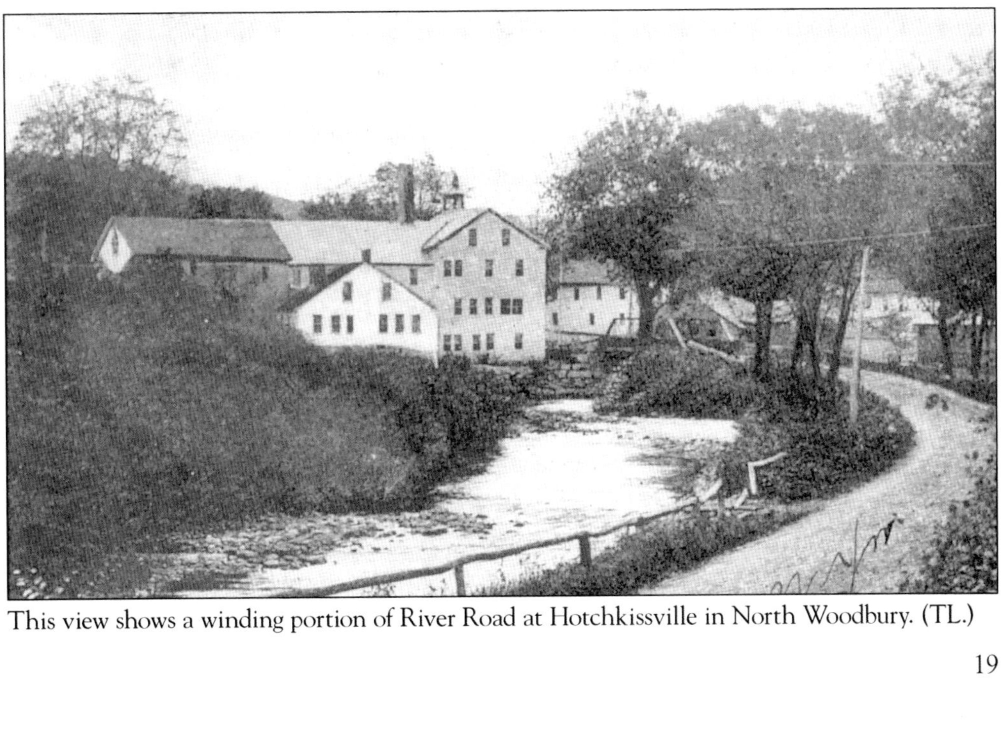

This view shows a winding portion of River Road at Hotchkissville in North Woodbury. (TL.)

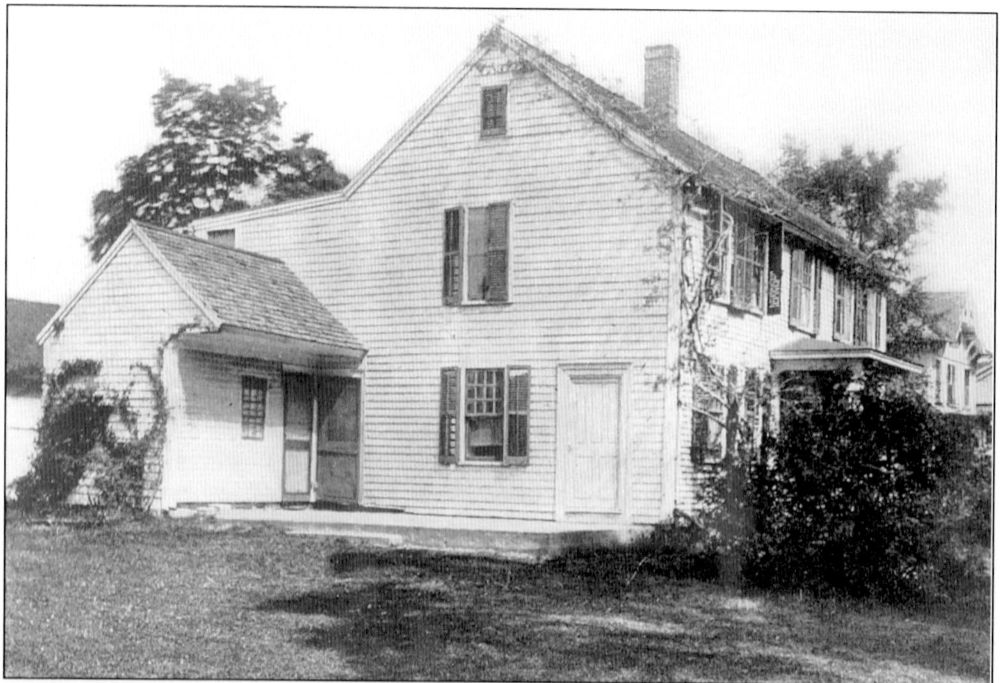

This is the Jonathan Platt House in Woodbury. The photograph was taken in the early 1900s, prior to World War I. (WP.)

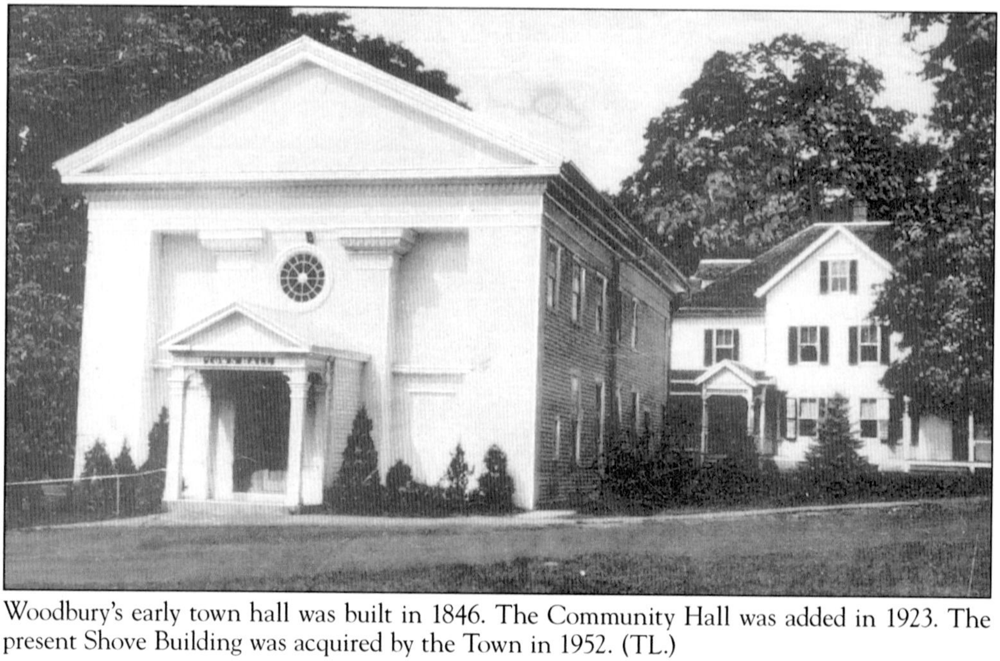

Woodbury's early town hall was built in 1846. The Community Hall was added in 1923. The present Shove Building was acquired by the Town in 1952. (TL.)

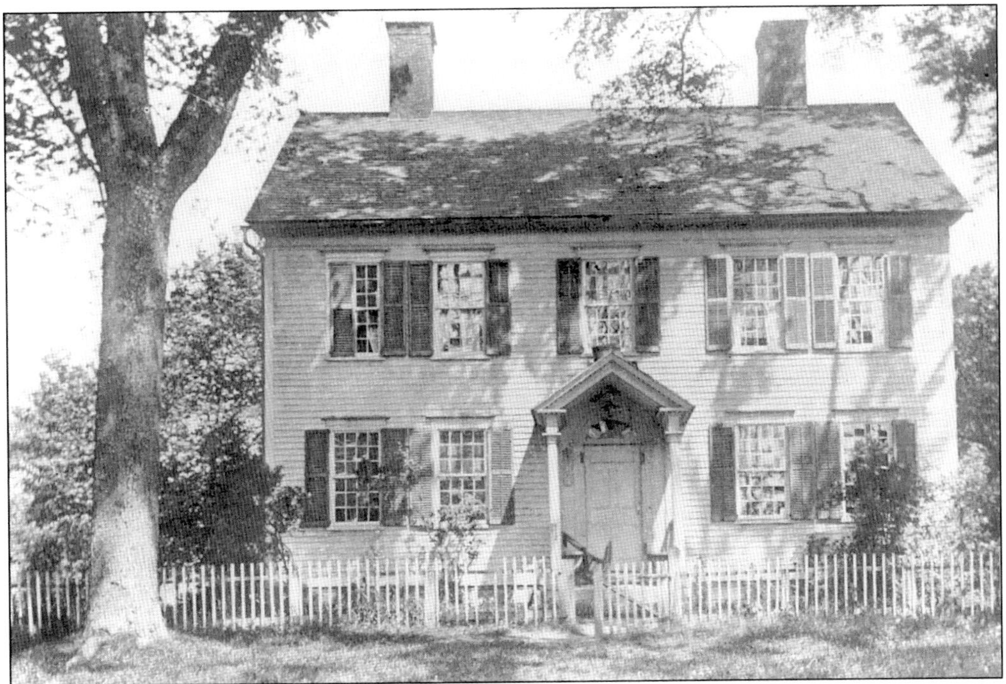

This elegant structure is the Bostwick House in Southbury. It later became a parsonage for the Congregational Church. (W.P.)

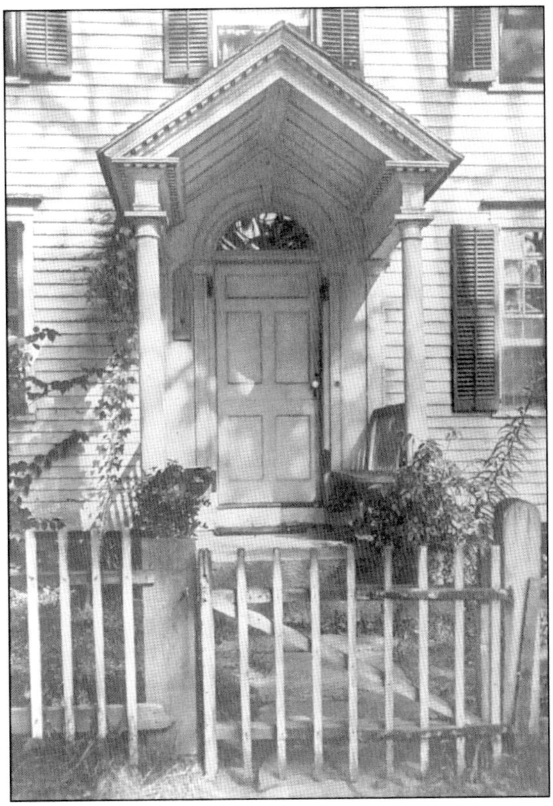

This view shows some of the interesting detail on the front porch and door of the Bostwick House. (W.P.)

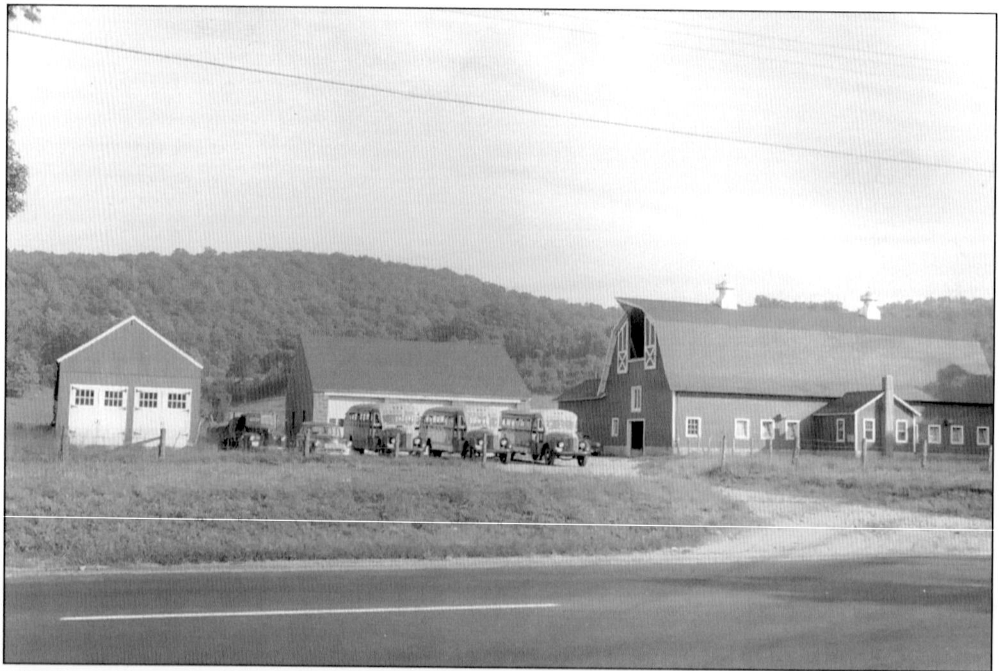

The former Pumpkin Patch Farm is now the site of the Southbury Mall. (SHS.)

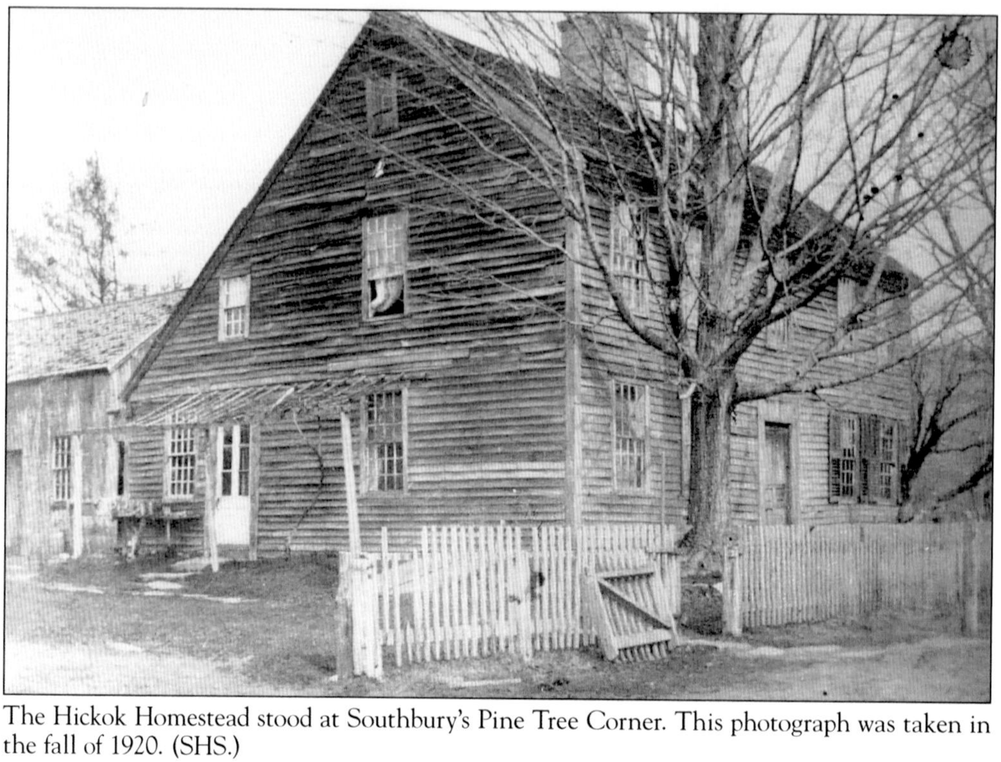

The Hickok Homestead stood at Southbury's Pine Tree Corner. This photograph was taken in the fall of 1920. (SHS.)

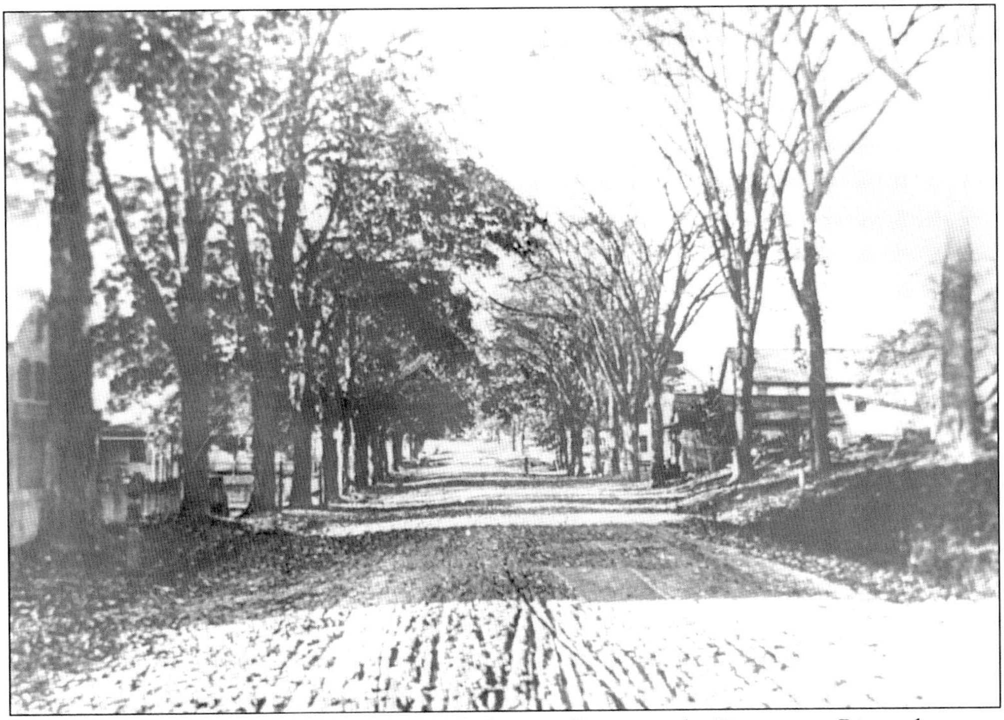

This early view shows Main Street in South Britain. Being on the Pomperaug River, the town of South Britain was more active in manufacturing than was Southbury itself. (SHS.)

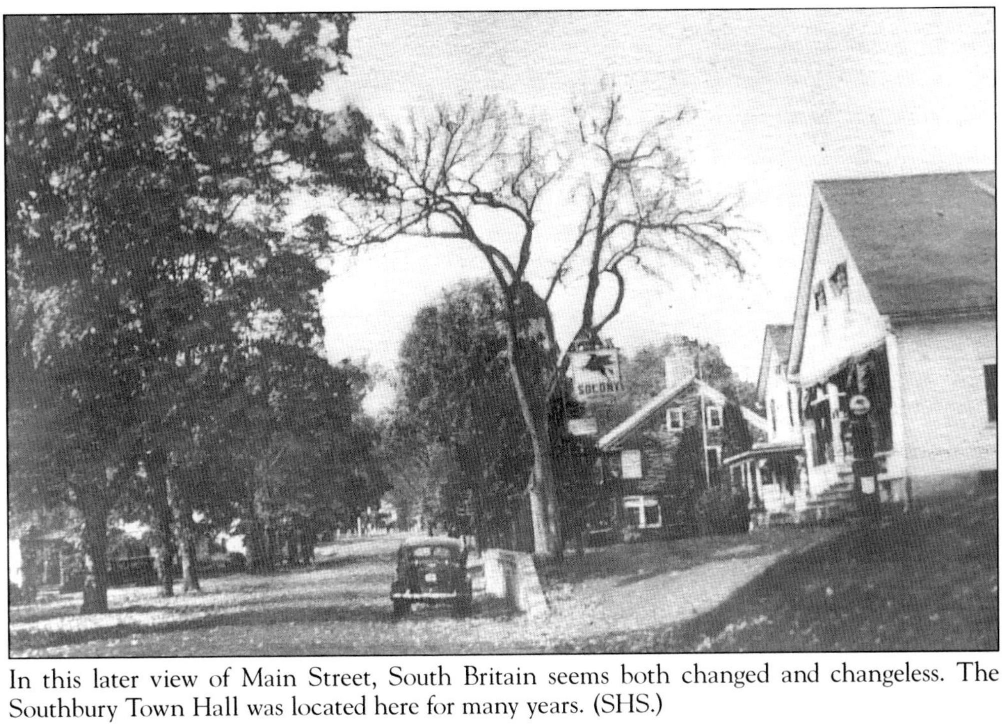

In this later view of Main Street, South Britain seems both changed and changeless. The Southbury Town Hall was located here for many years. (SHS.)

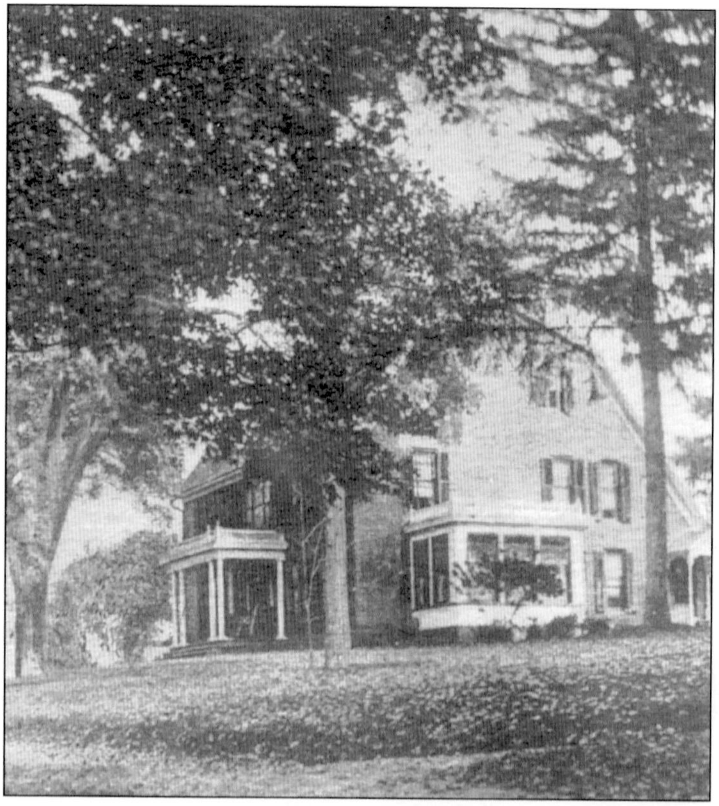

Southbury's Parley Place was built of local brick. Originally a family residence, it later became the noted Lutheran Home. (SHS.)

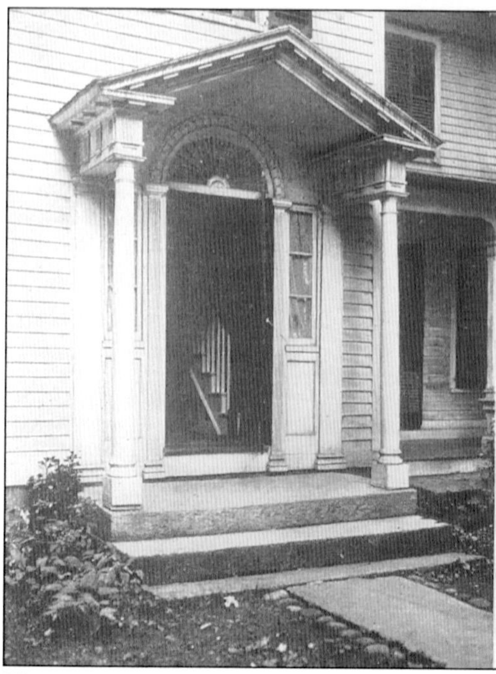

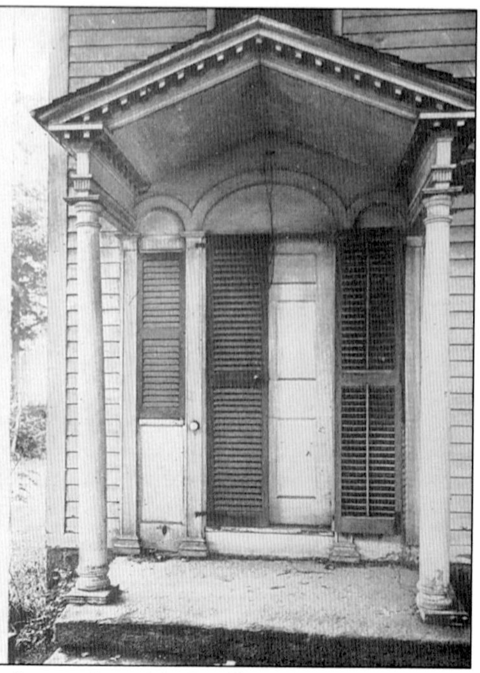

These two views are of the pillared front porches of some fine old Woodbury homes. (W.P.)

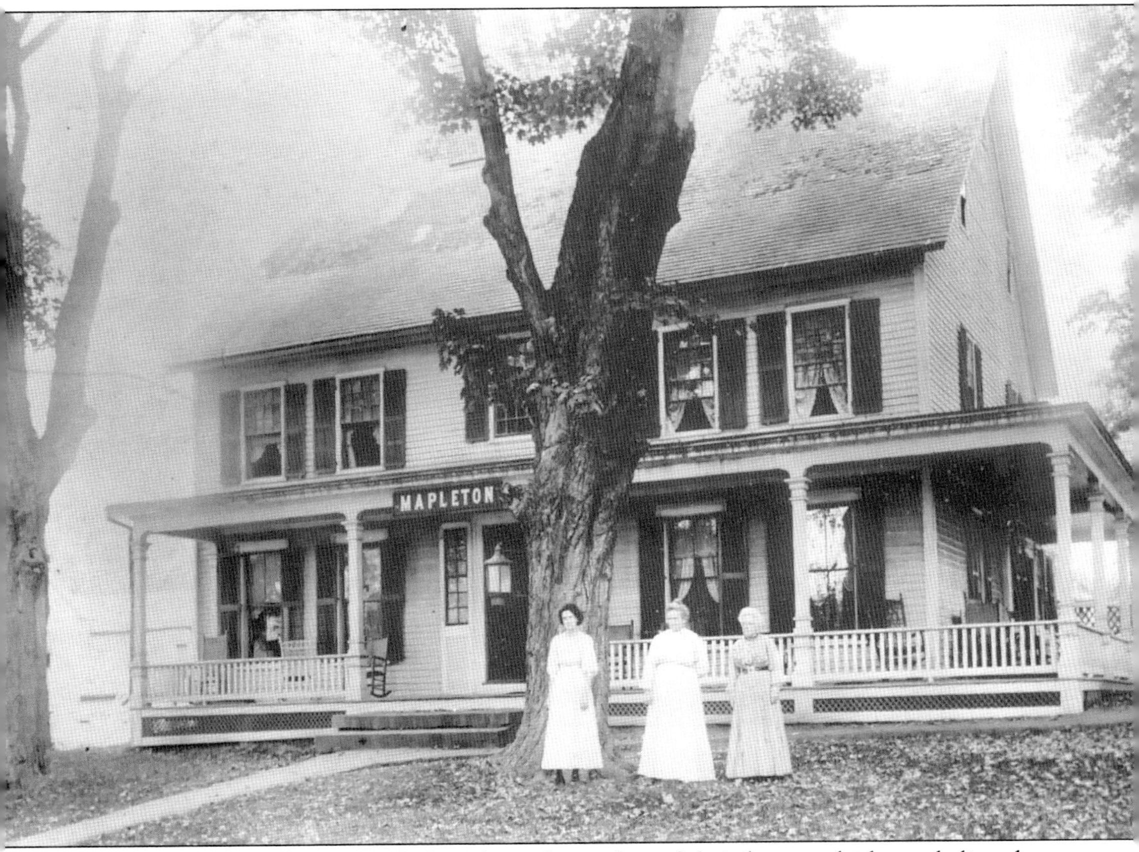

The residents of Mapleton pose before the wide porches of their home, which was believed to be on Pleasant Street in Woodbury. (C-H.)

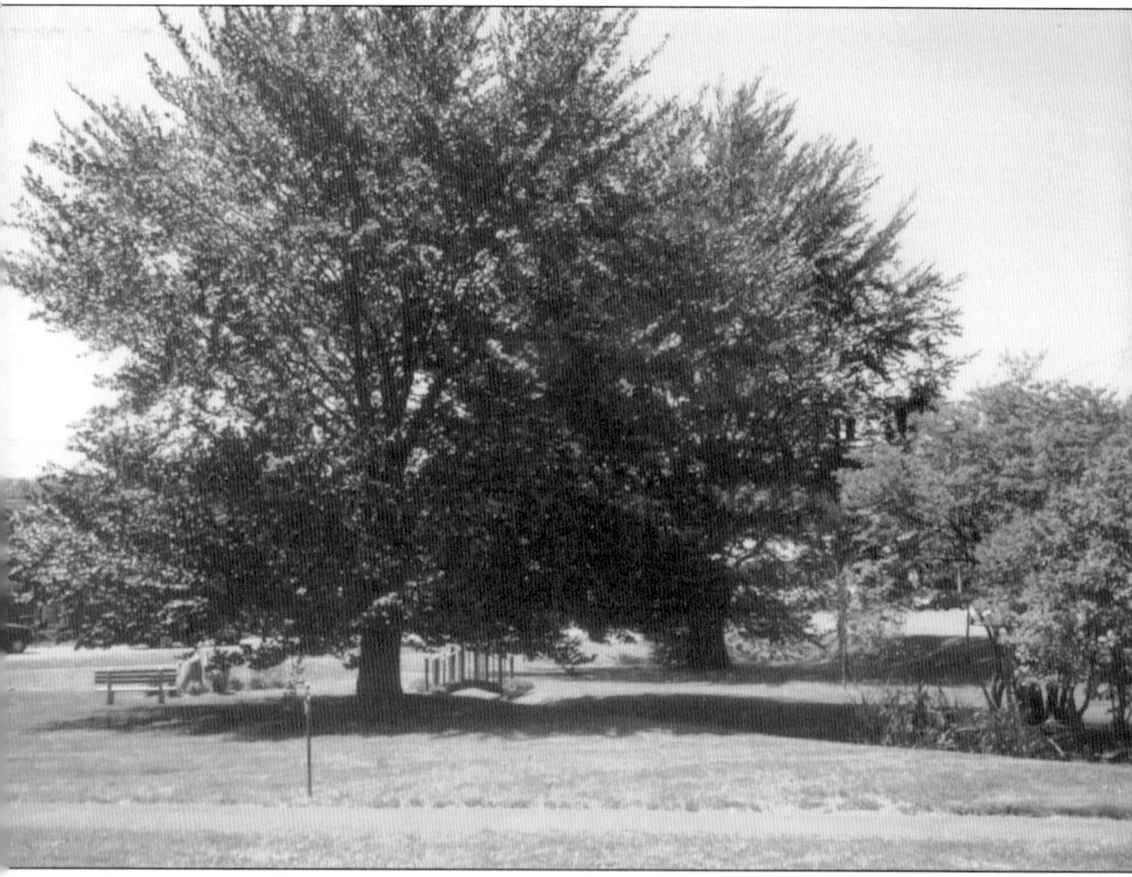

The great copper beech trees at the bottom of Sherman Hill seem little changed from the way they appeared in photographs taken well over 50 years ago. Along with a 1932 commemorative plaque, they stand as living memorials to Gens. George Washington and Jean-Baptiste Rochambeau. (FWC.)

Two

At Work

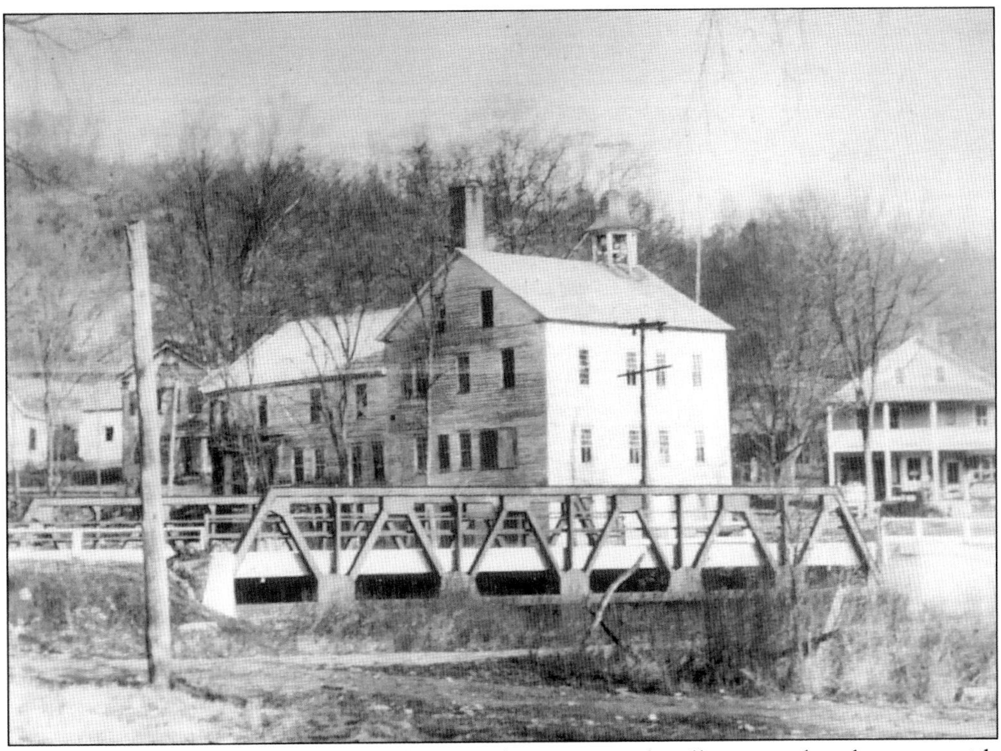

Basic agriculture was the original and essential occupation for all area settlers; however, with succeeding generations, diversification brought new and important activities, culminating in textile and metal fabrication. This photograph shows the back of the Woolen Mill and the Weekeepeemee Bridge at Hotchkissville. (C-H.)

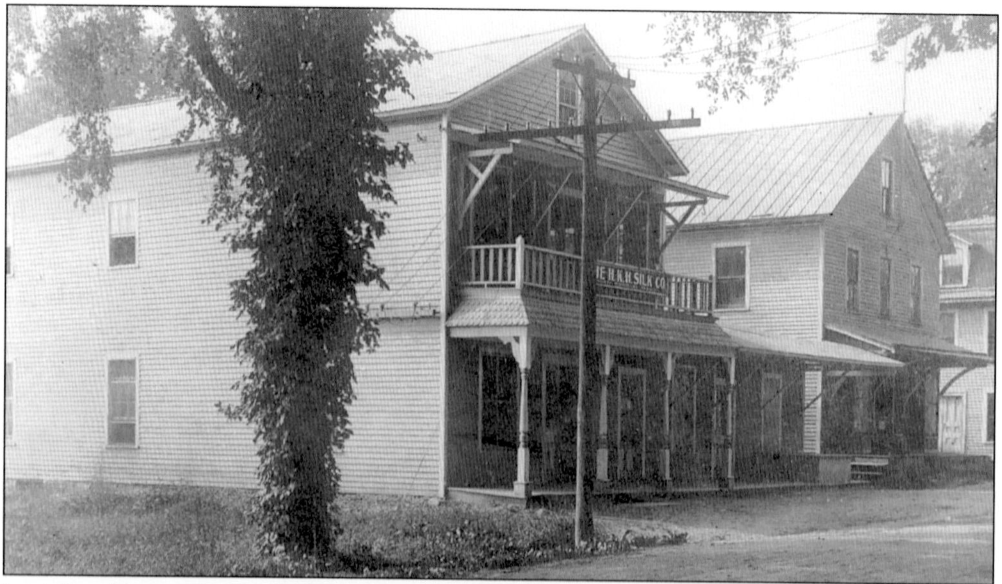

Initially, sheep were the most common livestock raised, 10,000 being reported grazing in Woodbury when the Revolutionary War drove up the demand for uniforms. Daniel Curtis operated a large complex at Pomperaug Mills in the mid-1800s. Satinet and other wool fabrics grew in importance with the Civil War's insatiable demand for uniforms and blankets, and local flocks multiplied accordingly. Other textiles, including linen, cotton, and silk were also manufactured over the years. This 1921 photograph shows the H.K.H. Silk Company in North Woodbury. (C-H.)

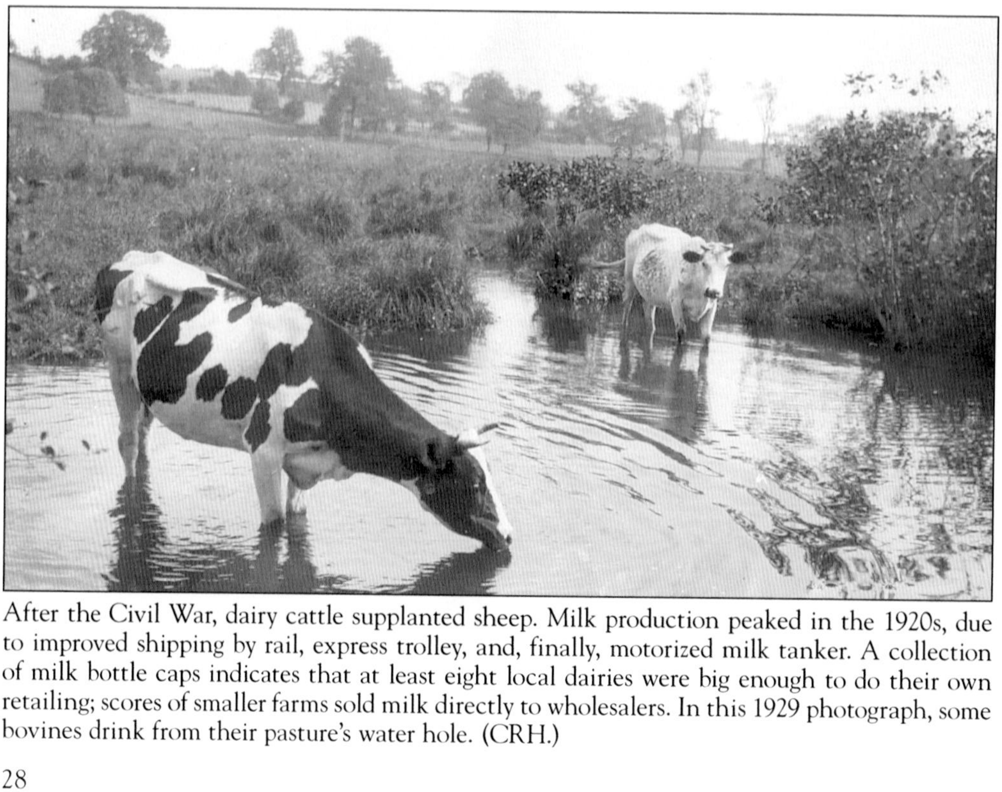

After the Civil War, dairy cattle supplanted sheep. Milk production peaked in the 1920s, due to improved shipping by rail, express trolley, and, finally, motorized milk tanker. A collection of milk bottle caps indicates that at least eight local dairies were big enough to do their own retailing; scores of smaller farms sold milk directly to wholesalers. In this 1929 photograph, some bovines drink from their pasture's water hole. (CRH.)

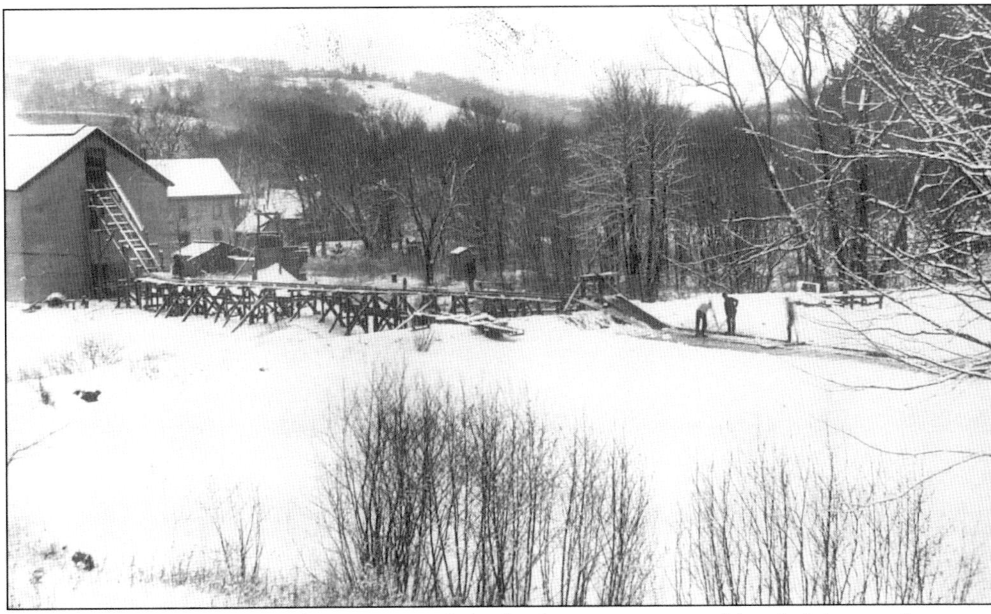

Before refrigeration, natural ice was vital for both preservation of local dairy products and as an export item. Ice cutting was thus an important seasonal business for years on local ponds. Bantam Lake had an extensive icehouse complex, complete with several railroad sidings. (FWC.)

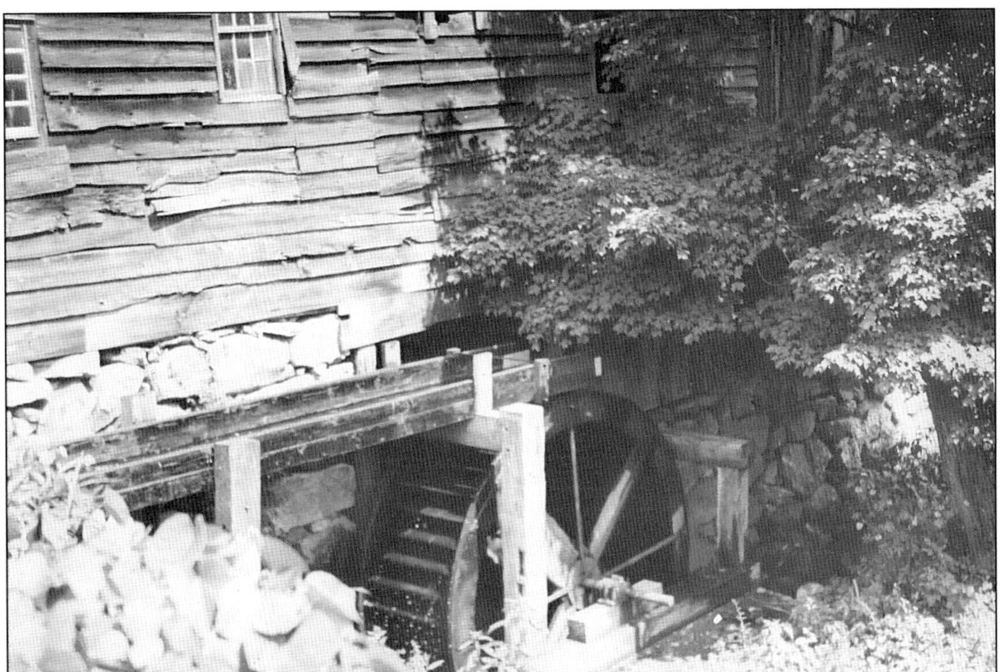

The massive stone foundation of this mill hardly hints at how labor intensive early American life was. (FWC.)

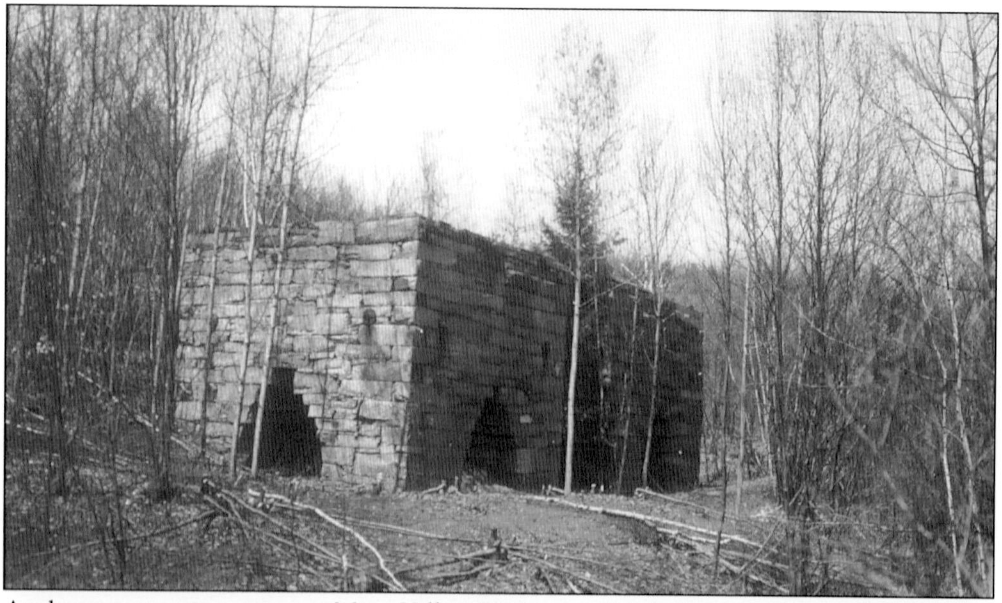

At these ore-roasting ovens on Mine Hill in Roxbury, a "Little Pittsburgh" struggled for a few years after the Civil War. The prize was siderite, an iron ore especially suited for conversion into steel. However, there were many problems: the ore bound up in granite and quartz was difficult to mine, the elegantly built furnace was cranky and inefficient, and the on-site steel mill proved to be unworkable. This photograph dates from 1934. (CRH.)

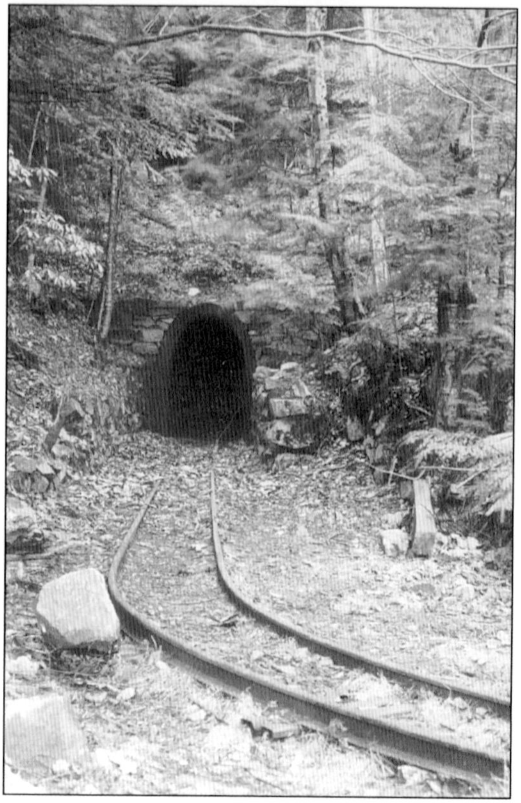

This was the main entrance to the Roxbury Iron Mine. Between 1915 and 1925, the Columbia School of Mines used the tunnels for a summer course of hands-on mining experience. Students lived at Camp Columbia, near the south end of Bantam Lake. The photograph was taken in 1934. (CRH.)

This 1934 photograph shows the northeast corner of Roxbury Furnace. Now a part of the Roxbury Land Trust, the roasting ovens and furnace have been carefully preserved. (CRH.)

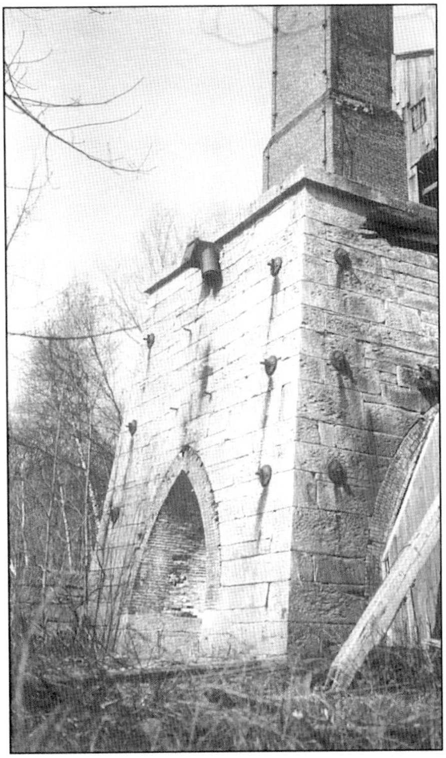

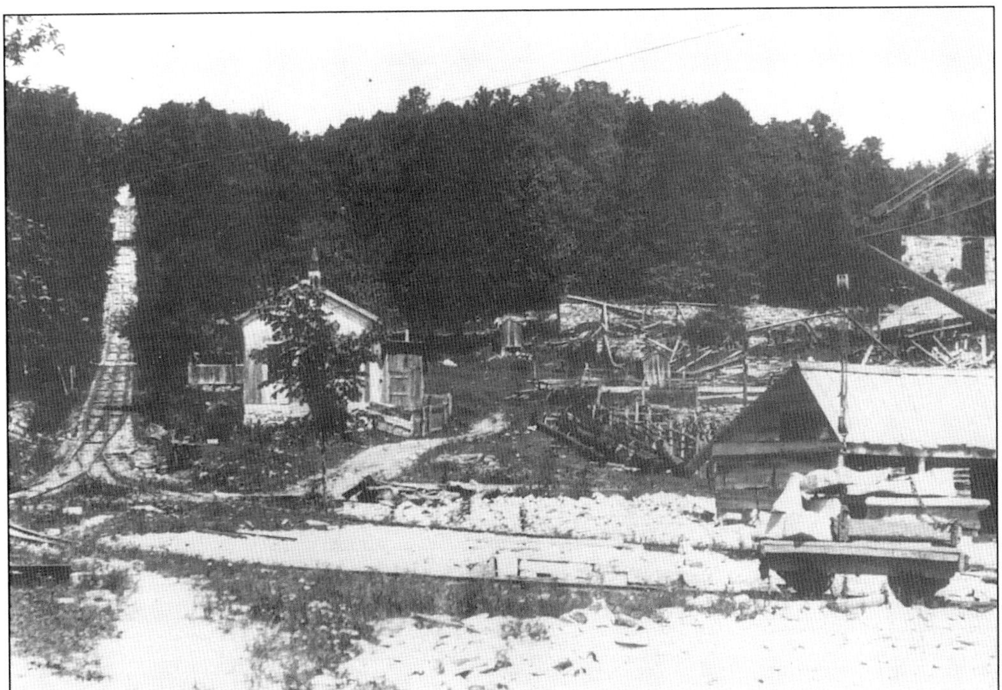

After the demise of the iron operation, two granite quarries operated until the early 1900s. The dual-tracked incline, shown c. 1910, conveyed cut blocks from the upper Rockside Quarry down to a loading dock at Roxbury Station. (FWC.)

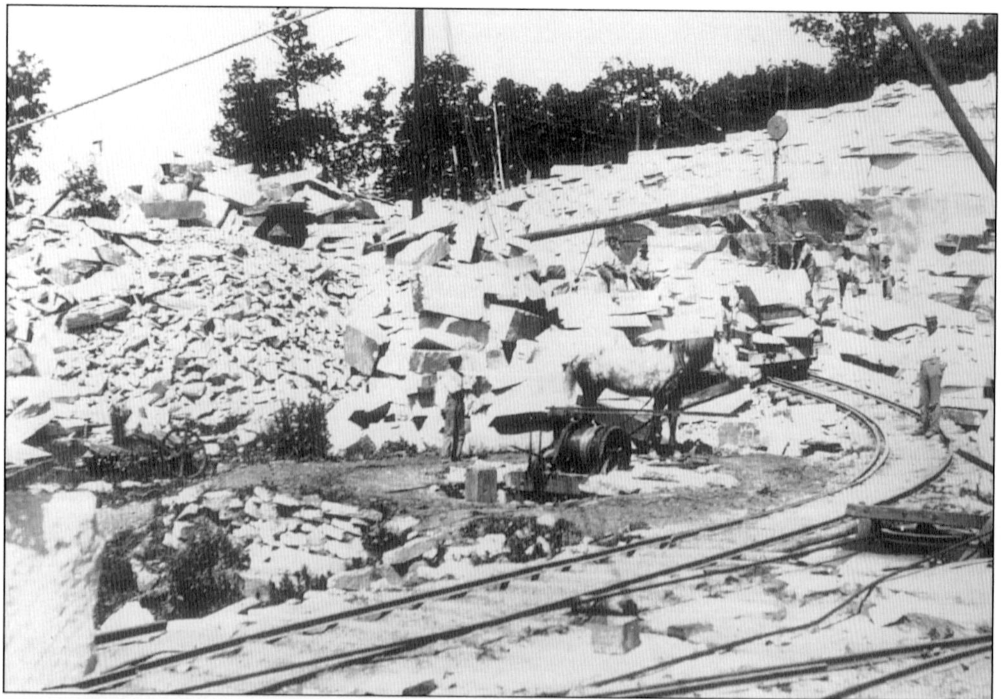

The Upper Quarry on Mine Hill used the descending loaded cars to haul the empties back up. Near the north end of Mine Hill, a special siding on the Shepaug Railroad loaded great granite slabs for New York City building projects. One block, 40 feet long, was shipped to New York City on special flatcars. Use of reinforced concrete ended operations *c.* 1910. (FWC.)

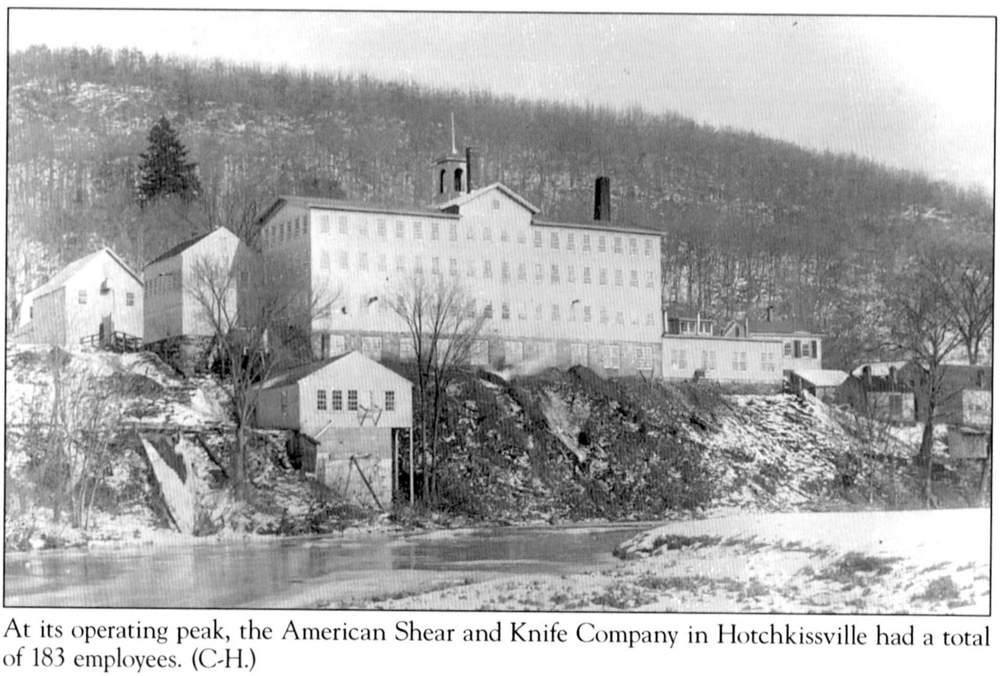

At its operating peak, the American Shear and Knife Company in Hotchkissville had a total of 183 employees. (C-H.)

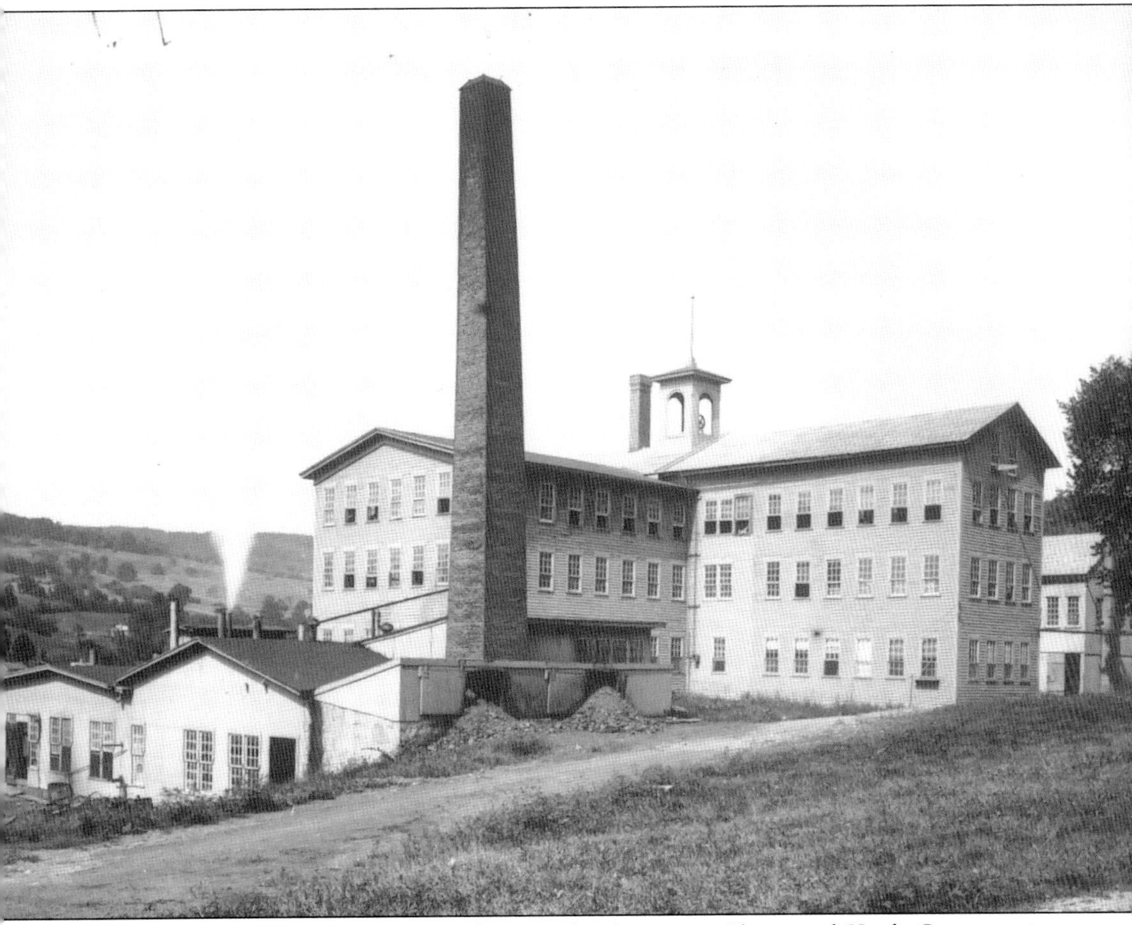

This is a view of Woodbury's largest factory, the American Shear and Knife Company in Hotchkissville. In 1896, the plant employed some 200 hands. Other area factories made steel traps and a host of iron and brass items for hardware, dress goods, and harness fittings. (C-H.)

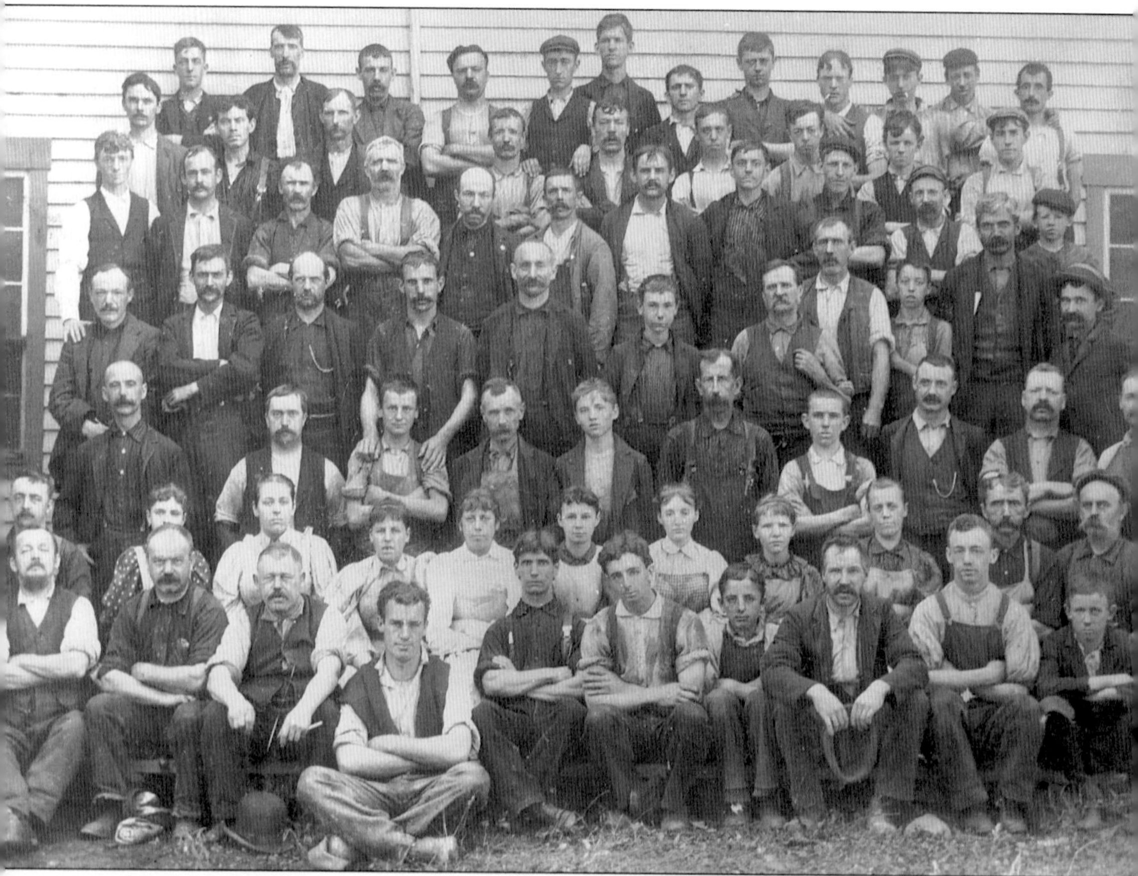

Cutlery workers had special trades, which they took individual pride in. A man who could rapidly turn out a sharp quality blade was regarded as a valuable asset, especially in an era when labor and management lived relatively side by side. Trades included cutler, grinder, polisher, and shear maker. (C-H.)

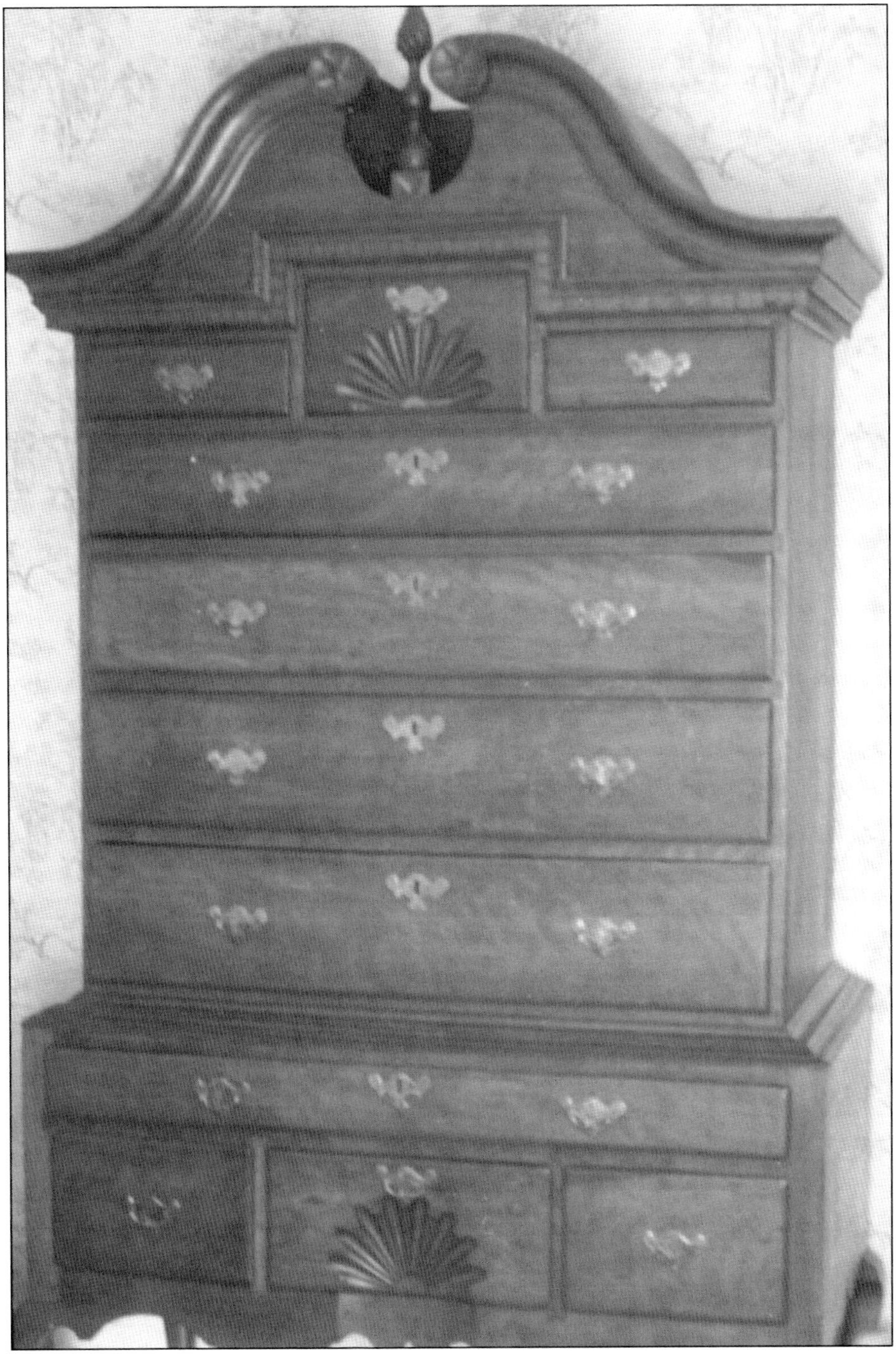

Woodbury had its own cabinet-making period, competing with Newtown and other fine-furniture centers. Silas Butler, originally from Martha's Vineyard, Massachusetts, signed this elegant Queen Anne highboy, proudly dating it "March ye 23rd, 1755." Butler was probably completing his apprenticeship requirements for a "master-piece" before becoming a journeyman. He later moved to the Stockbridge area and died in Sheffield, Massachusetts. (FWC)

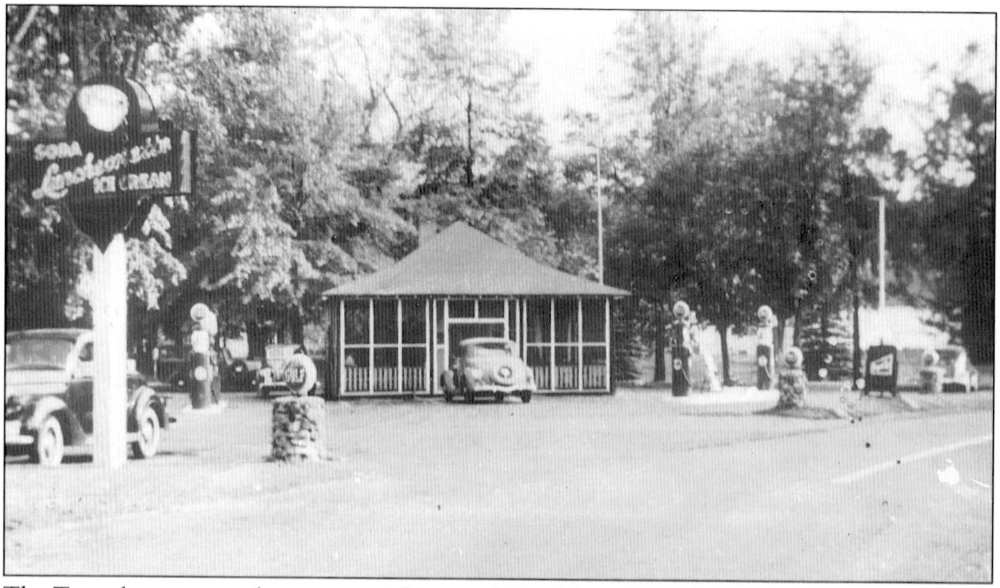

The Triangle was once the commercial heart of Southbury. (SHS.)

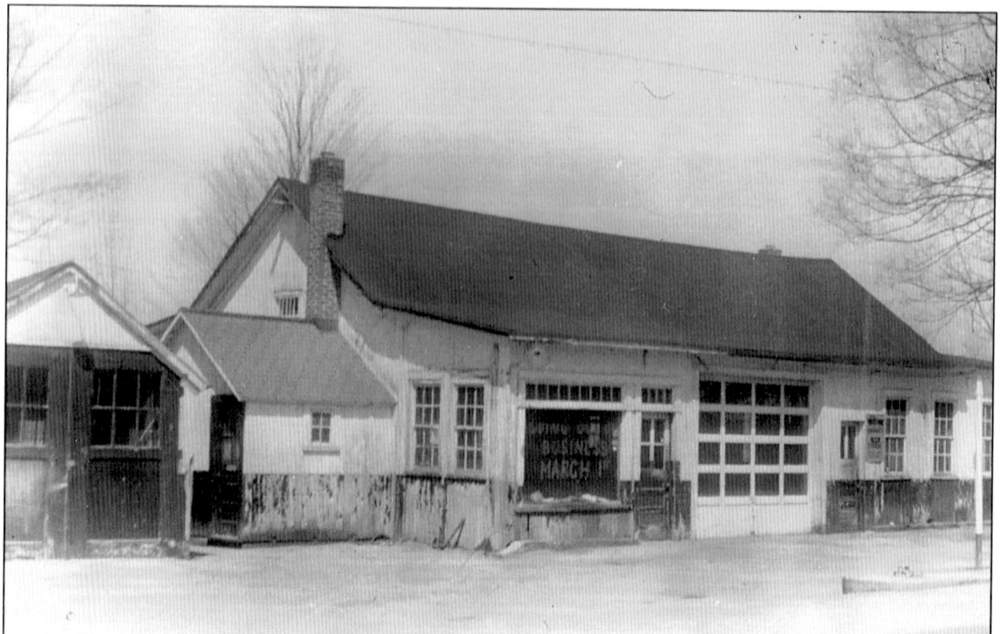

This building once housed the old Bennett Garage in Southbury. The photograph was taken after the garage went out of business. (SHS.)

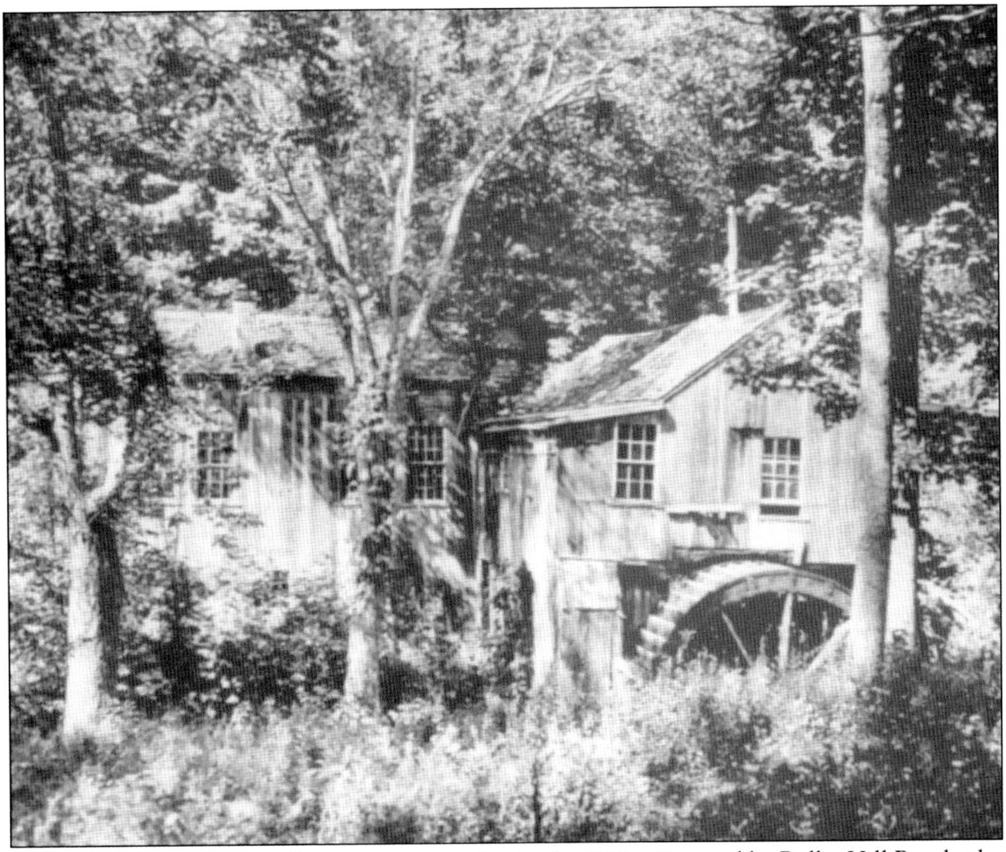

The Old Bullet Hill Plow Shop was in operation in the 1870s. Powered by Bullet Hill Brook, the Wakely Mill made the Southbury plow. At the same time, Bronson's Foundry on Jack's Brook turned out the Roxbury plow. (FWC.)

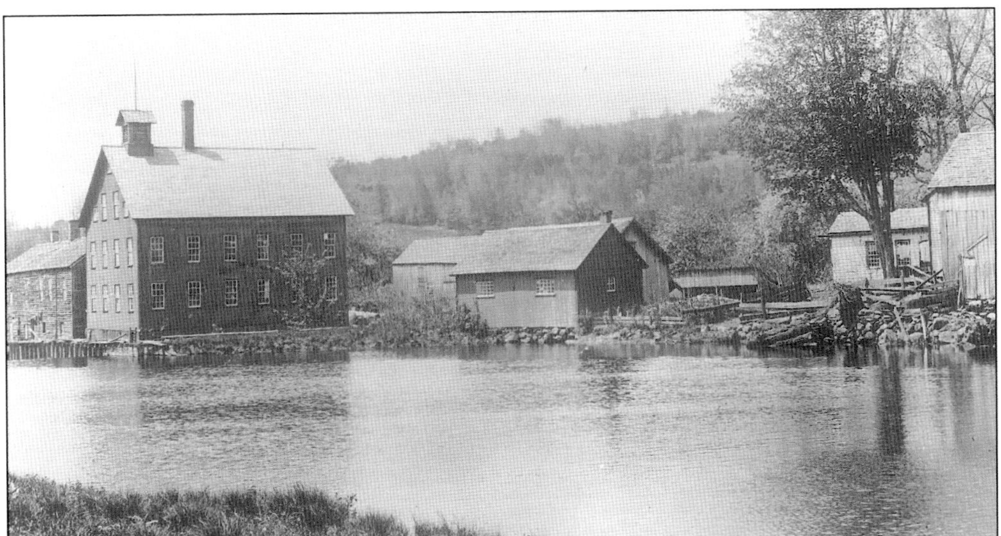

The Guild Carriage Shop was Bethlehem's largest enterprise. (BHS.)

ST. PIERRE OIL COMPANY, INC.

SOLE DISTRIBUTORS OF GULF OIL PRODUCTS SINCE 1909

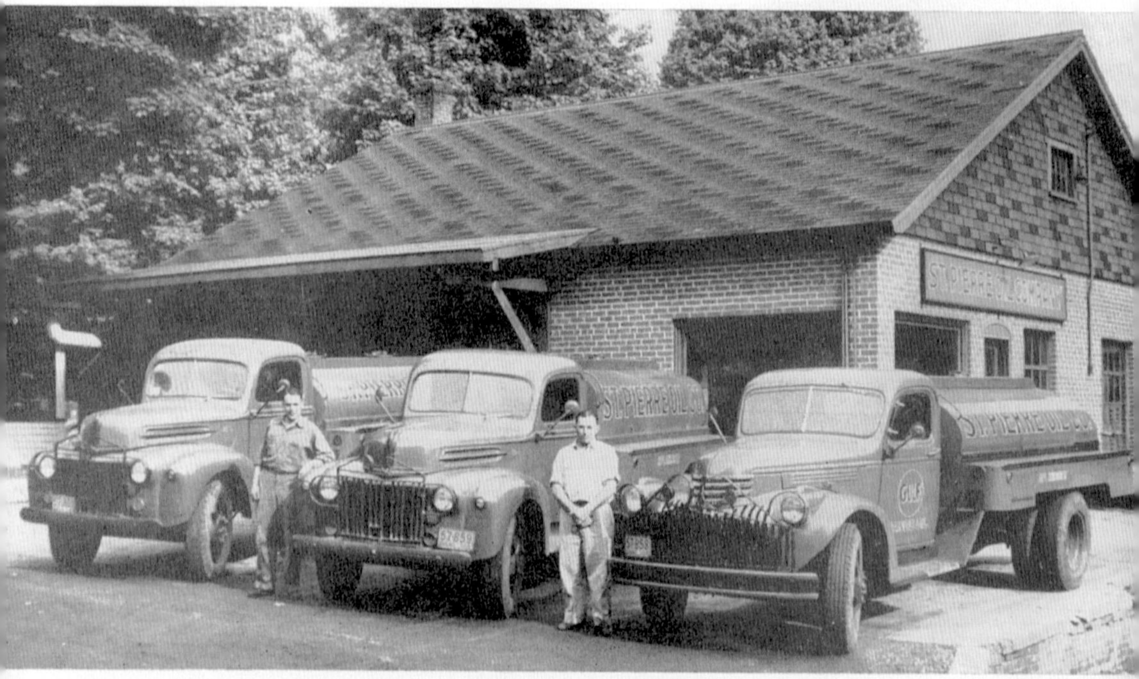

Part of our truck fleet serving Woodbury, Southbury, Middlebury, Oxford, Bethlehem, Roxbury and Washington. Fred C. St. Pierre and E melee shown in the picture and Townsend D. Hauxhurst are veteran drivers.

GASOLINE — MOTOR OILS — RANGE and FURNACE OILS — STO CK and HOUSEHOLD SPRAY

BULK PLANT AT SOUTHBURY — MAIN OFFICE AT WOODBURY

Telephone 142-2 Fortuna J. St. Pierre, President

Oil and gasoline were the life blood of the internal combustion age. This 1949 advertisement shows the men and equipment of the area's largest fuel supplier. (ETT.)

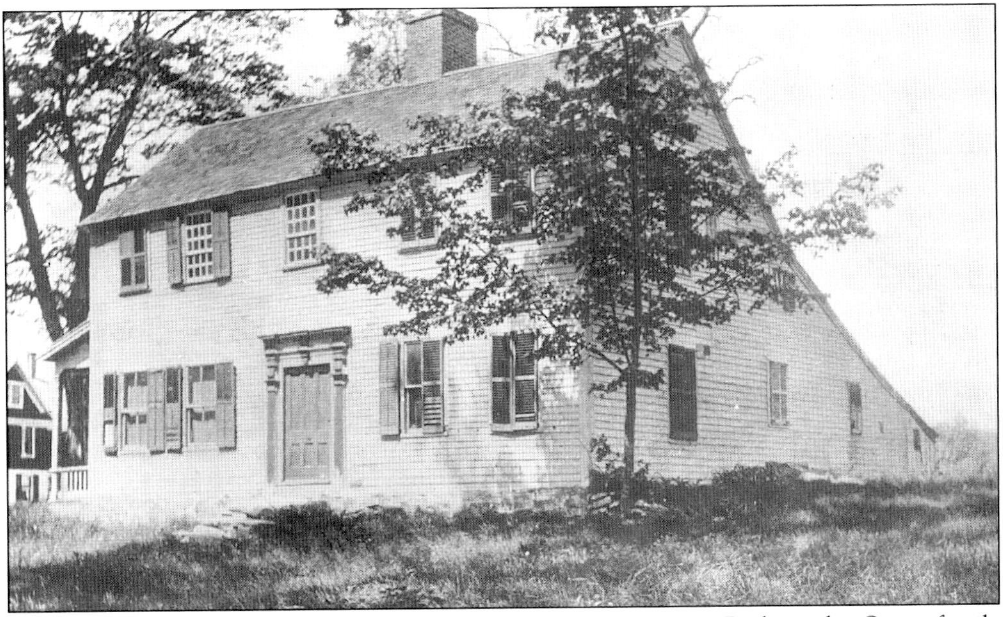

The Orton Tavern was probably the earliest of Woodbury's inns. Built as the Orton family homestead in 1711, it served as a supply depot for the Continental army and was a noted inn during stagecoach days. The building, pictured c. 1914, was dismantled in 1923, and part of the land became occupied by St. Teresa's Church. (WP.)

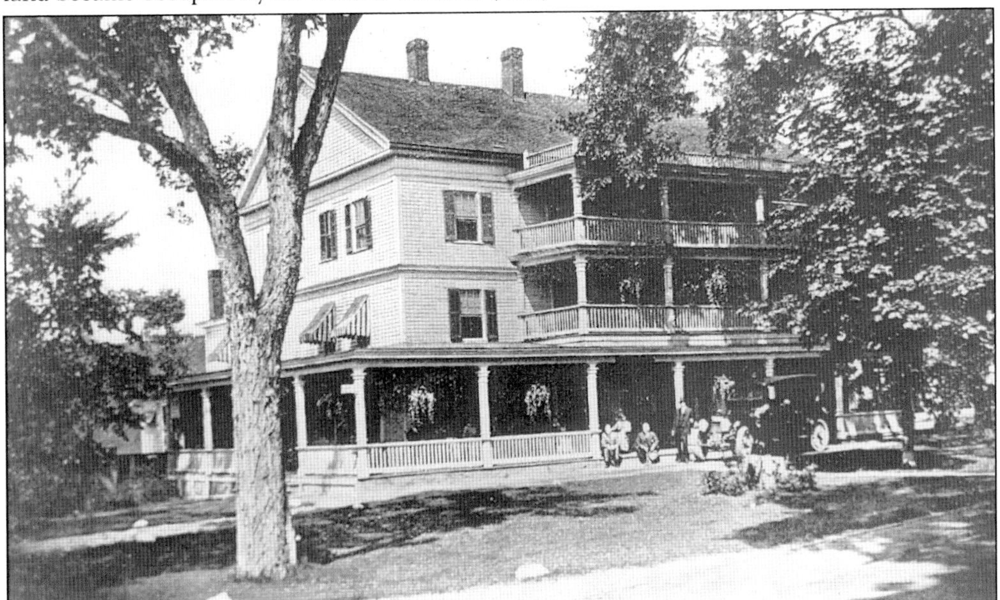

The Curtis House had its inn-keeping origins back in 1754, when Peter Gilchrist leased the Stoddard residence and commenced offering hospitality to travelers in the spirit of "Entertainment for Man and Horse." After many changes of ownership and name, the hotel settled on the present title in 1882. In 1900, Levi Curtis celebrated the new century by adding a third story to his hostelry. A local newspaper advertisement c. 1910 proclaimed, "Stable your horse here, while you take the trolley into Waterbury." This photograph shows the Curtis House in the early automobile age. (C-H.)

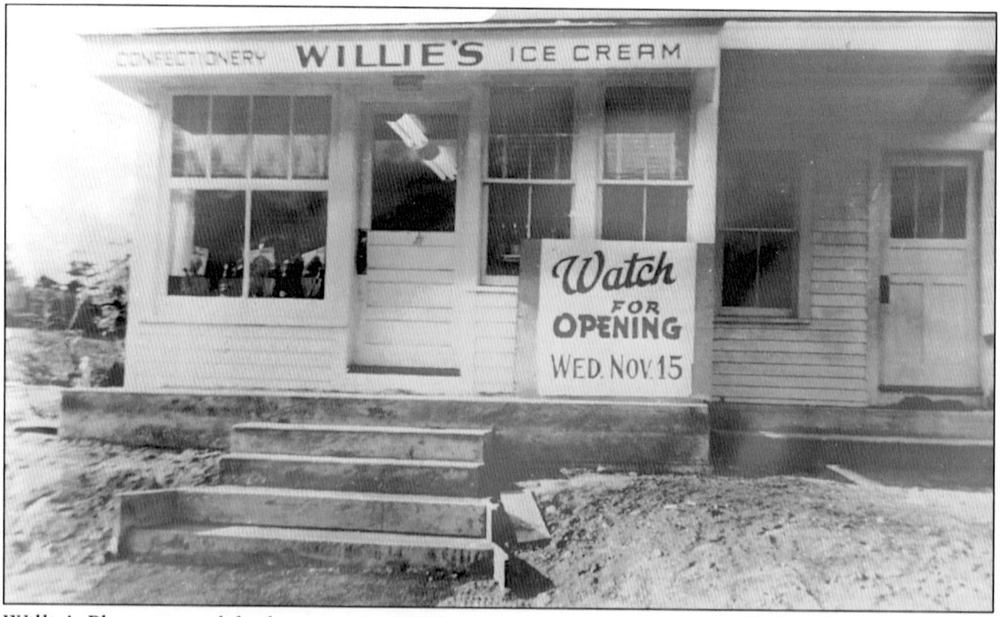

Willie's Place opened for business on Wednesday, November 15, 1950. It offered "ice cream all winter long." (C-H.)

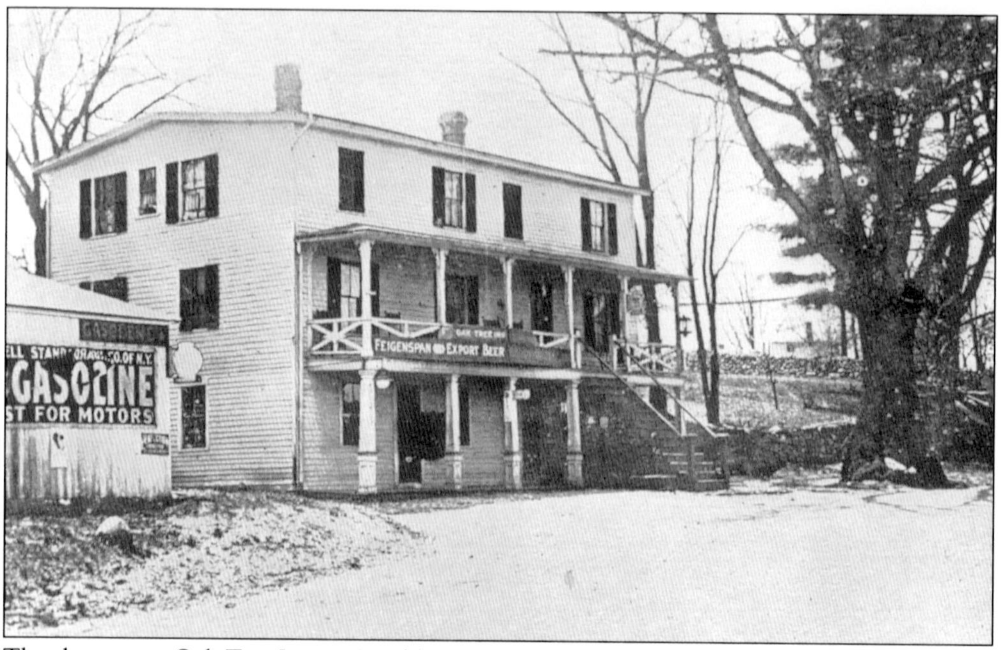

The three-story Oak Tree Inn in Southbury served Feigenspan Export Beer. Other long-noted area eateries were the Chanticleer, the Mayflower Inn, Phillips Diner, the Charcoal Chef, the Tollgate Inn, and the Oak Tree Inn. One former Southbury stagecoach stop, the Old Hundred Inn, had an ice-cream operation that long outlasted the popular restaurant. Finally, atop Sherman Hill was Briarwood, with its unique and long-lost logo: a neon-outlined tilted teacup, complete with animated descending amber drops. (SHS.)

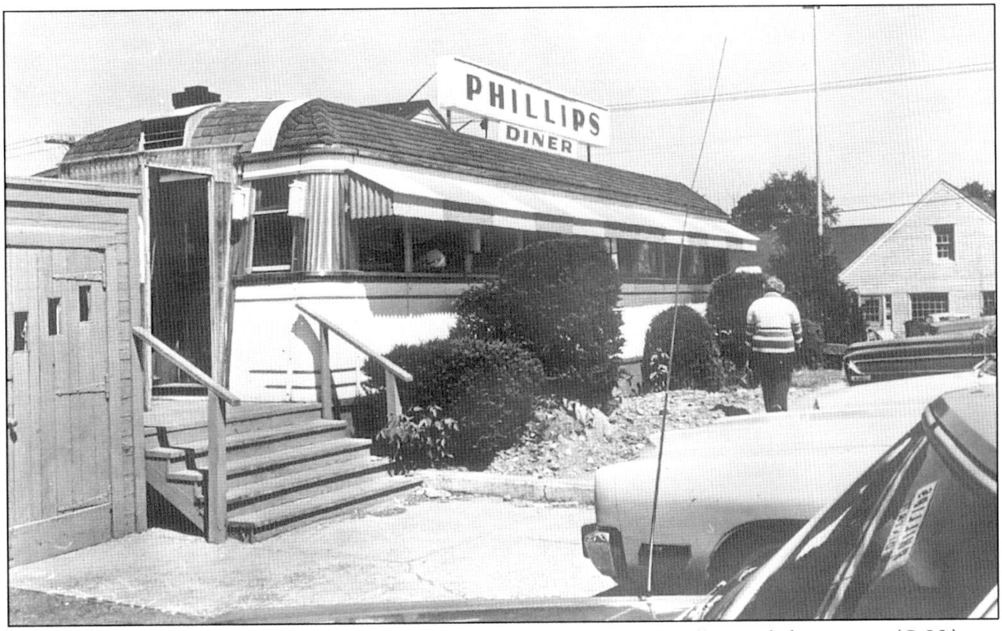

The original Phillips Diner was housed in this classic Art Deco all-metal dining car.(C-H.)

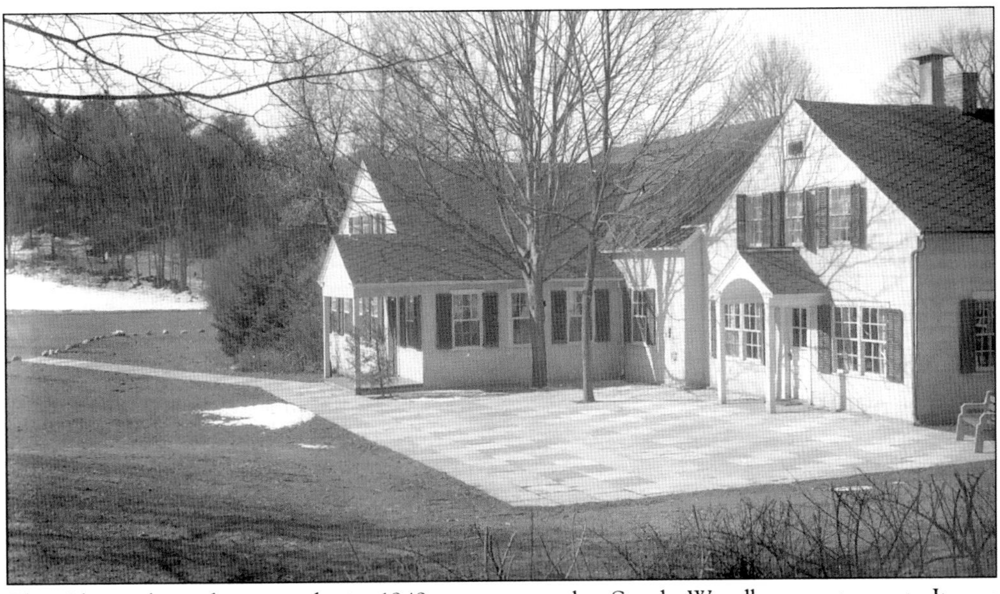

The Chanticleer, shown early in 1949, was a popular South Woodbury restaurant. It was destroyed by fire in 1960. (C-H.)

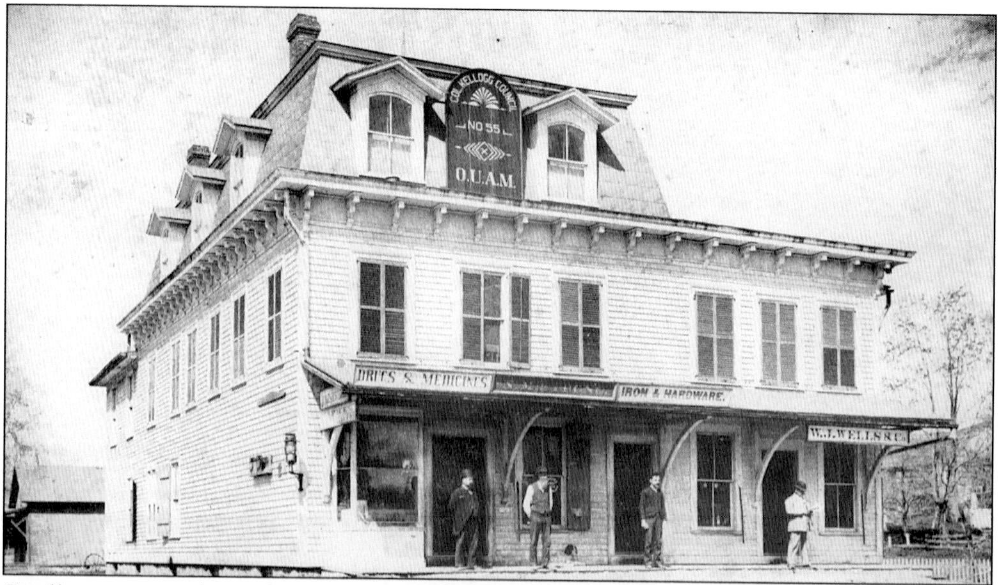

Small in size, numbers of employees, and net worth, these local businesses were nevertheless big to the needs of Woodbury area residents. This structure was built *c.* 1876 and housed the N.M. Strong store and W.J. Wells & Company. The photograph dates from *c.* 1884. (C-H.)

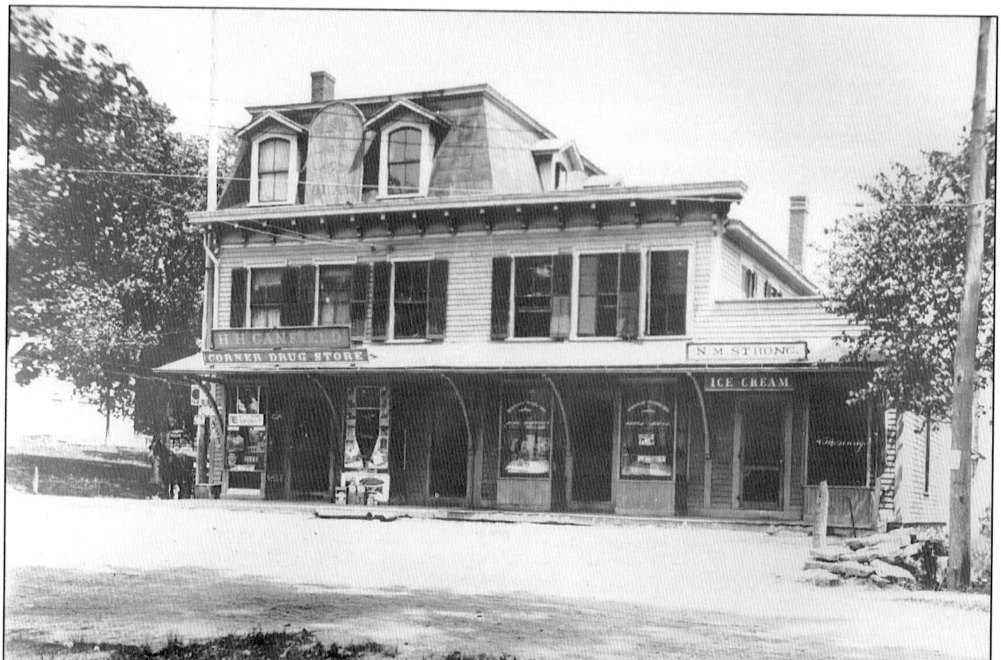

Canfield Corner, with the H.H. Canfield Corner Drug Store, became a commercial center for the north end of Woodbury. This photograph was taken *c.* 1910. Some 40 years later, John F. Schwartz was the drugstore's registered pharmacist. (C-H.)

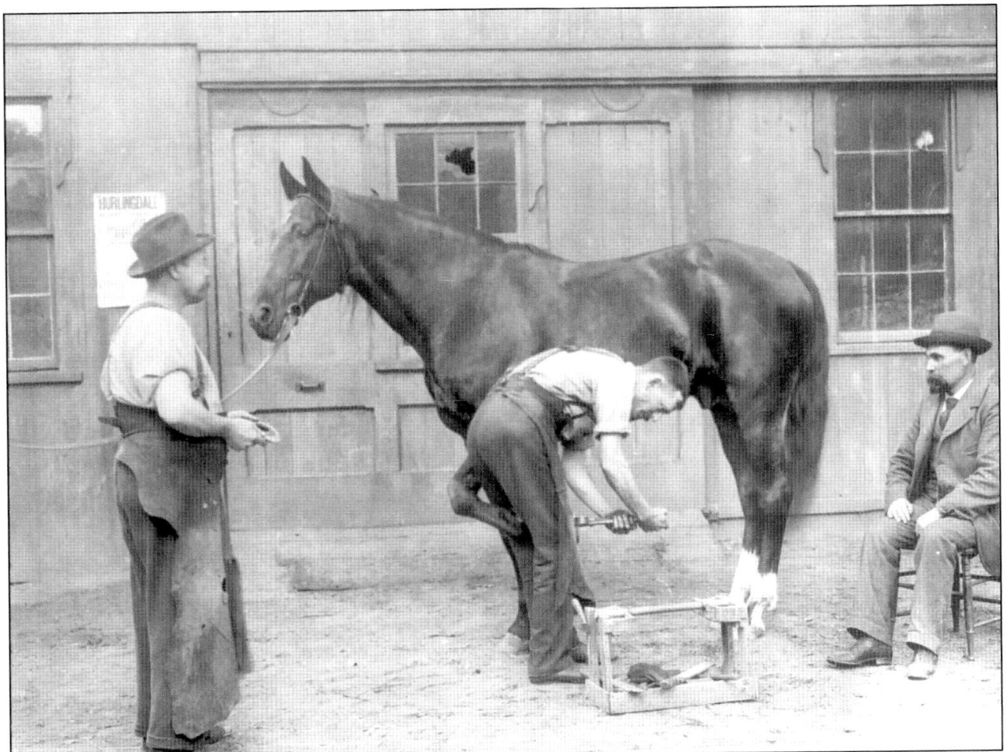

Blacksmiths were an essential part of every small town. In this c. 1905 scene, Fred Parkins shoes an amiable Woodbury horse. With him are Joe Hall, left, and Joe Atchison, seated. (C-H.)

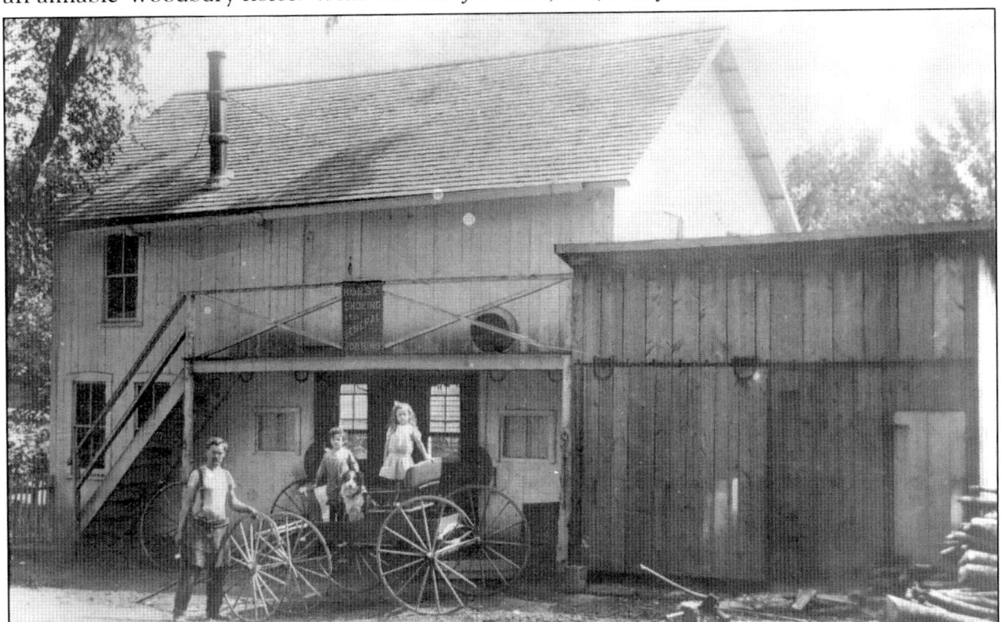

Stuart Hall's blacksmith shop was a Southbury feature for many years. The business advertises "Horse Shoeing and General Jobbing." Holding a carriage wheel is Stuart Hall, with two children and a dog in the carriage. Note the ax in the chopping block at the right. (C-H.)

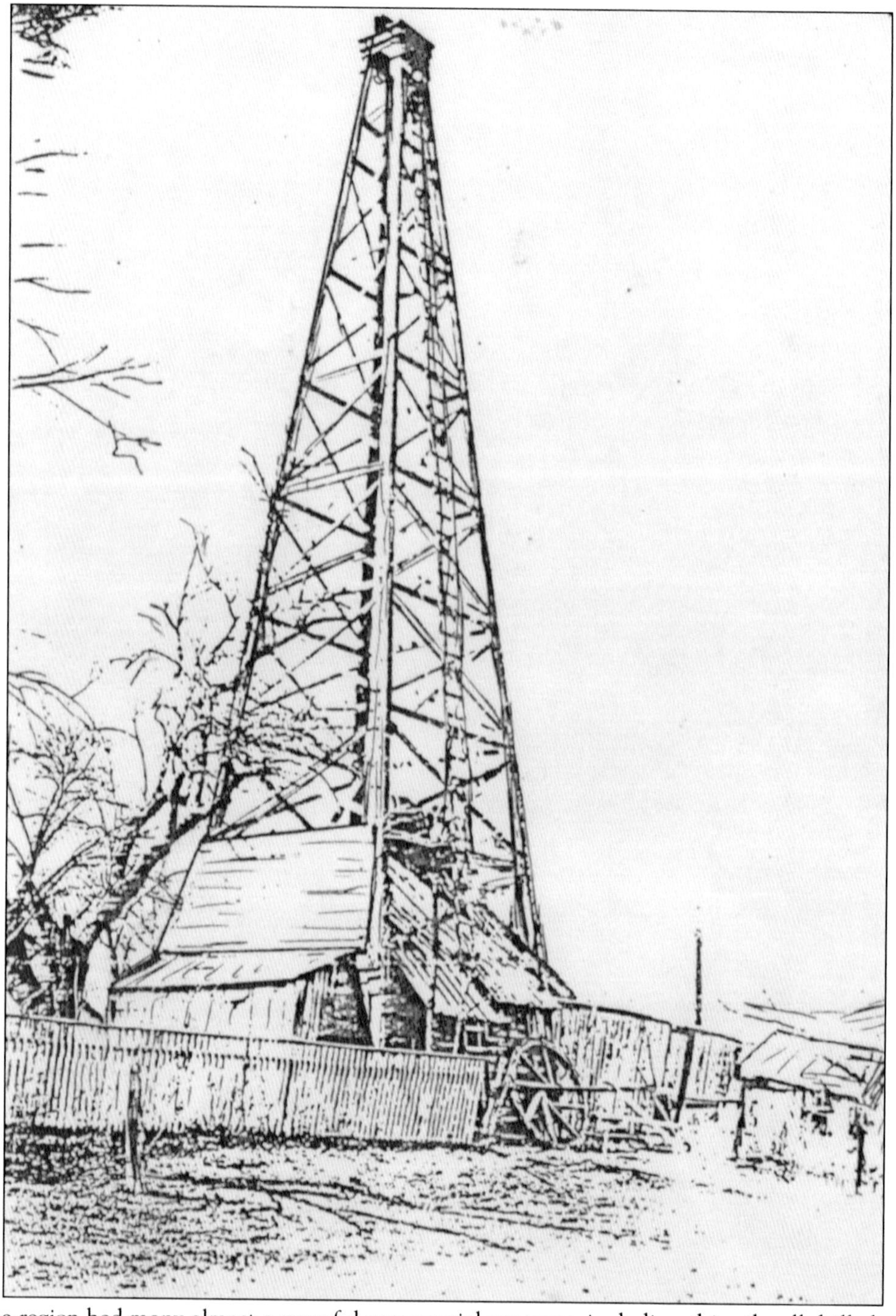

The region had many almost successful commercial ventures, including this oil well drilled on Poverty Road in 1888–99. The closest it came to being a gusher was at 1,400 feet, where Triassic shales yielded a tantalizing sample of "black gold," giving Southbury temporary boomtown status. However, at 1,535 feet drilling ended, with only a virtual "dry hole" to show for the investors' financial efforts. Some 60 years later, in the early Cold War period, a local mine for beryllium ore—vital for high-tech metallurgy—had some success. (SHS.)

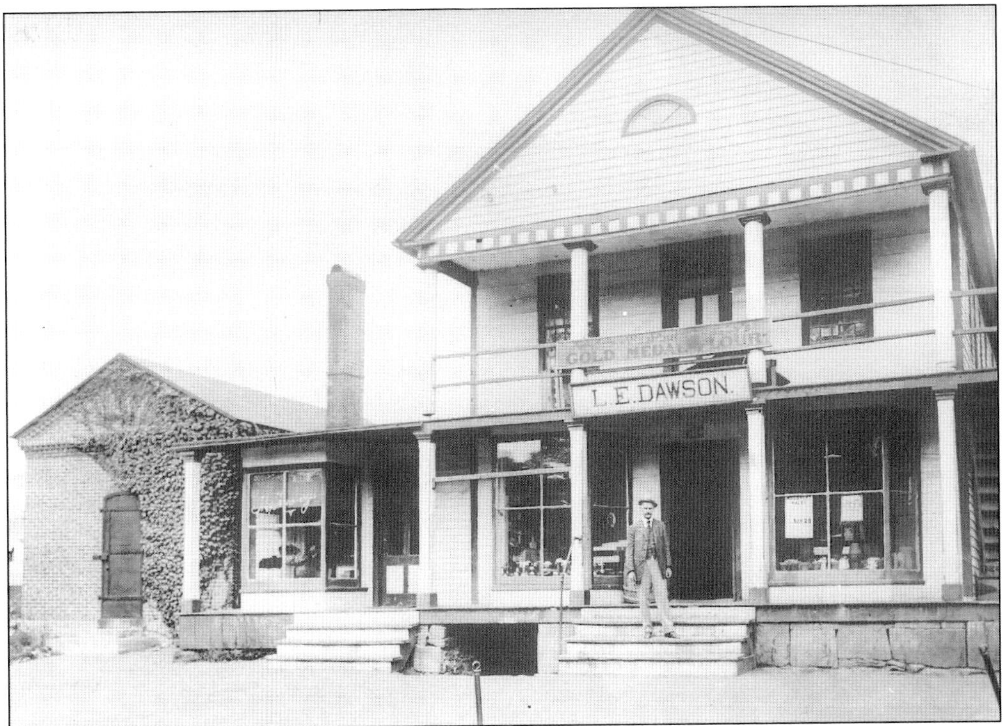

Across from Canfield Corner were the L.E. Dawson store and the Town Records Vault, left. The store advertises Gold Medal Flour and, in the window, a sign announces that Woodbury Races will be held on September 28. The photograph dates from c. 1900. (C-H.)

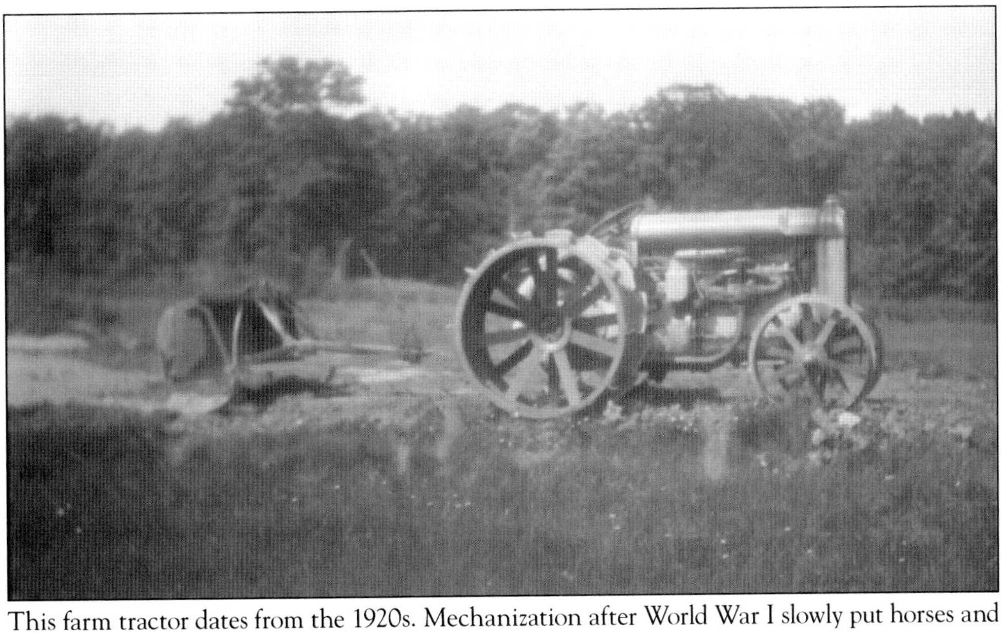

This farm tractor dates from the 1920s. Mechanization after World War I slowly put horses and oxen out to pasture. (CRH.)

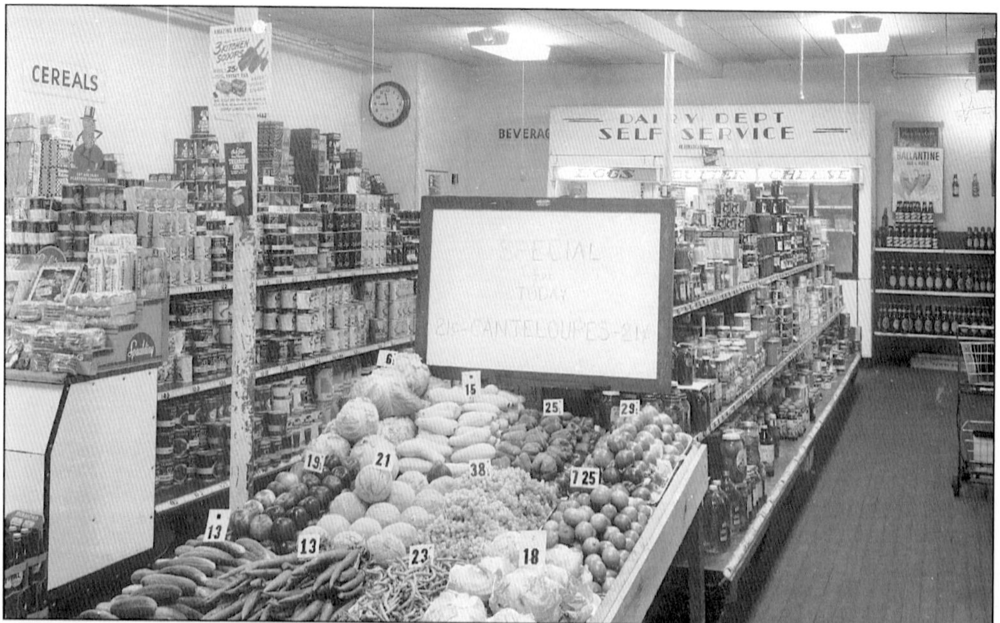

Cantaloupes are on special for 21¢ at George Tomey's market in Woodbury in the 1940s. A head of lettuce costs 18¢, and a cucumber 13¢. Per-pound prices for other produce include apples 19¢, green peppers 25¢, grapes 38¢, string beans 23¢, and cabbage 6¢. (C-H.)

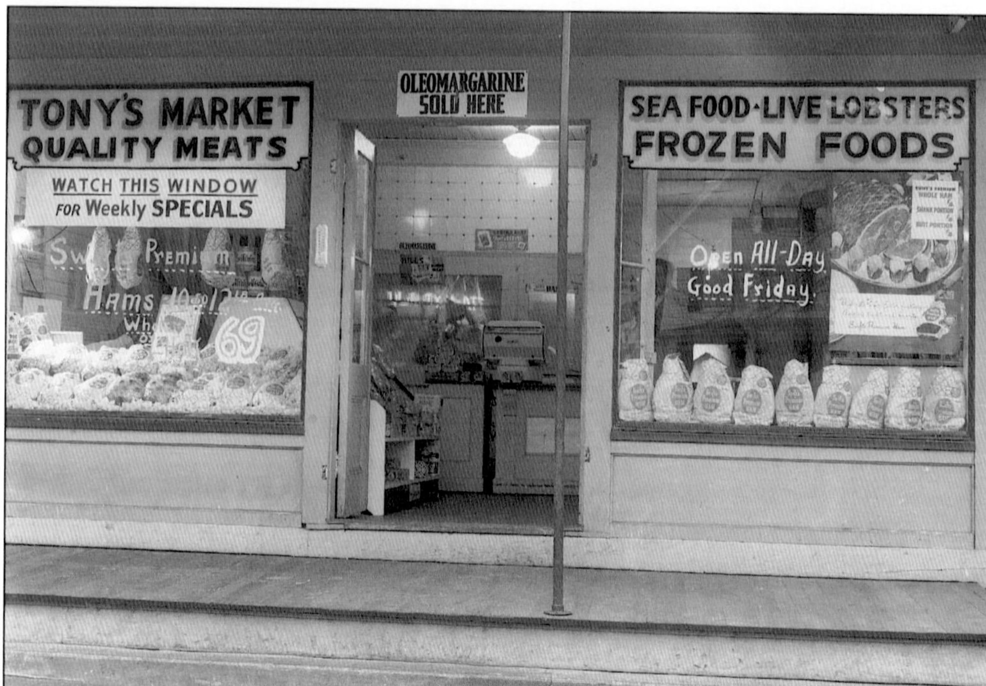

Tony's Market is well stocked with Easter hams, other quality meats, and oleomargarine. The store announces that it is going to be open all day on Good Friday. (C-H.)

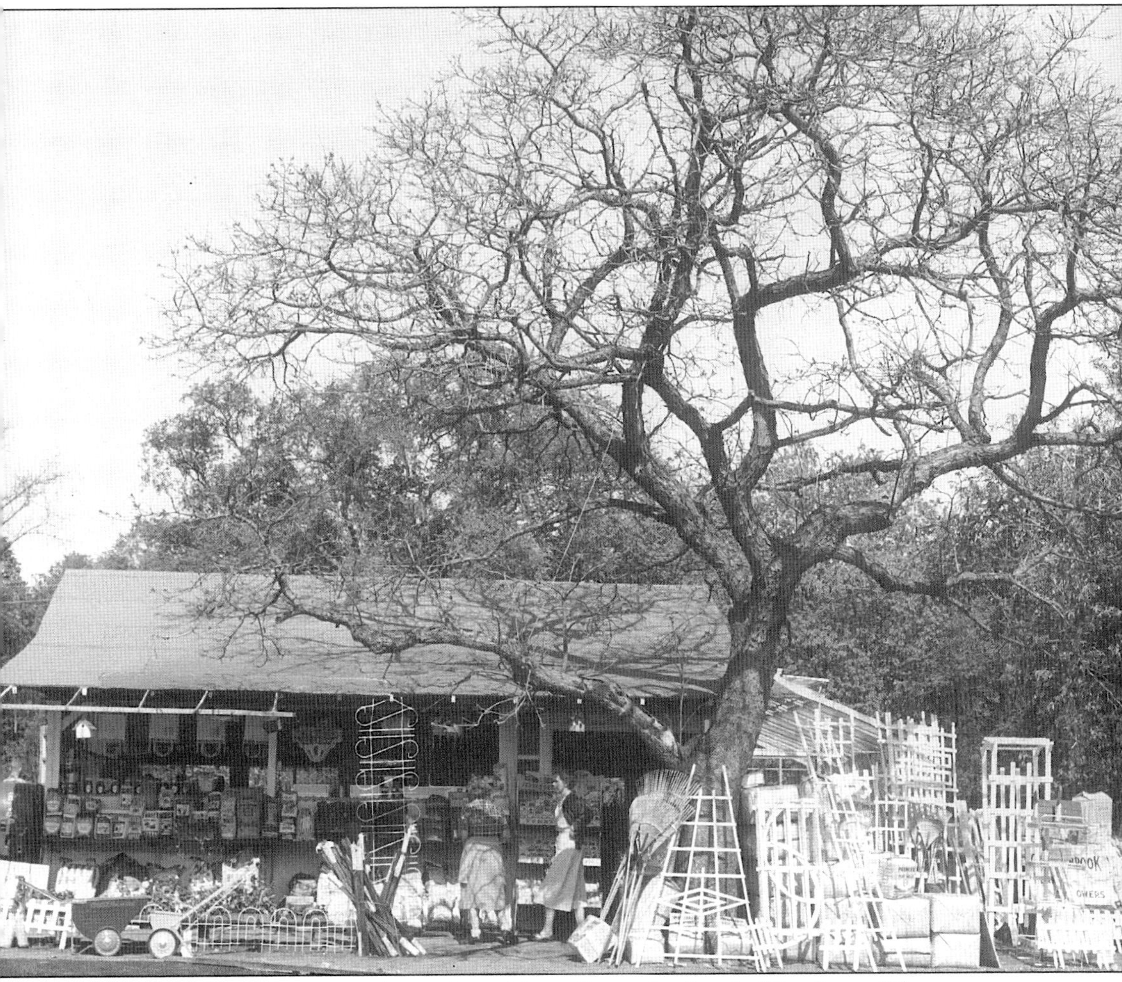

Abbott's Garden Center was located on Main Street in South Woodbury. The owner was nurseryman H. Ellsworth Abbott. (ETT.)

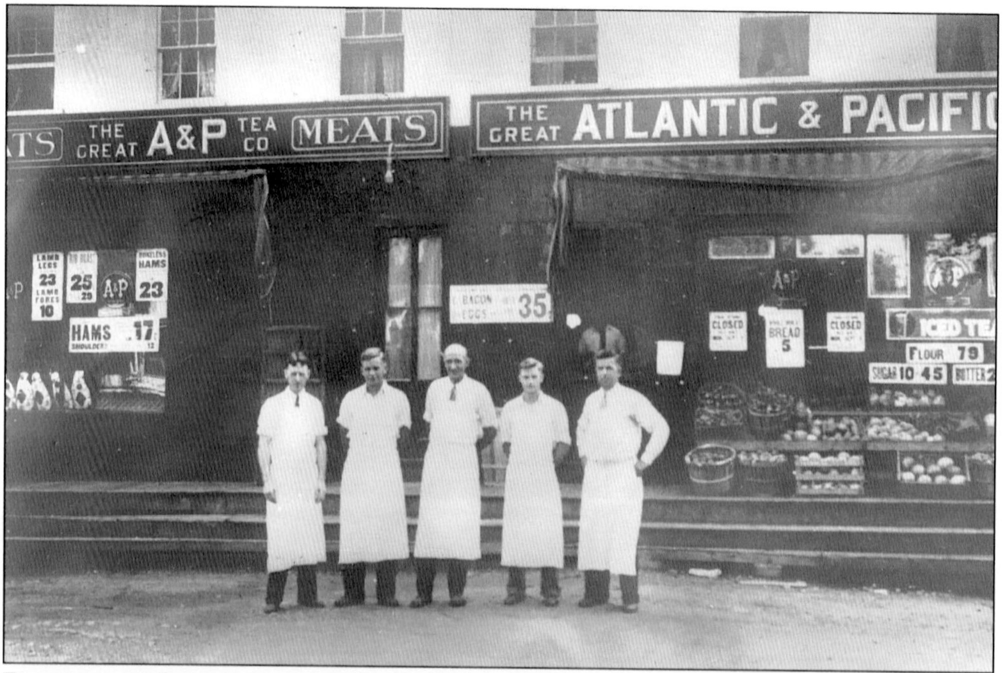

Five apron-clad men pose outside the Great Atlantic & Pacific Tea Company. They are identified, from left to right, as Jim McConville, James Tomlinson, Lester Cable, Kenneth Allen, and Paddy Atwood. In 1934, Tomlinson was grocery manager and Henry Donovan was meat manager. During World War II, the A & P became Carl & Walt's tire shop. (C-H.)

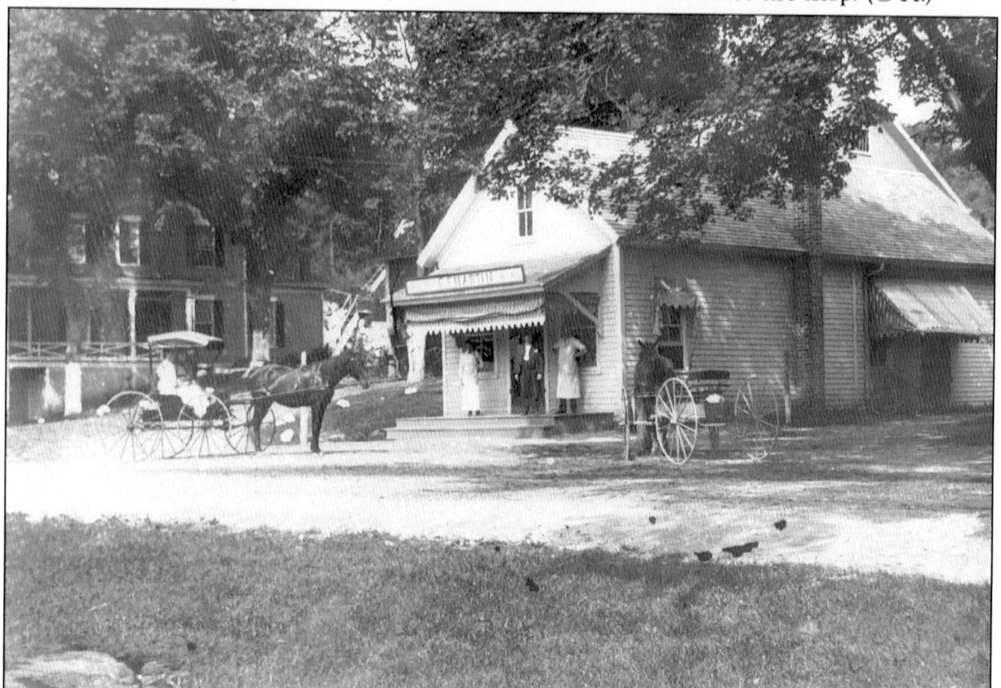

This c. 1904 photograph shows the C.F. Martin market on the right and the Central Hotel on the left. (C-H.)

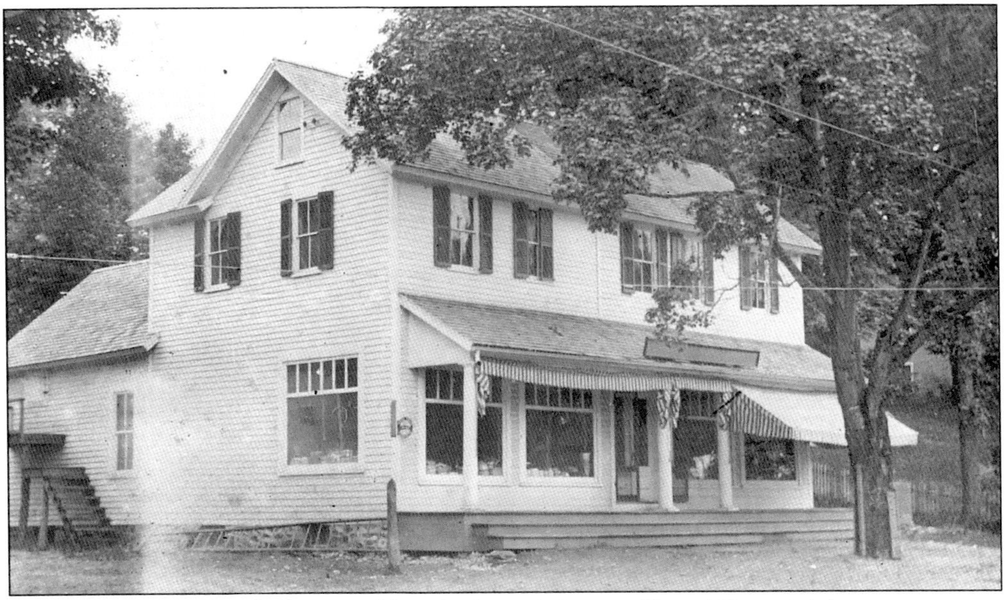

Martin's store eventually became Mrs. Anderson's Louise Shop. The mini-department store was very popular with women of the area, as it carried a variety of dressmaking fabrics and notions. (C-H.)

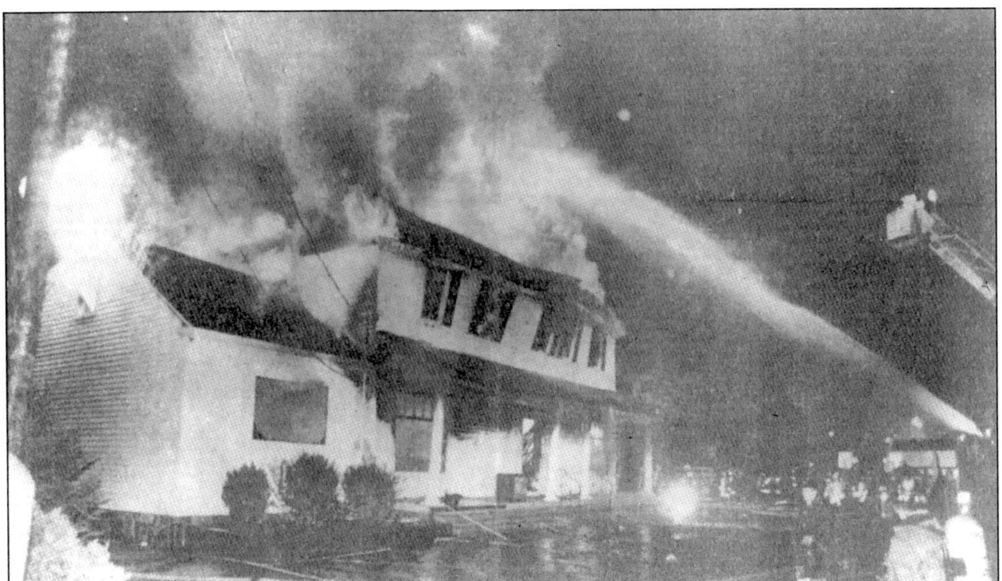

In November 1980, a spectacular nighttime fire, attributed to arson, completely destroyed the building. (C-H.)

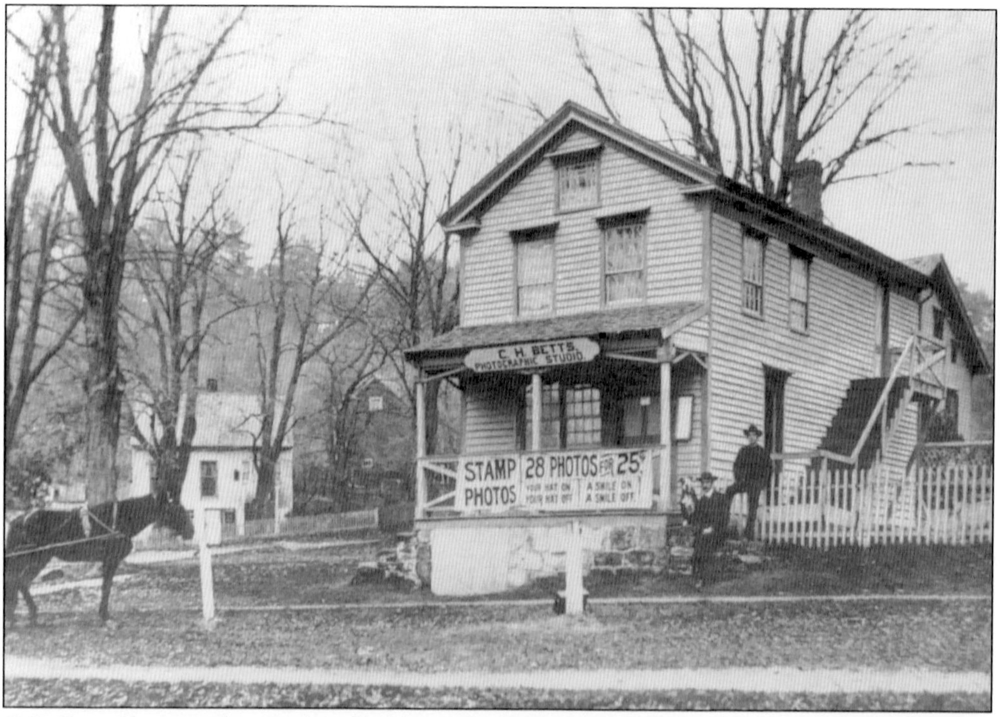

C.H. Betts Photographic Studio offered popular stamp-sized photographs. The studio advertised 28 photographs for 25¢, with the following choices: "Your hat on, your hat off" and "A smile on, a smile off." (C-H.)

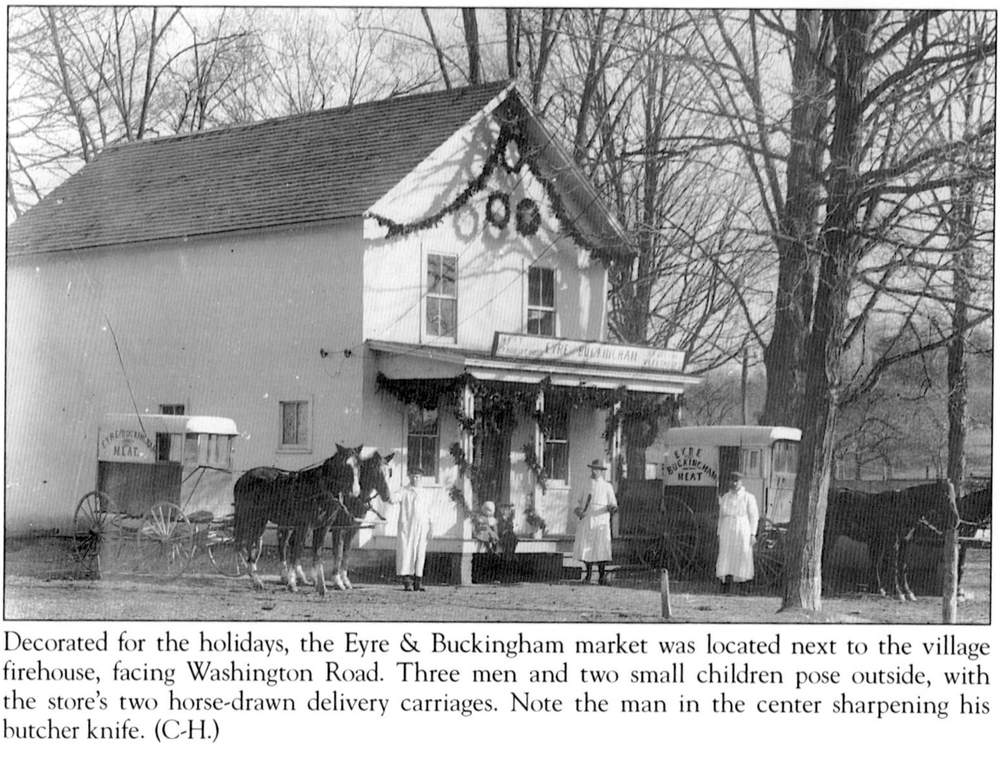

Decorated for the holidays, the Eyre & Buckingham market was located next to the village firehouse, facing Washington Road. Three men and two small children pose outside, with the store's two horse-drawn delivery carriages. Note the man in the center sharpening his butcher knife. (C-H.)

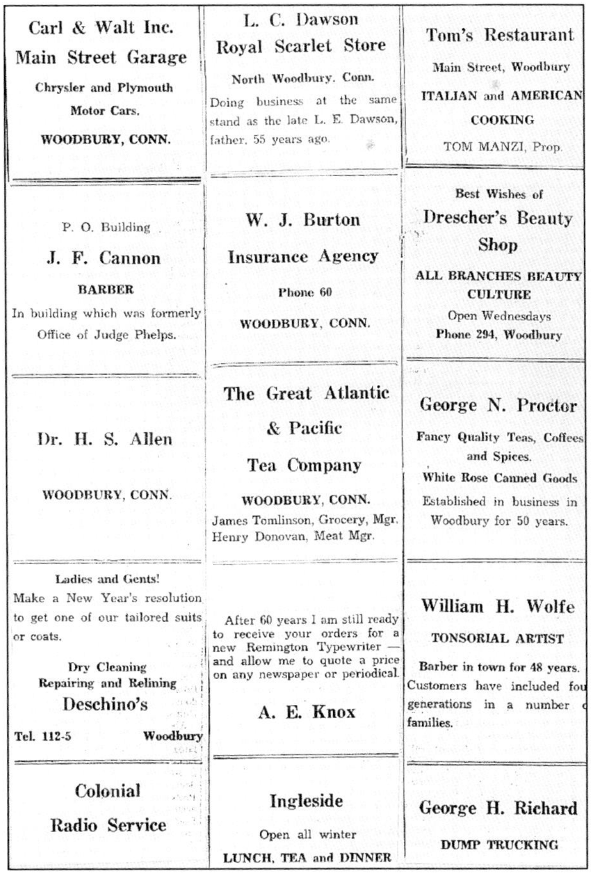

Carl & Walt Inc.
Main Street Garage
Chrysler and Plymouth Motor Cars.
WOODBURY, CONN.

L. C. Dawson
Royal Scarlet Store
North Woodbury, Conn.
Doing business at the same stand as the late L. E. Dawson, father, 55 years ago.

Tom's Restaurant
Main Street, Woodbury
ITALIAN and AMERICAN COOKING
TOM MANZI, Prop.

P. O. Building
J. F. Cannon
BARBER
In building which was formerly Office of Judge Phelps.

W. J. Burton
Insurance Agency
Phone 60
WOODBURY, CONN.

Best Wishes of
Drescher's Beauty Shop
ALL BRANCHES BEAUTY CULTURE
Open Wednesdays
Phone 294, Woodbury

Dr. H. S. Allen
WOODBURY, CONN.

The Great Atlantic & Pacific Tea Company
WOODBURY, CONN.
James Tomlinson, Grocery, Mgr.
Henry Donovan, Meat Mgr.

George N. Proctor
Fancy Quality Teas, Coffees and Spices.
White Rose Canned Goods
Established in business in Woodbury for 50 years.

Ladies and Gents!
Make a New Year's resolution to get one of our tailored suits or coats.
Dry Cleaning
Repairing and Relining
Deschino's
Tel. 112-5 Woodbury

After 60 years I am still ready to receive your orders for a new Remington Typewriter — and allow me to quote a price on any newspaper or periodical.
A. E. Knox

William H. Wolfe
TONSORIAL ARTIST
Barber in town for 48 years.
Customers have included fou generations in a number families.

Colonial
Radio Service

Ingleside
Open all winter
LUNCH, TEA and DINNER

George H. Richard
DUMP TRUCKING

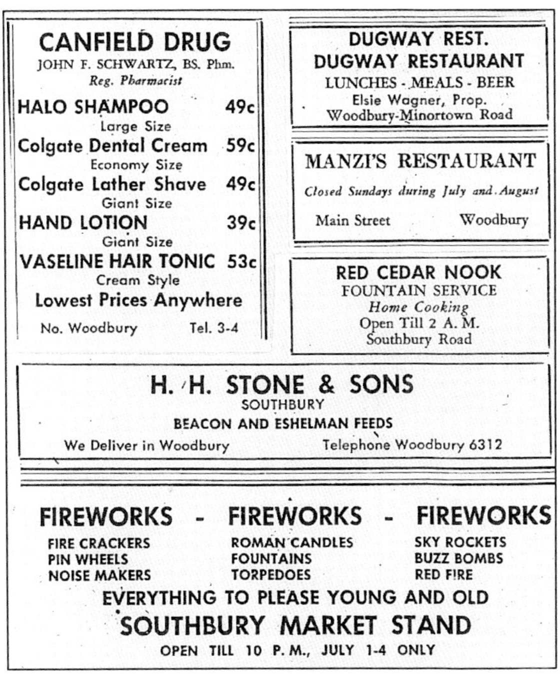

CANFIELD DRUG
JOHN F. SCHWARTZ, BS. Phm.
Reg. Pharmacist
HALO SHAMPOO 49c
Large Size
Colgate Dental Cream 59c
Economy Size
Colgate Lather Shave 49c
Giant Size
HAND LOTION 39c
Giant Size
VASELINE HAIR TONIC 53c
Cream Style
Lowest Prices Anywhere
No. Woodbury Tel. 3-4

DUGWAY REST.
DUGWAY RESTAURANT
LUNCHES - MEALS - BEER
Elsie Wagner, Prop.
Woodbury-Minortown Road

MANZI'S RESTAURANT
Closed Sundays during July and August
Main Street Woodbury

RED CEDAR NOOK
FOUNTAIN SERVICE
Home Cooking
Open Till 2 A. M.
Southbury Road

H. H. STONE & SONS
SOUTHBURY
BEACON AND ESHELMAN FEEDS
We Deliver in Woodbury Telephone Woodbury 6312

FIREWORKS - FIREWORKS - FIREWORKS
FIRE CRACKERS ROMAN CANDLES SKY ROCKETS
PIN WHEELS FOUNTAINS BUZZ BOMBS
NOISE MAKERS TORPEDOES RED FIRE
EVERYTHING TO PLEASE YOUNG AND OLD
SOUTHBURY MARKET STAND
OPEN TILL 10 P. M., JULY 1-4 ONLY

These advertisements were placed in the *Woodbury News*. Those above are from a 1934 edition, and those on the left from 1950. Note the ad for fireworks at the lower left. Before a statewide ban went into effect c. 1952, many rural volunteer fire departments added to their income by setting up stands and selling fireworks a few days before the Fourth of July. (ETT.)

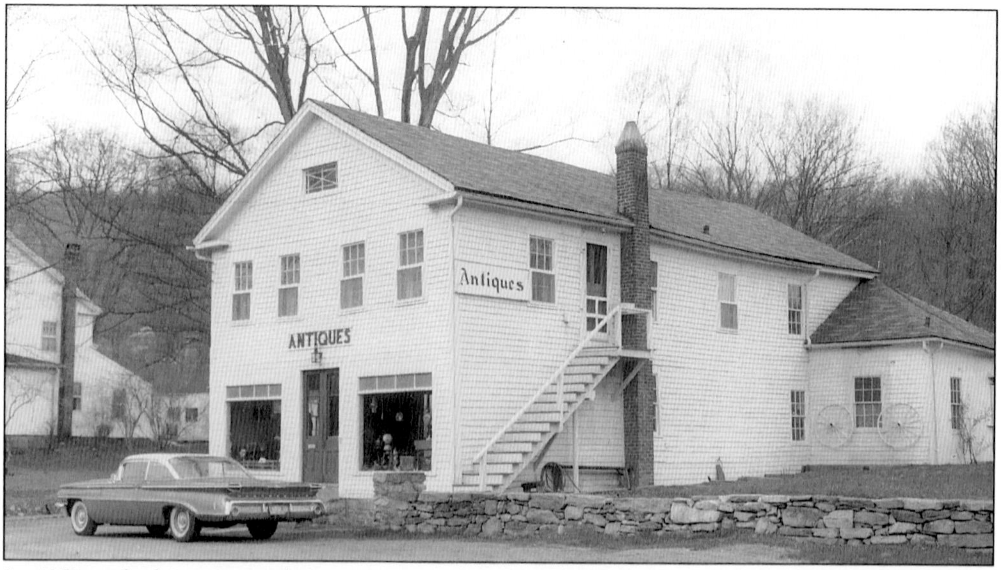

In 1959, only four antique businesses were listed in Woodbury, with two in Southbury. After Interstate 84 was built, tourists and antique seekers arrived in the area, looking for leisurely rides through interesting and relatively uncrowded secondary roads. As a result, the antique business expanded considerably along old Route 6 through Southbury and Woodbury. Over the years, the route became known as "Antique Alley." This photograph shows Henry Read's Antique Shop in 1963. (C-H.)

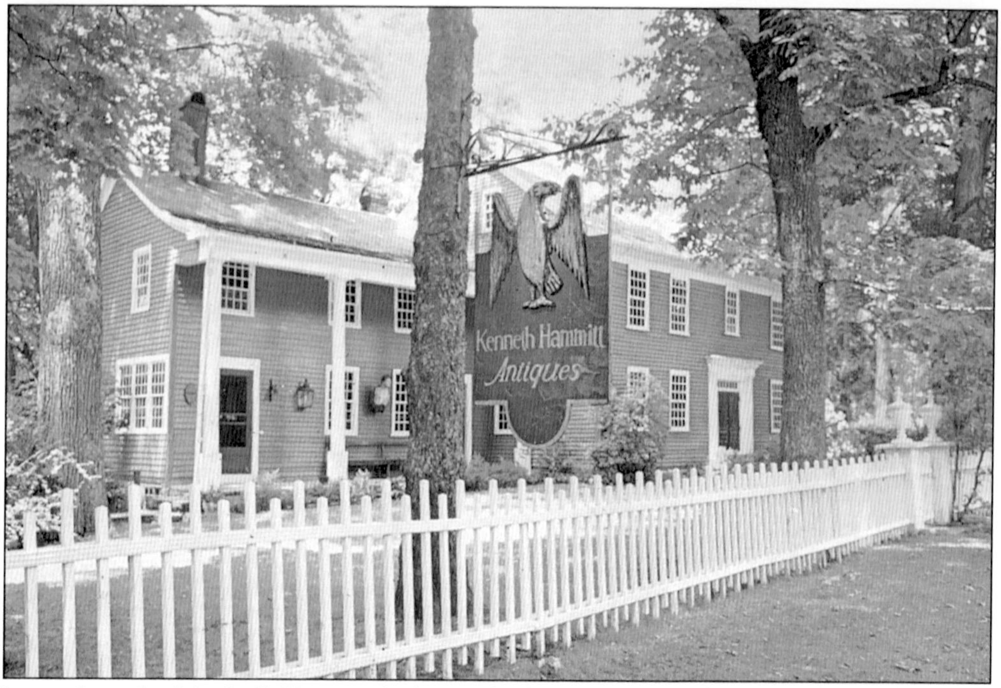

Located in the Marshall House, which was built in 1668 and enlarged in 1753, Kenneth Hammitt Antiques was one of the pioneers in the business. Along with this shop on Main Street in Woodbury, other local antique dealers included Moira Wallace, Wayne Pratt, and the Mill House. (TL.)

Three

At School

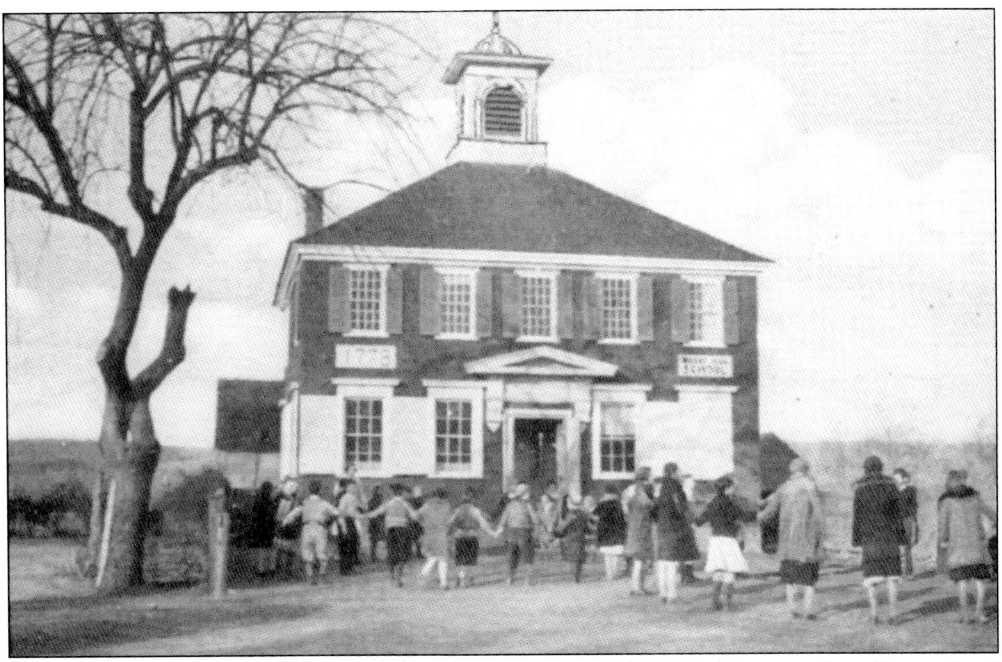

In 1960—and perhaps even today—Southbury had the honor of having the oldest school building in continuous use. The building is the Bullet Hill School, named for the spent lead bullets salvaged from a Revolutionary War training site. It was built of brick c. 1762 and became part of a group of one-room schoolhouses covering such widely spaced districts as Hull's Hill, Kettletown, Pierce Hollow, Pootatuck, Purchase, South Britain, Southford, White Oak, Strongtown, and Wapping. (FWC.)

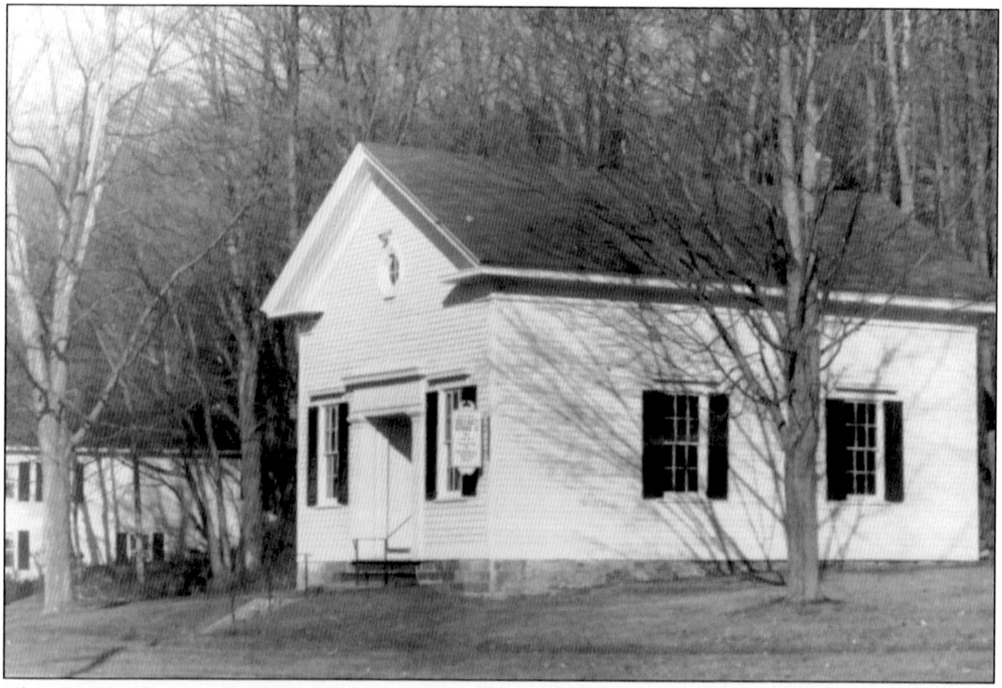

The South Center District School 2 has been restored by the Old Woodbury Historical Society. (C-H.)

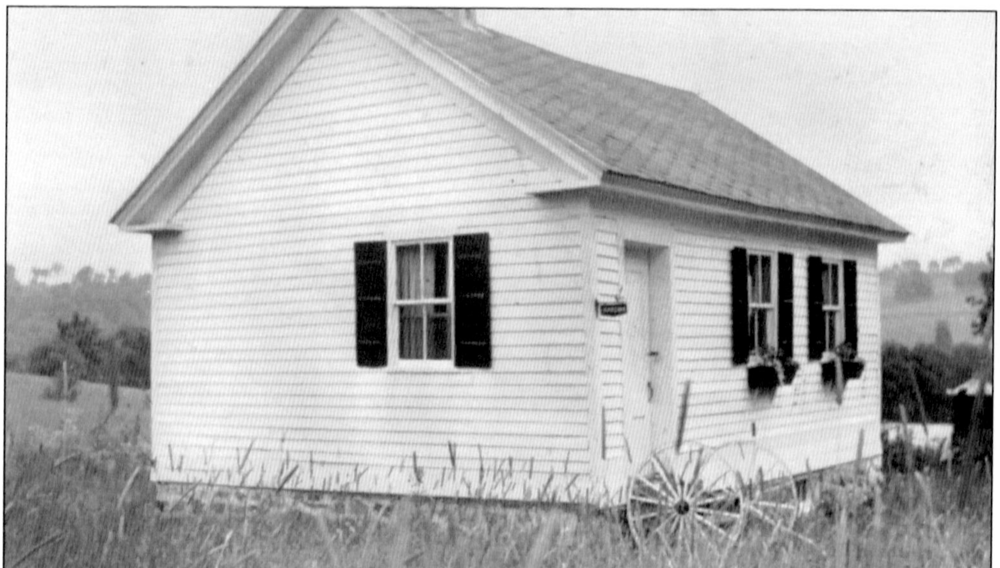

Woodbury's *Directory of 1896* listed the following named school districts: Middle Quarter, South Center, North Center, Puckshire, Minortown, Nonnewaug, Flanders, Weekeepeemee, Hazel Plain, West Side, Transylvania, Quassapaug, Cat Swamp, and Hotchkissville. There were two private schools and the Parker Academy, educating nearly 400 students. Bethlehem had nine districts, all consolidated in 1923. Roxbury also had nine, with its central Booth Free School established in 1890. This photograph shows the Weekeepeemee District School *c.* the 1950s. (C-H.)

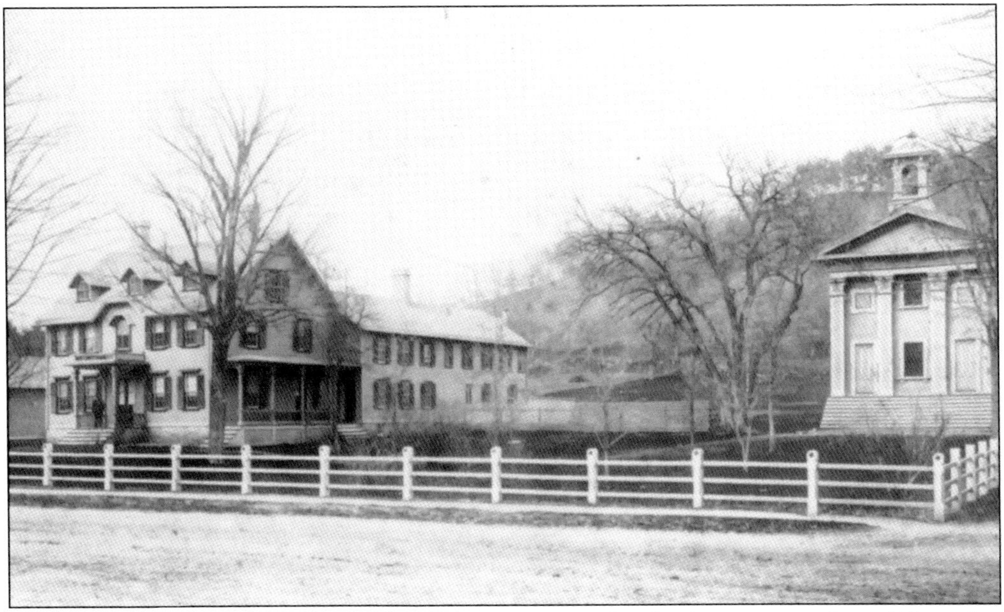

Parker Academy was one of Woodbury's two private schools. It was erected in 1851 as "an institution of higher education," a form of prototype high school. This photograph shows the academy on the right and Phelps House on the left. (C-H.)

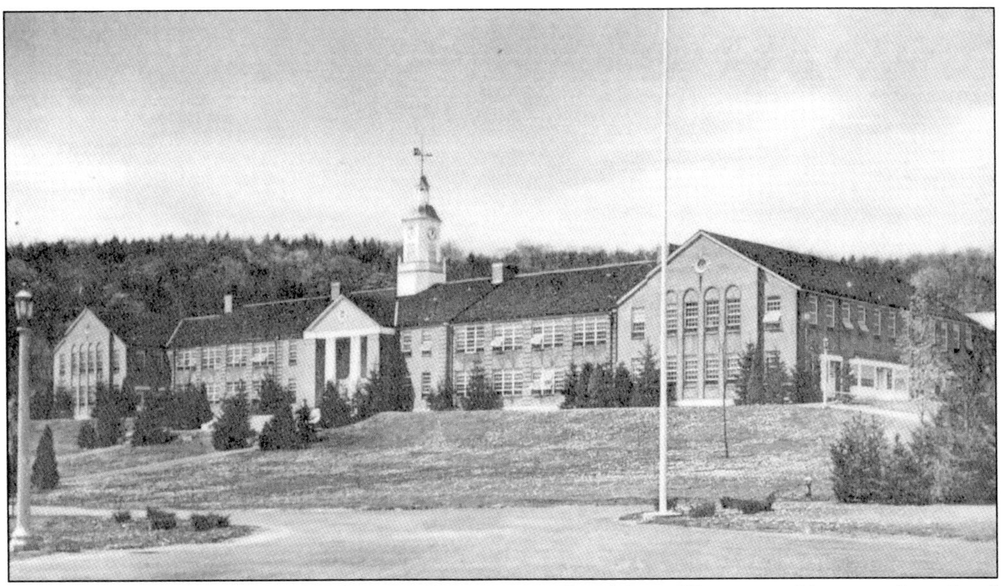

The Southbury Training School opened in 1940 in Southbury. For some 60 years, the school provided employment to Woodbury area residents. In 1964, there were 764 full-time staff and just over 2,000 residents. (FWC.)

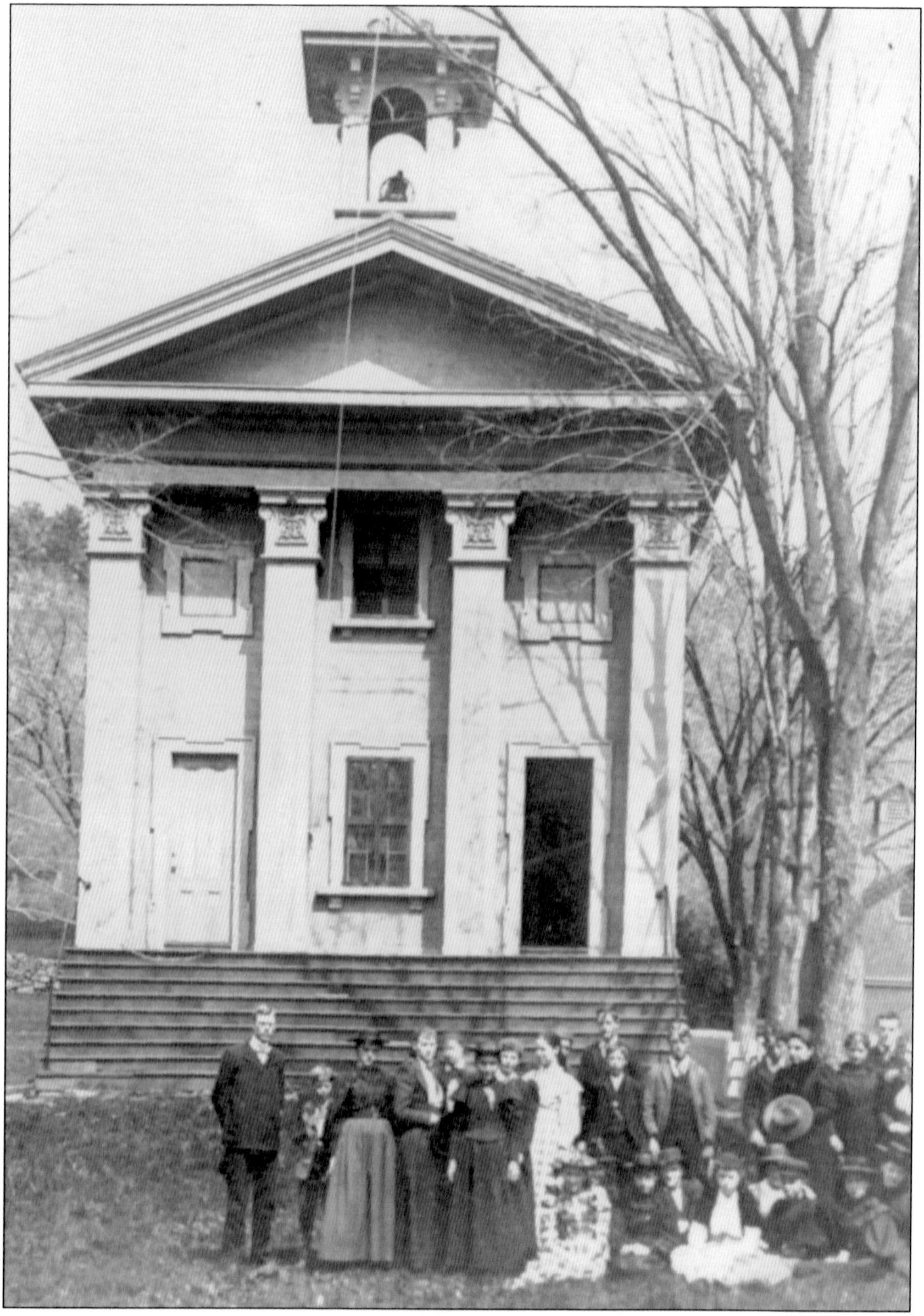

The Parker Academy had both an extensive educational and architectural effect on Woodbury. In 1902, the building became the town library; today, it serves as the Gallery Annex to the new library built in the 1960s. In this photograph, students and others pose in front of Parker Academy. (C-H.)

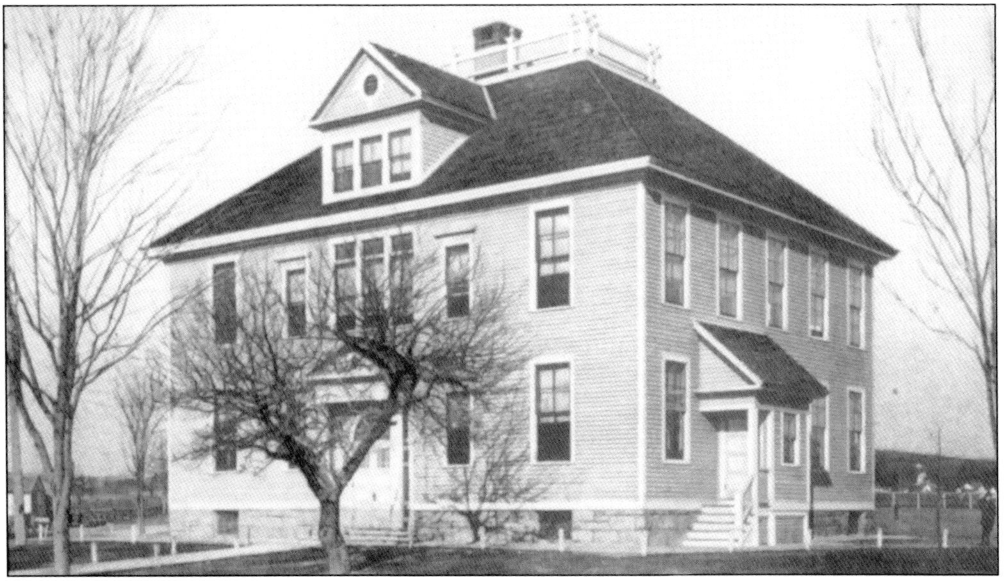

This early view shows the Mitchell School in Woodbury. Opened in 1898 with 200 students, Mitchell was intended as a central high school. Graduating students in the Class of 1947 were Josette Marie Boglio, Marian Elsie Cooper, Lorraine Spaulding Cristofano, Carl Wilfred Drescher Jr., John Paul Ford, Rosemary Catherine Ford, Nina Tamara Grecenko, Samuel Green Jr., Gladys Ruth Hicock, Virginia Lee Hicock, Hazel Ada Holleran, Arthur Nelson Johnson Jr., Dorothy Jane Lawrence, Alice Mae Mackowitz, Donald William Terrell, and George Henry Underhill Jr. Supt. Carroll F. Johnson presented them with diplomas during commencement exercises, held on Wednesday, June 11, 1947, at the Woodbury Town Hall. As the one-room district schools were closed, more elementary pupils needed space. After several additions of classrooms proved insufficient, Woodbury High School moved into its own building in 1954. (C-H.)

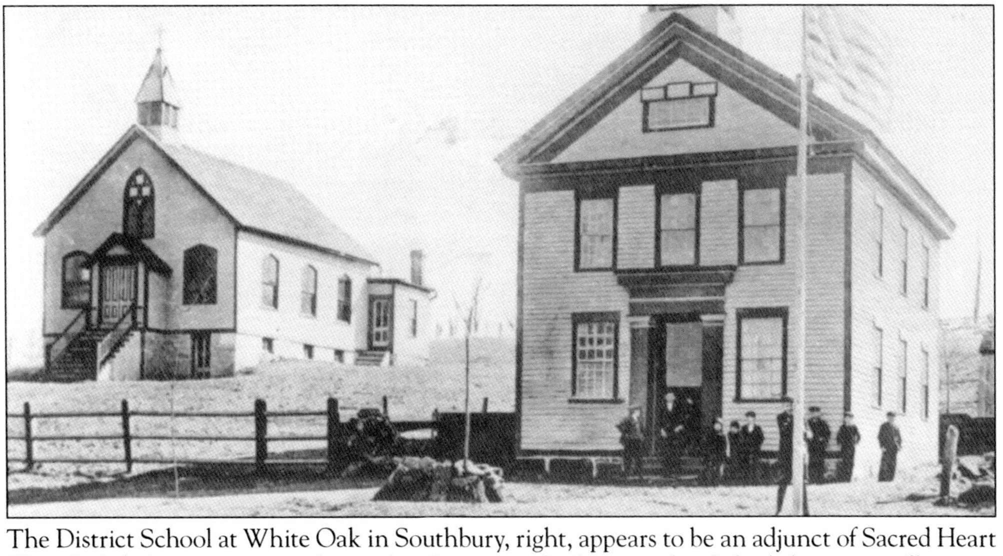

The District School at White Oak in Southbury, right, appears to be an adjunct of Sacred Heart Church, left, but it was entirely secular. Private and religious schools had their own adherents. Washington was noted for two independent academies: the Gunnery, established in 1850, and Rumsey Hall, 1949—both now providing coeducation. (SHS.)

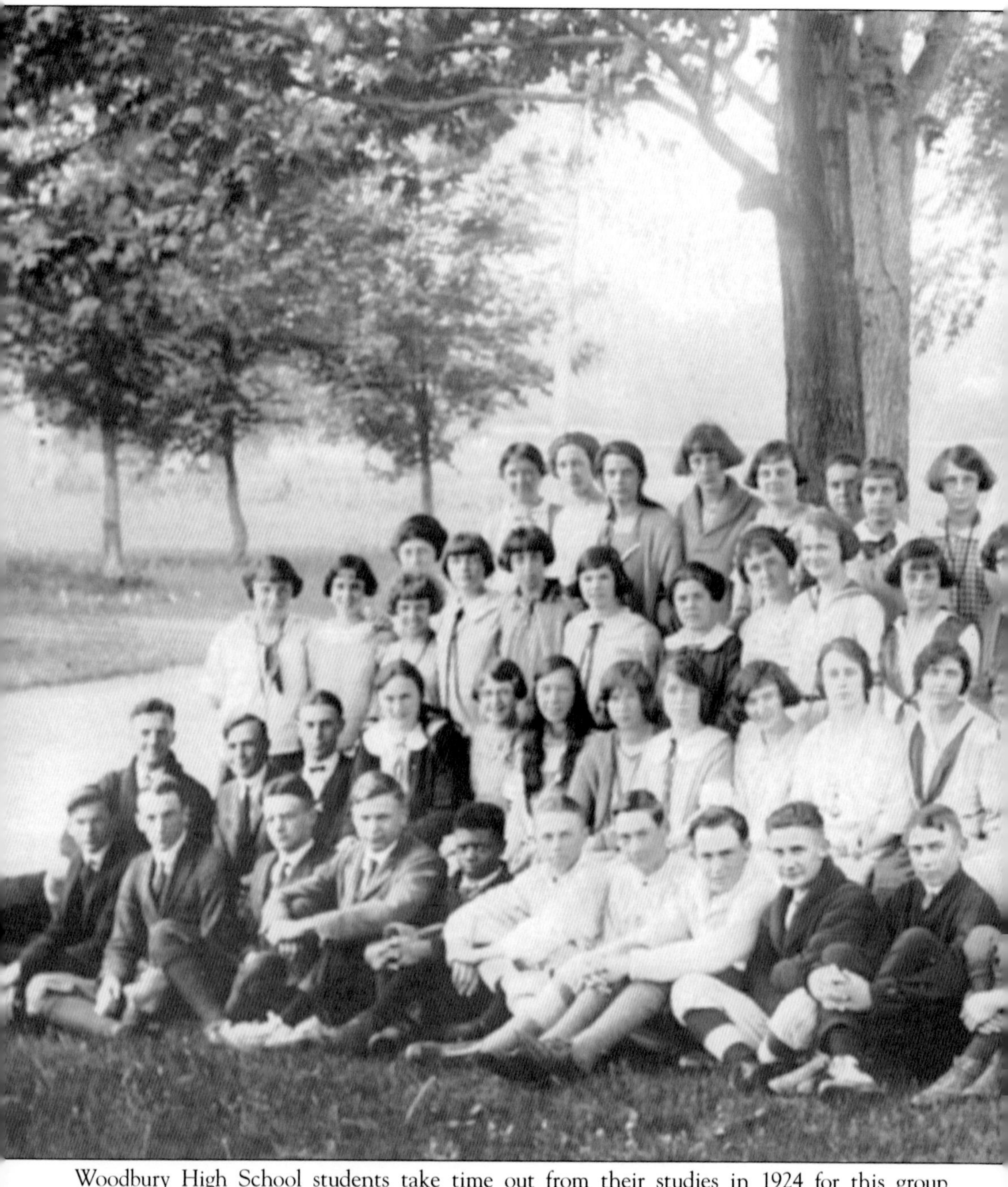

Woodbury High School students take time out from their studies in 1924 for this group photograph. They are identified, from left to right, as follows: (first row) Clive Somerset, Rufus Munsell, Curtis Hitchcock, James Tomlinson, Elliott Balcolm, Gordon Schulk, Sherwood Allen, Gutherie Luf, Walter Dixon, Ralph Parmelee, Merwin Mitchell, Gerald Hall, Charles Adams, Frank Reichenbach, Karl Warner, Herbert Fowler, and Wilfred Leslie; (second row) Minor Cartwright, Stedman Hitchcock, Porter Hubbell, Myra Coad, Vella Leslie, Mildred Parkins, Evelyn Atwood, Shirley Dawson, Agnes Carroll, Elizabeth Fowler, Elizabeth Pogdenski, Peggy Bryant, Mary Bansefen, Priscilla Moore, Marjorie Frazier,

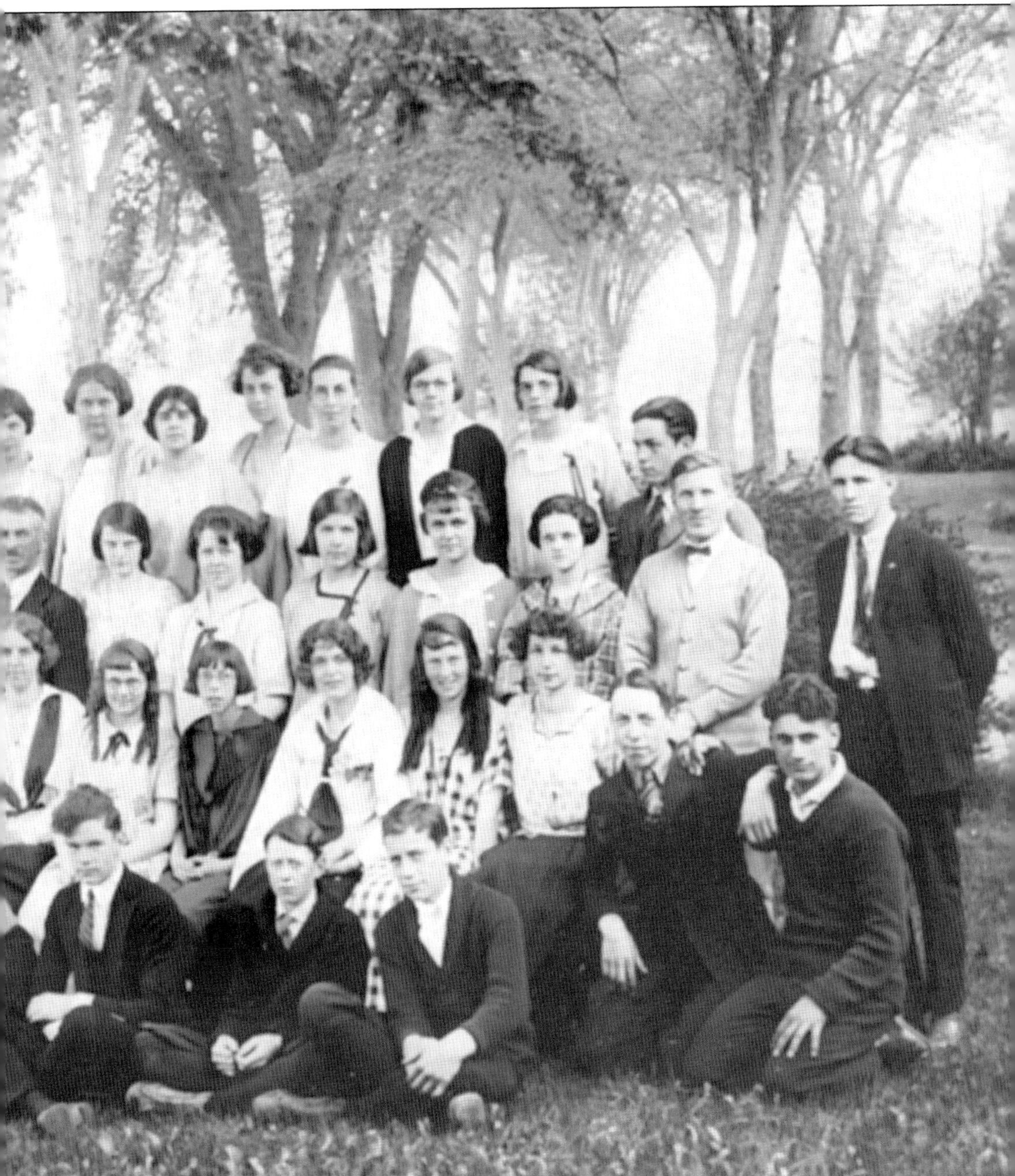

Esther Clark, Jeanie Adams, and Viola Stratman; (third row) Ethel Martus, Esther Stone, Jean Creighton, Miss Vaill (in back), unidentified, Eunice Creighton, Harriett Minor, Dorothy Murray, Rosamond Platt, Estella Cole, Julie Mitchell, Edith Brewer, Mr. Burnap, Pearle Capewell, Eva Roswell, Elberta Rich, Corrine Cartwright, Lena Smith, and Mr. Clark; (fourth row) Miss Clark, Josephine Perro, Dot Roswell, Lannie Nickok, Irene Swanson, Edla Judson, Evelyn Curtis, ? Leslie, Martha Reichenbach, Louise Judson, Evelyn Wheeler Strong, Marjorie Canfield, Marilla Randall, Harriett Isham, Emily Tomlinson, Jennette Hitchcock, and Robert Crane. (ETT.)

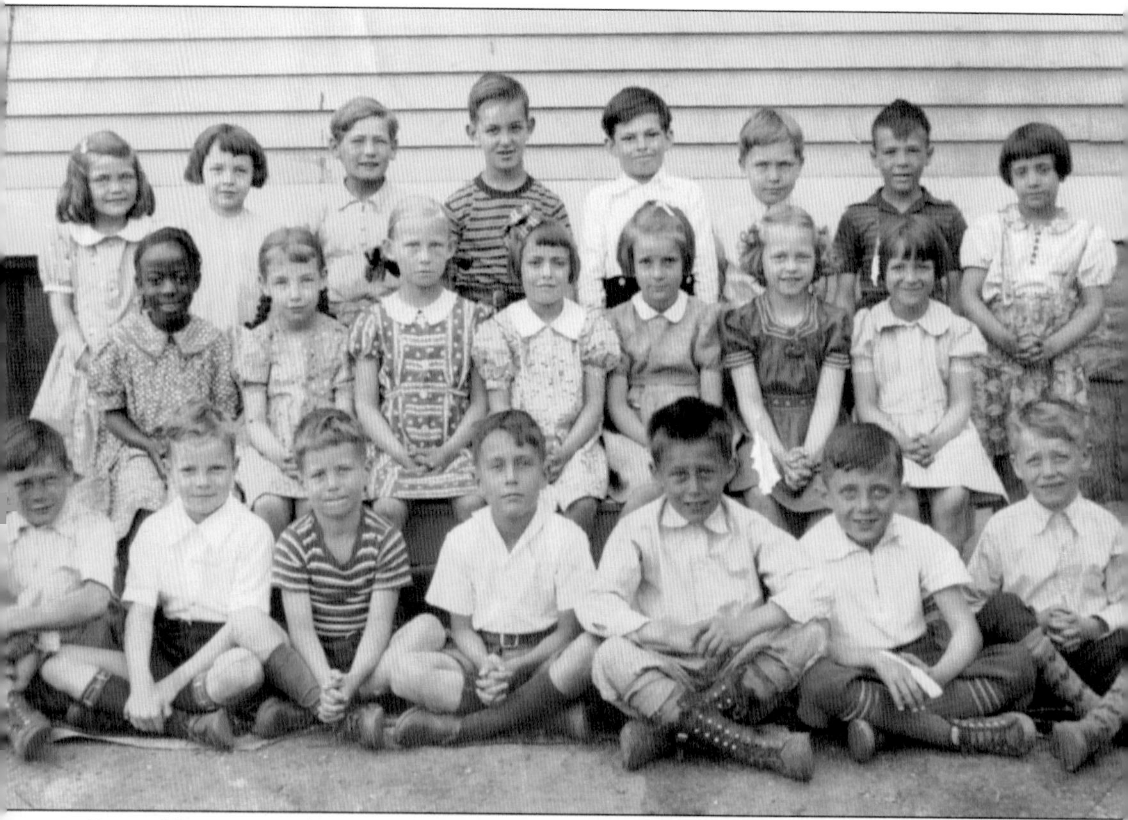

Dressed for summer, these Mitchell School second-graders look quite ready to end their 1937–38 school year with promotion into the third grade. The only students identified on the back of the photograph are those in the back row, who are, from left to right, Esther Terrell, Joyce Bice, Norman Cole, Anthony Calbrese, Edmond Lucas, Bobby Paden, George Fray, and Nainanie Clements. (ETT.)

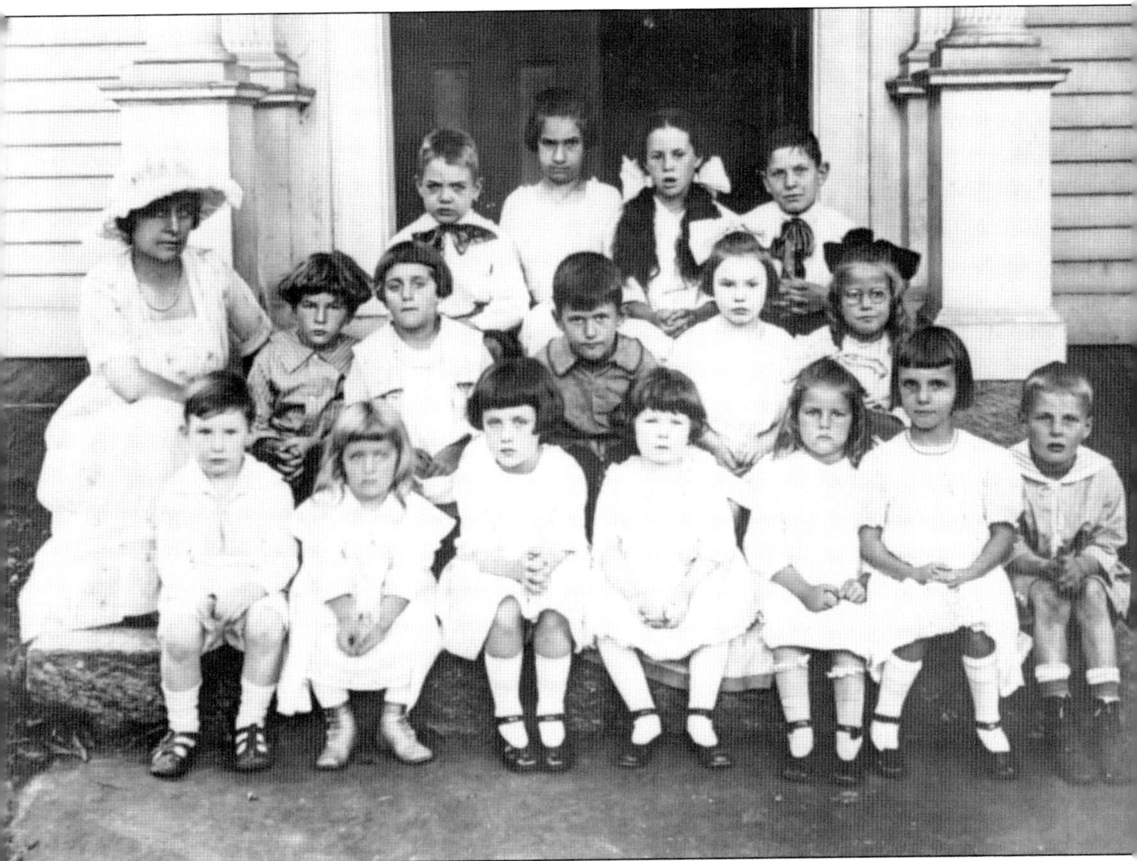

Church school was part of most children's education in 1916. Mrs. O'Neil, left, taught this group of youngsters, dressed in their Sunday best, probably around Easter. Some of the students in the back row do not look pleased to be posing. (C-H.)

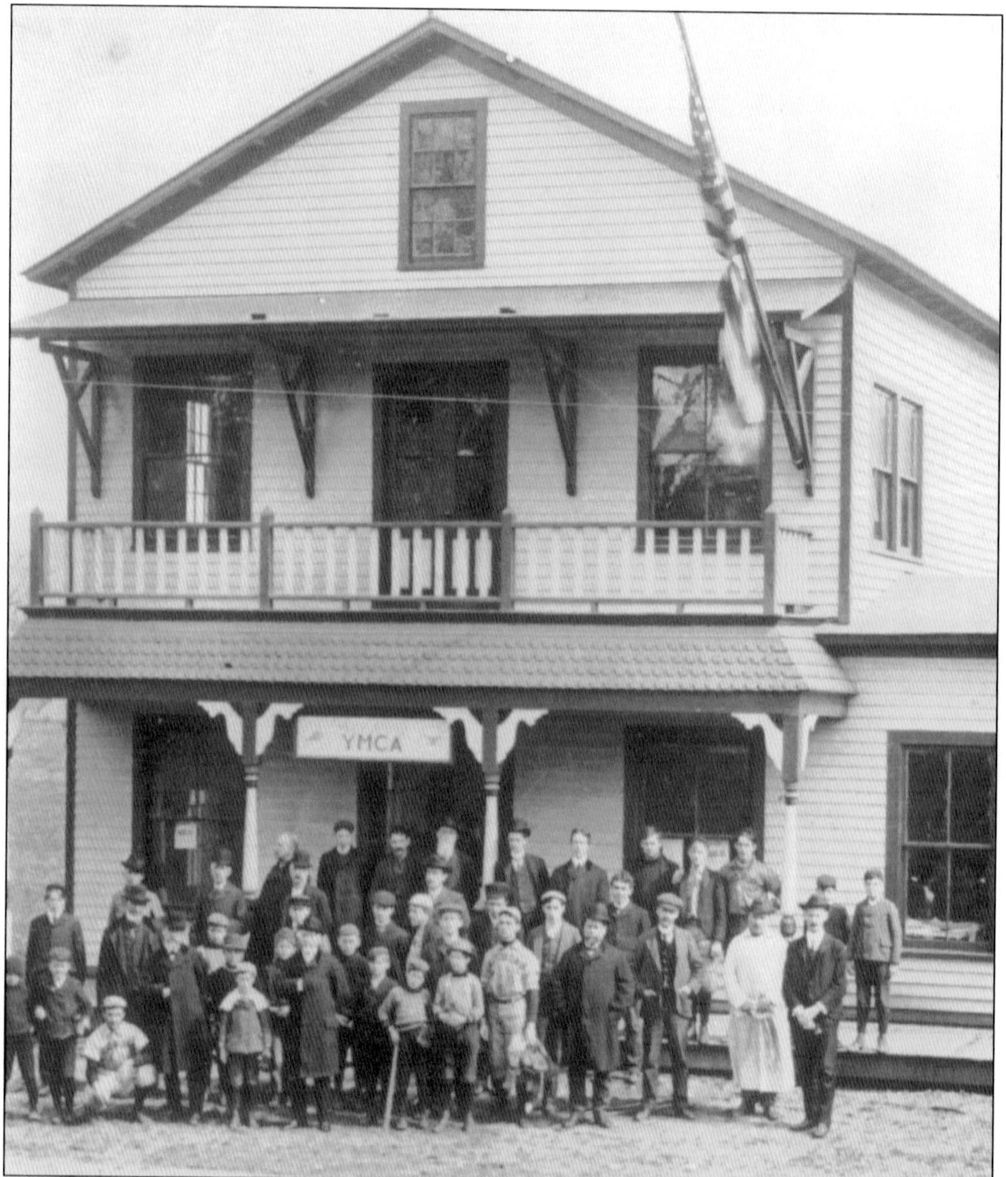

In 1906, a former silk factory was converted to a YMCA facility, offering both physical education and cultural programs to Woodbury's boys and young men. (C-H.)

Four

Bridges to the Past

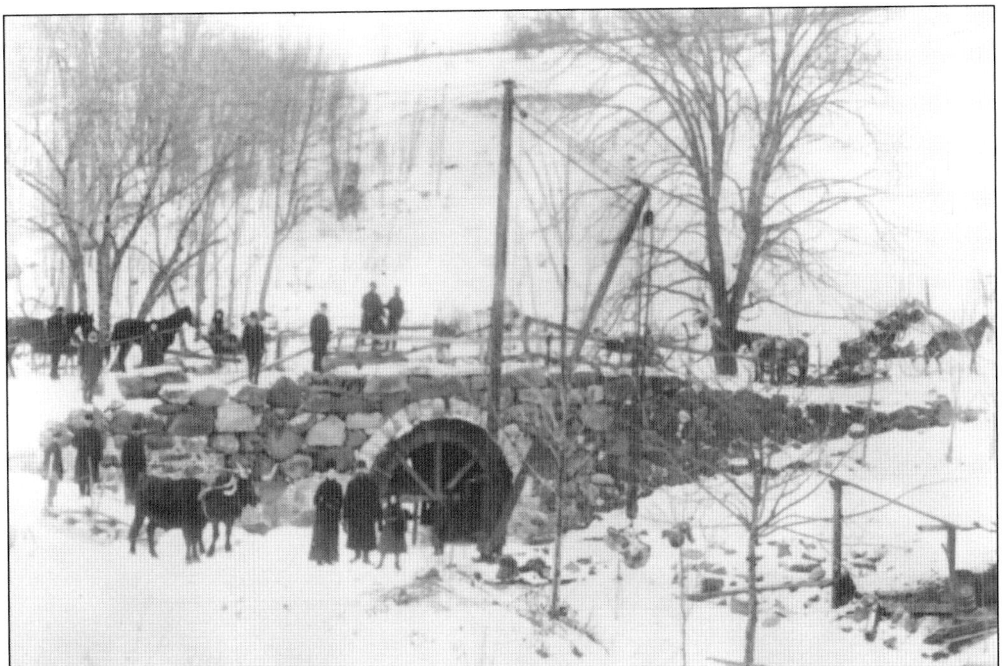

The Wood Creek Bridge in Bethlehem was built during the winter of 1886–87. Men and oxen labored throughout the winter to complete the strong masonry span, which is still in service today. This photograph was taken in January 1887. (BHS.)

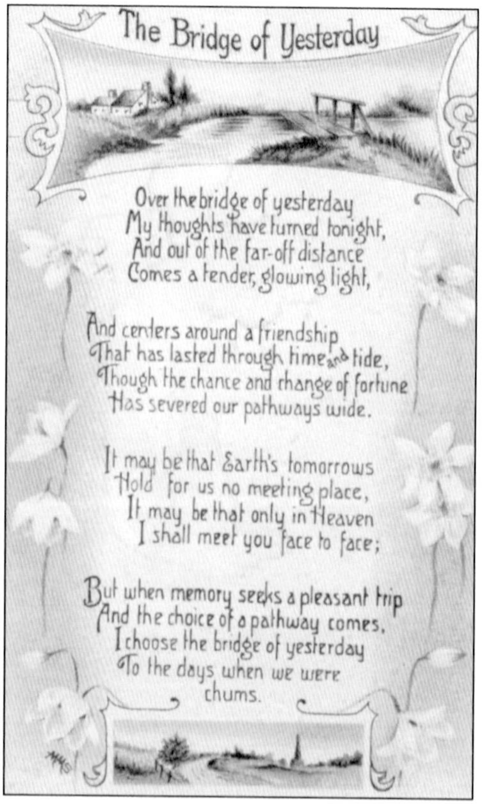

Although it lacked the tourist-exciting covered bridges of the upper Housatonic River, Greater Woodbury offered travelers a wide variety of spans, ranging from simple concrete-and-girder types to handcrafted masonry arches, elaborate highway bridges, and trolley and railroad structures. The early settlers, who drove cattle, sheep, and ox carts, depended upon shallow fords. As horse-powered wheeled traffic developed, rough wooden bridges were constructed, followed by increasingly sturdy structures of iron, steel, masonry, and reinforced and prestressed concrete. (FWC.)

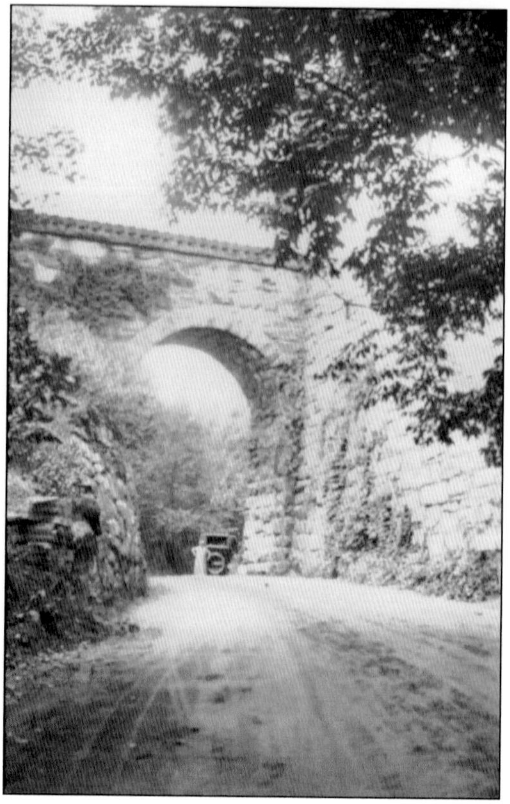

This handsome masonry arch was built near the Naugatuck-Middlebury line by the New York and New England Railroad *c.* 1880. It carried Waterbury traffic west to Southbury, Newtown, Hawleyville, and Danbury. In this September 1912 photograph, the bridge towers far above Mr. Harte and his touring car. With abandonment of the rail line *c.* 1940, the bridge became a traffic hazard. It stubbornly resisted its demolition down to the last massive block. (CRH.)

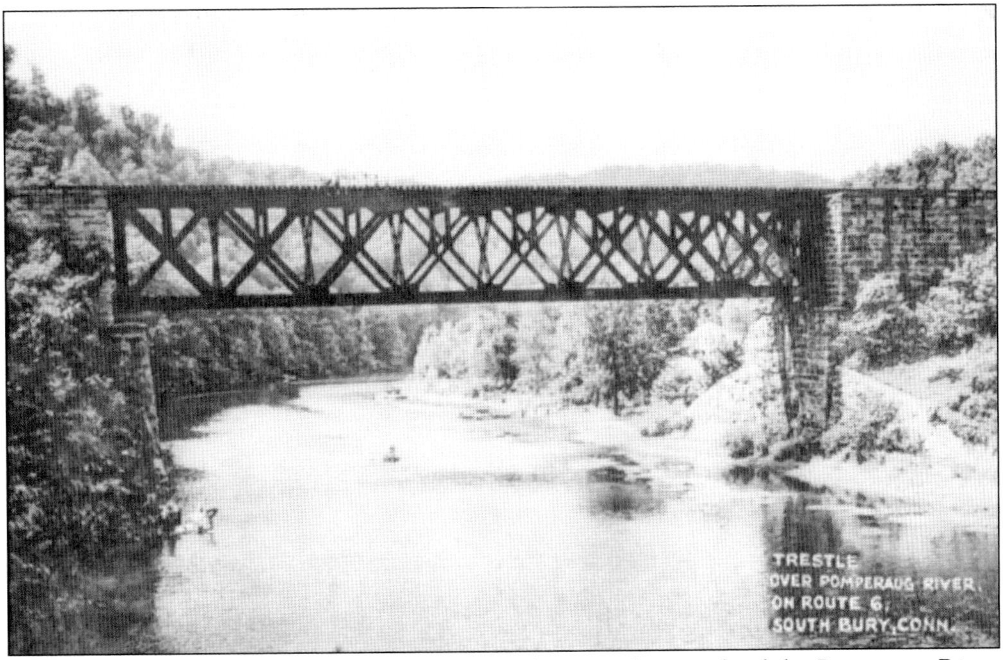

Leaving Southbury, trains crossed this girder bridge near the mouth of the Pomperaug River. Daring bathers once dove off its soaring deck and piers. (FWC.)

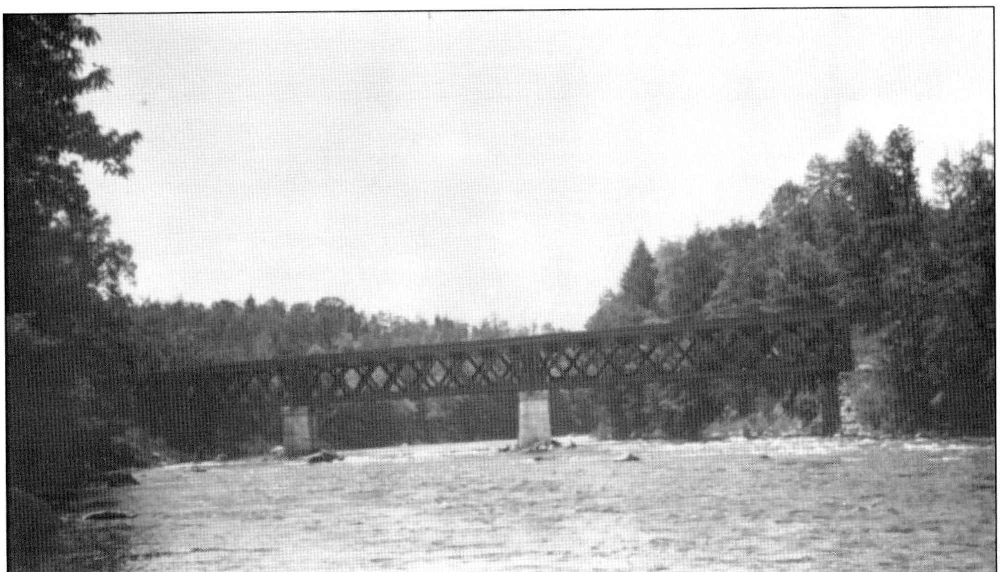

The long-vanished New Haven's Litchfield Division left Hawleyville, crossed the Housatonic River via the Shepaug railroad bridge, and headed up the Shepaug Valley to Roxbury. This photograph was taken on June 7, 1912. (CRH.)

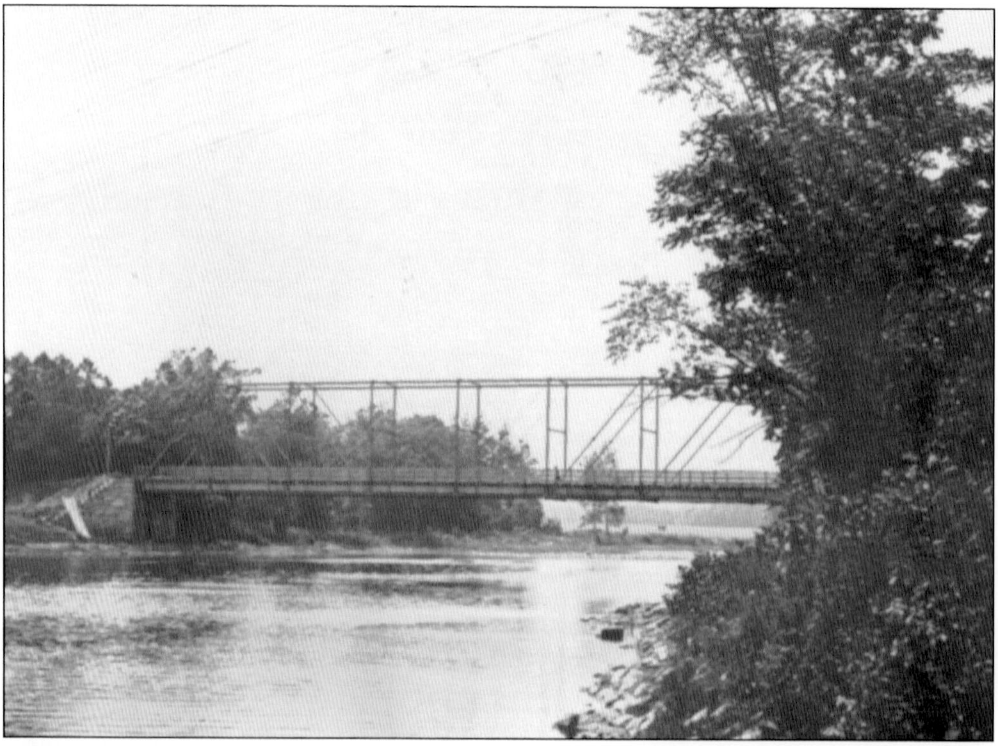

Babbitt's Bridge, photographed on July 6, 1912, was doomed by the damming of the Housatonic River to form Lake Zoar. (CRH.)

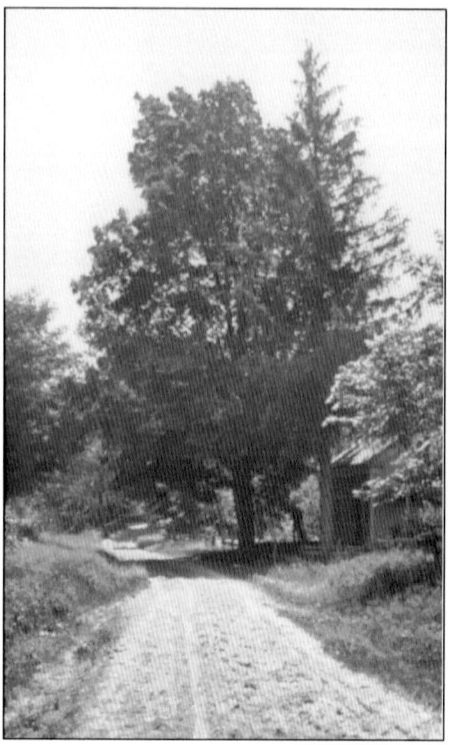

This June 1912 photograph shows a winding dirt road on the way to Babbitt's Bridge. (CRH.)

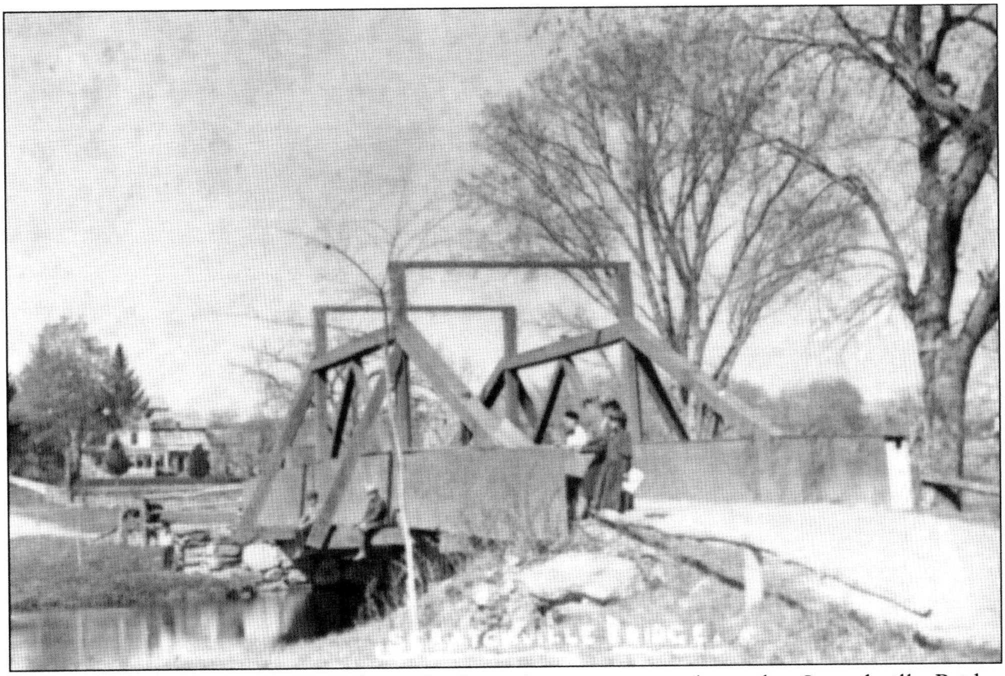

Most country bridges were simple girder-framed structures, such as the Scratchville Bridge across the Weekeepeemee River in North Woodbury. This photograph was taken in 1896, looking northward toward the Ford residence. (C-H.)

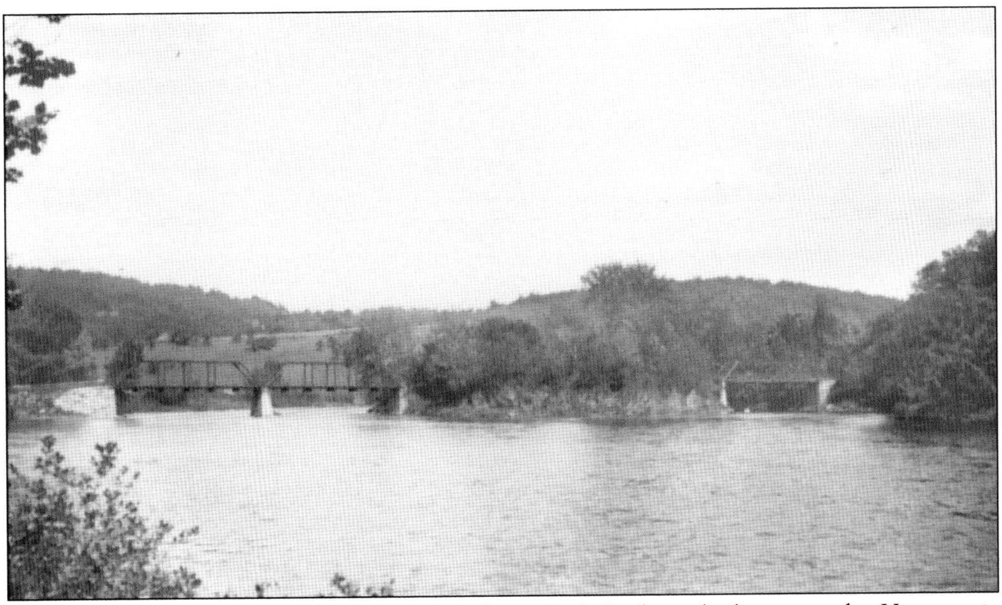

This view shows the multiple-girder spans of Bennett's Bridge, which crosses the Housatonic River. (CRH.)

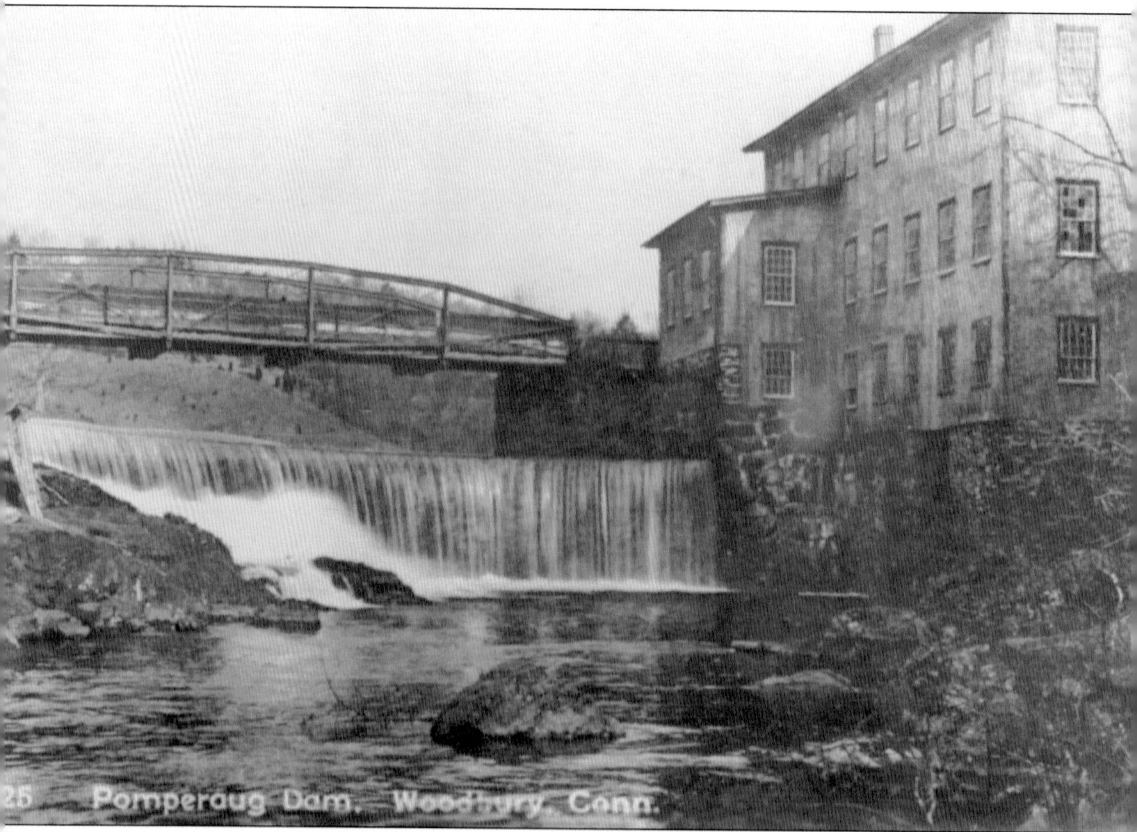

Sometimes a milldam required the building of a bridge, as was true in the Pomperaug section of Woodbury. This photograph shows the mill, the Pomperaug Dam, and the bridge above it. (C-H.)

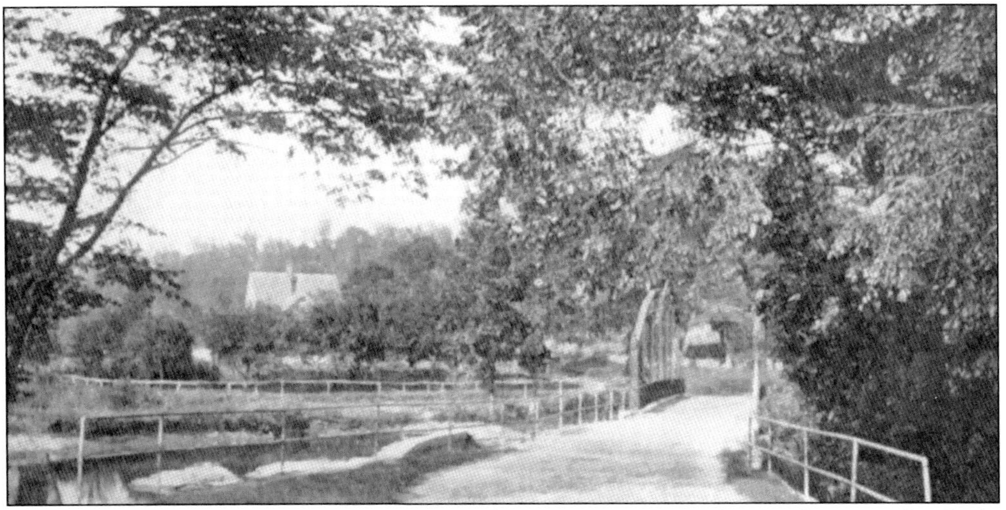

This bridge crosses the Shepaug River at Roxbury Station. It was frequently repaired, rebuilt, and relocated. (FWC.)

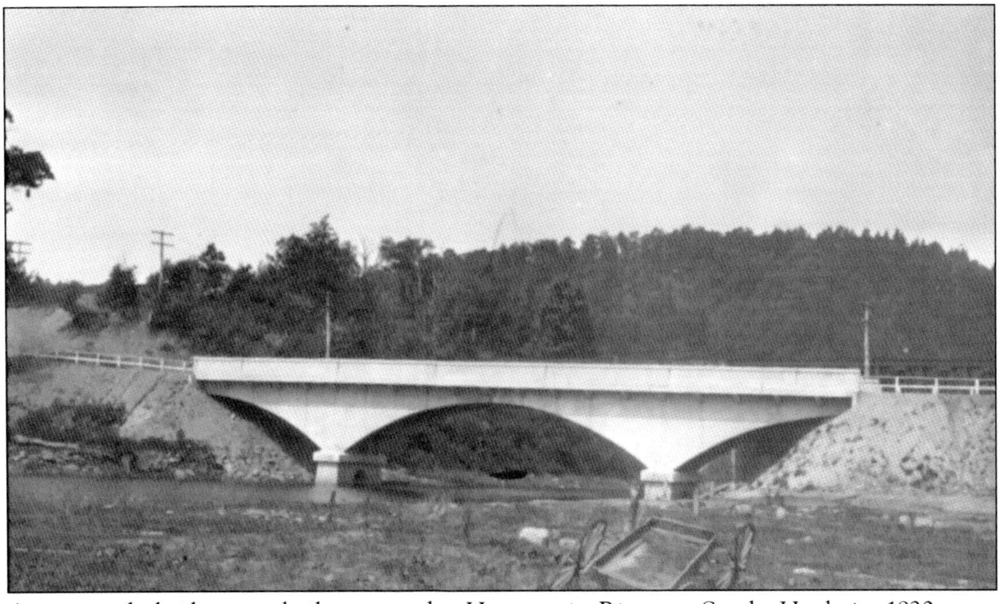

A new arch bridge was built across the Housatonic River at Sandy Hook in 1920, as a result of a substantial increase in motor traffic on Route 6. This photograph was taken on July 18, 1920. (CRH.)

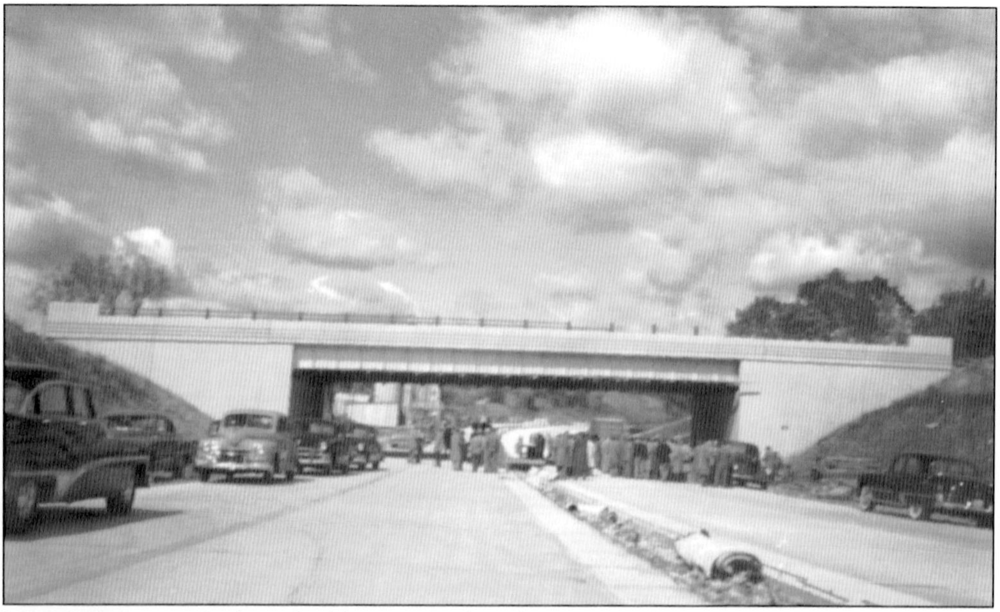

Mounting postwar highway building resulted in the New Rochambeau Bridge at Sandy Hook. The bridge opened on October 7, 1953. (CRH.)

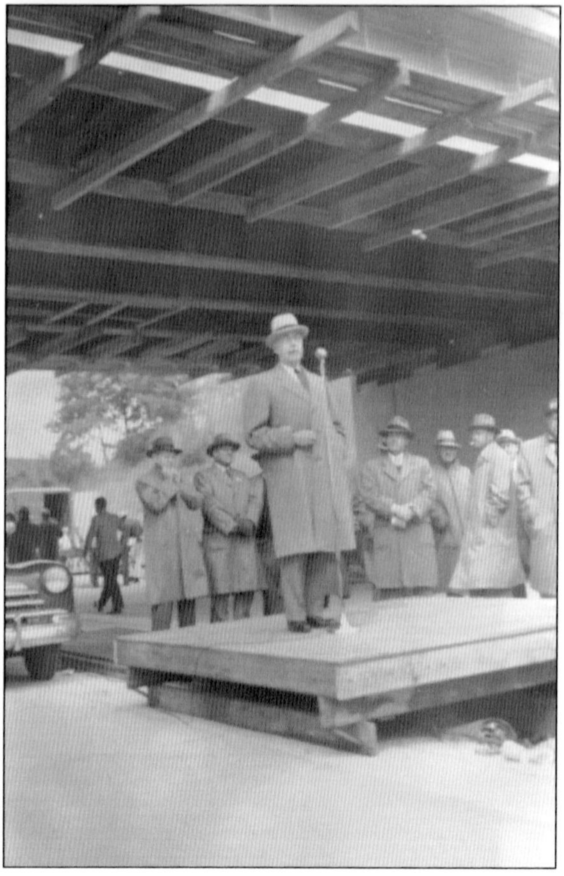

At the opening of the New Rochambeau Bridge, Highway Commissioner Hill was one of the key speakers. Civil engineer Charles Harte attended the October 7, 1953 ceremony and took this photograph. (CRH.)

Five

On the Move

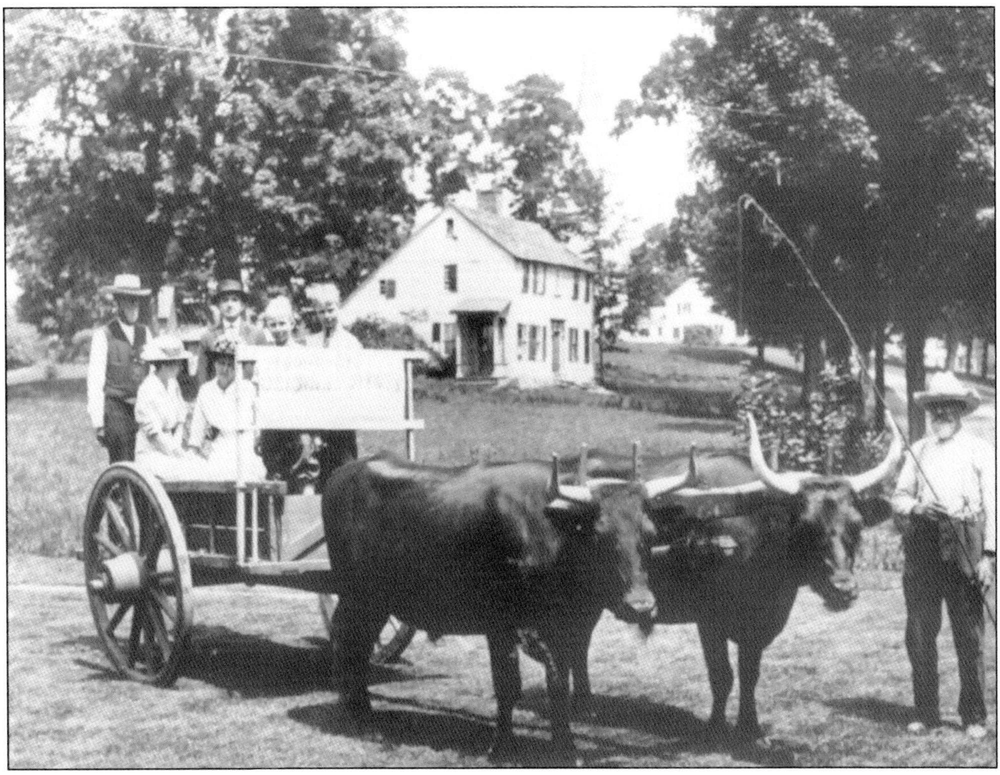

Early settlers relied more on oxen than on horses for transportation. Even into the 1900s, oxen were still used for heavy moving. This picture was taken in 1912, as automobiles were making their presence felt. The ox-powered cart bears six people and a sign proclaiming it to be "Woodbury's Original Jitney." (ETT.)

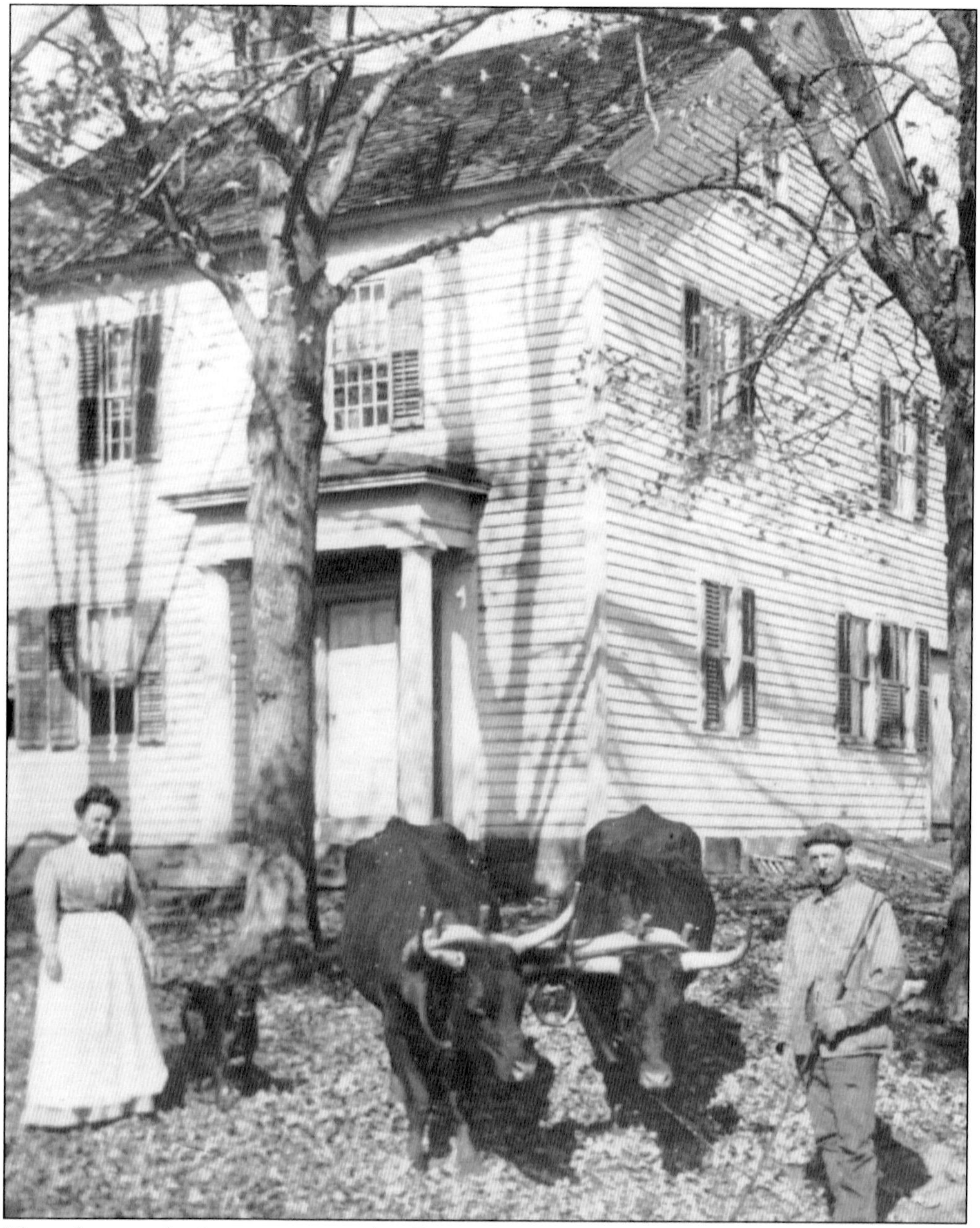

This photograph shows oxen at the Daury Farm, at 32 Good Hill Road. Pictured are Clara Allen Markam, the daughter of Llewelyn Allen, and "Old Jim," who was in charge of the ox team. (C-H.)

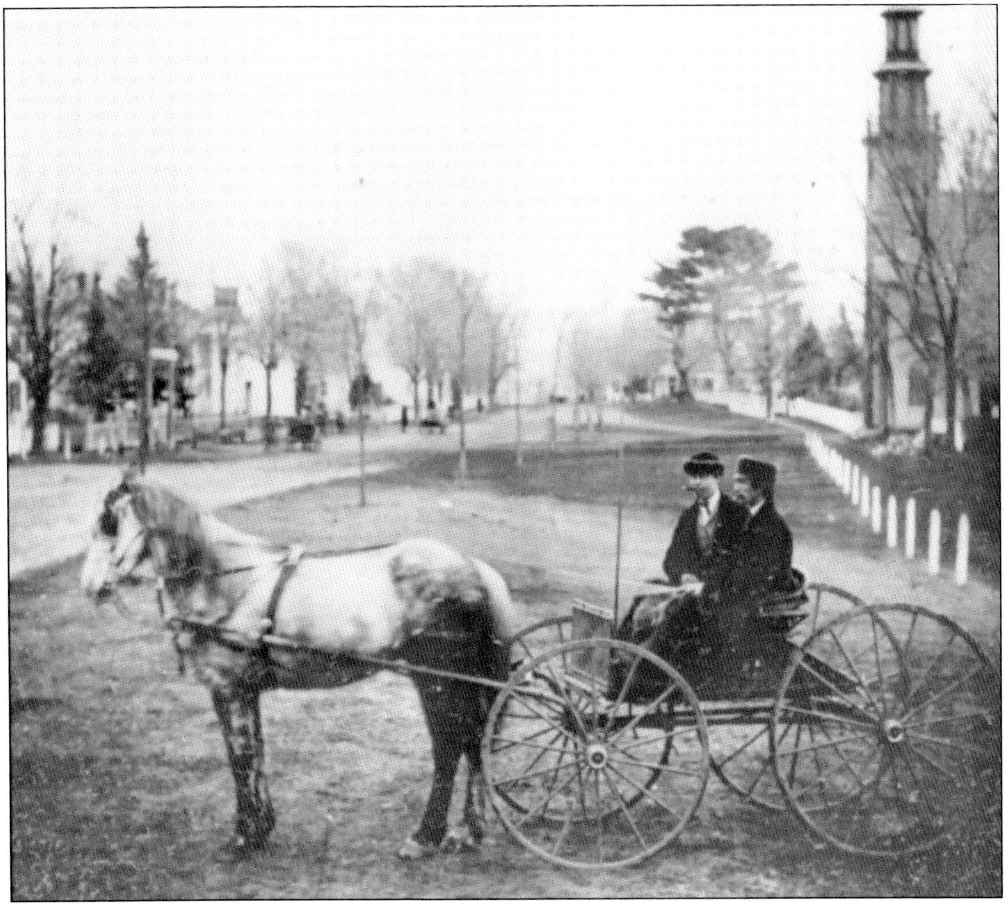

A horse and buggy pose on Main Street in 1864 for an unknown photographer. (C-H.)

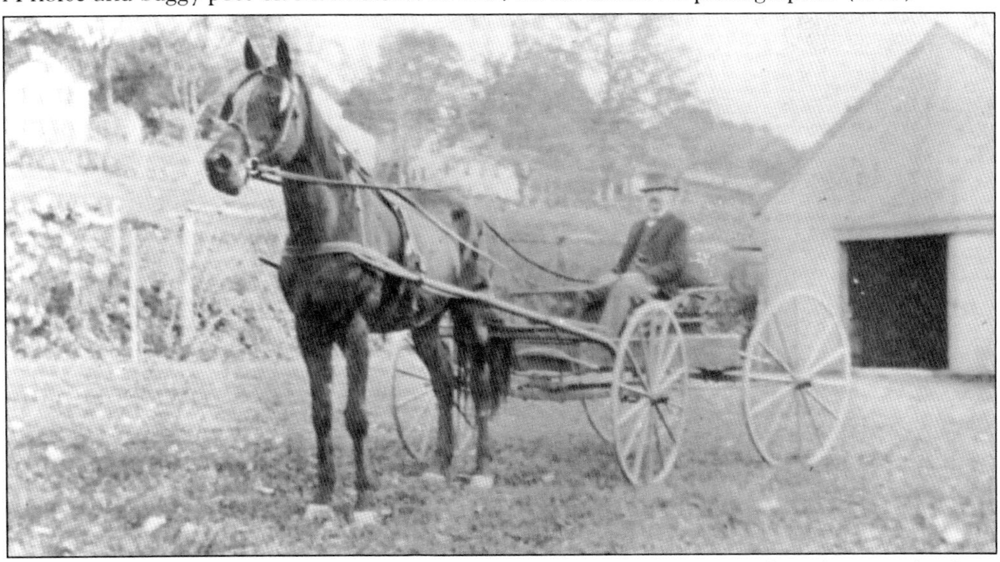

Emerson Atwood pauses with his fine horse on Spring Street. The photograph dates from 1908. (C-H.)

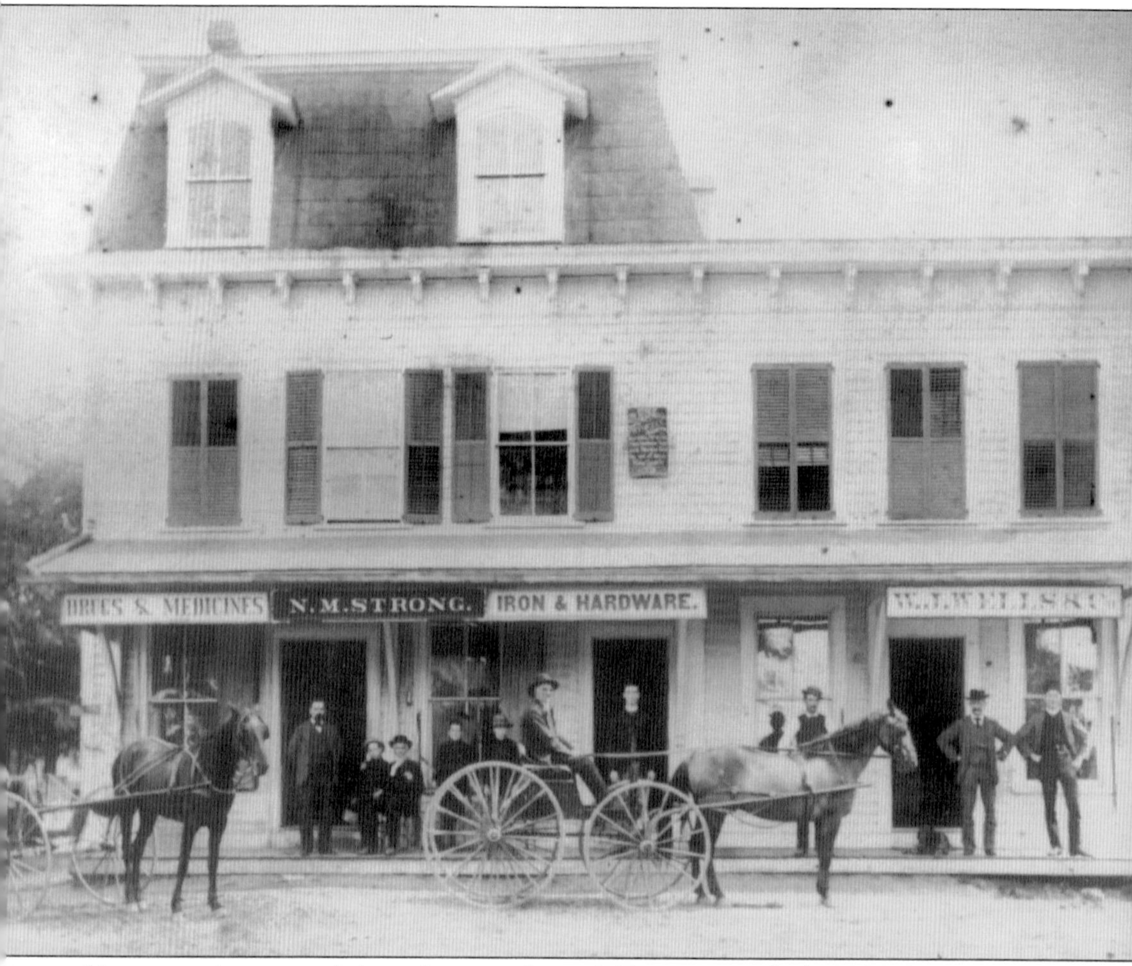

Horsepower is very much in evidence in this *c.* 1880 scene outside the N.M. Strong store and W.J. Wells & Company. (C-H.)

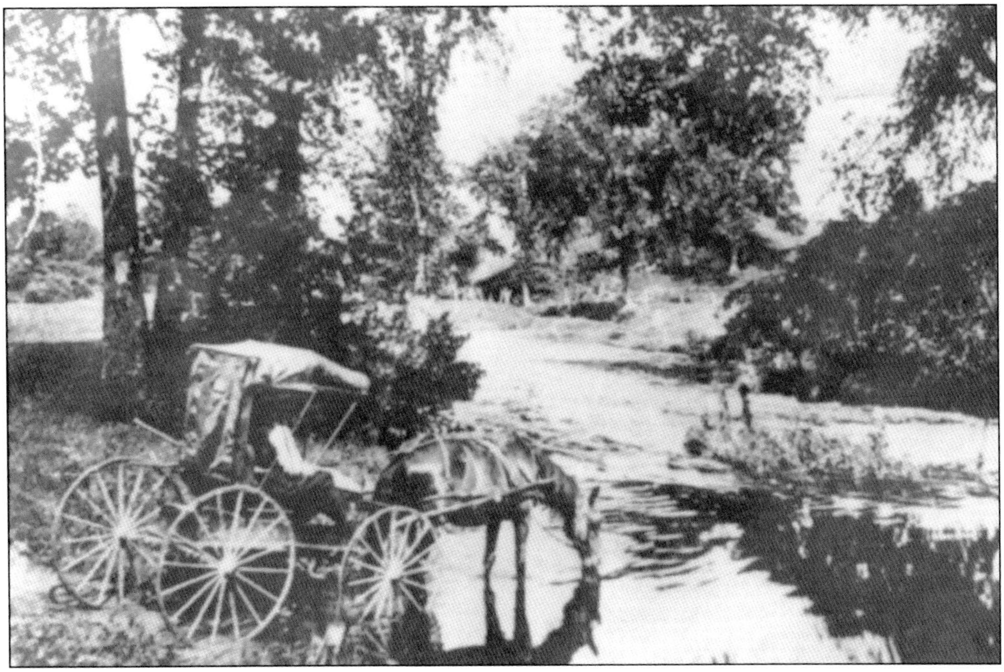

This harness horse drinks in the cool waters at the north end of the Nonnewaug River. The view was taken *c.* 1908, looking downstream from the North Bridge, just west of the Scratchville Bridge. (C-H.)

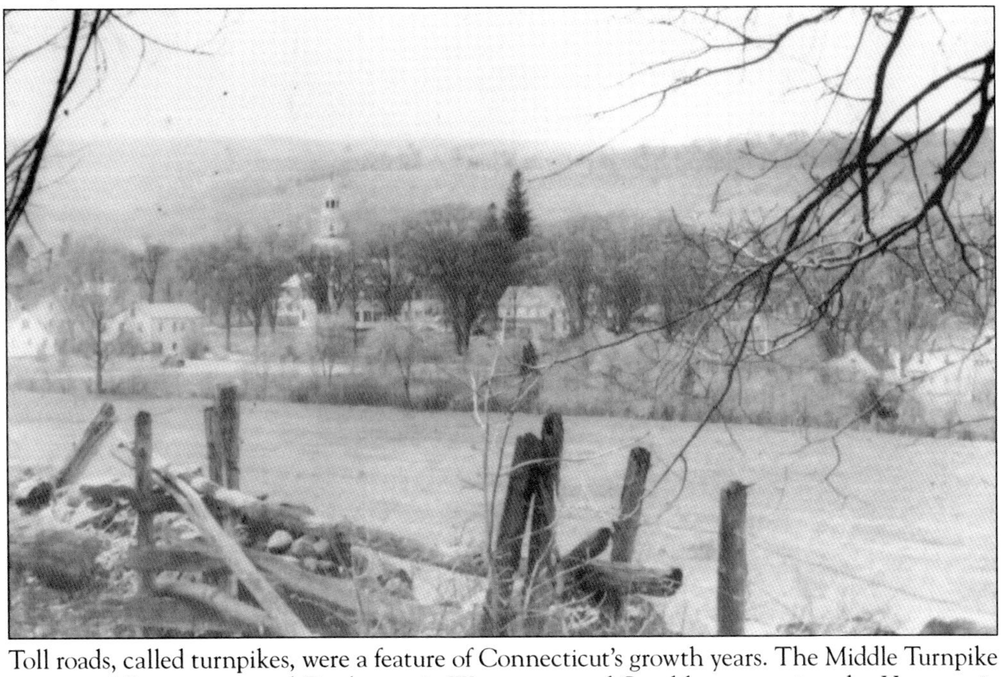

Toll roads, called turnpikes, were a feature of Connecticut's growth years. The Middle Turnpike connected Farmington and Danbury, via Watertown and Southbury, crossing the Housatonic River at Bennett's Bridge, which along with Zoar was a toll bridge, another source of civic and private income. This view of the Middle Turnpike in Woodbury was taken looking west toward the North Church. (C-H.)

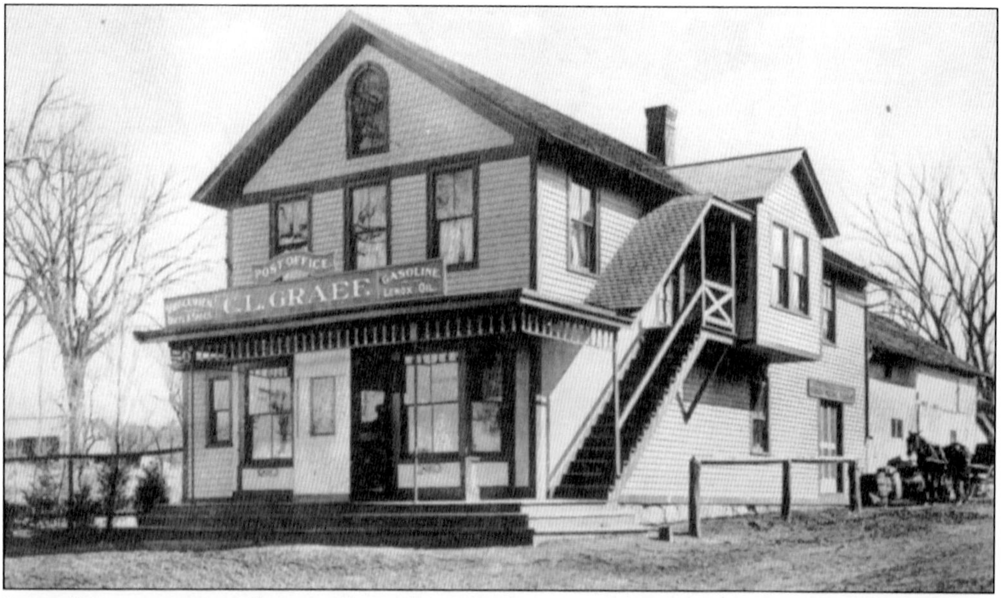

Post offices were generally located at a central town store. This one is at the C.L. Graef store in Southbury. Mail was delivered by stagecoach. The Woodbury Stage was established in 1854 and, by 1868, was making regular trips to Waterbury through Watertown and Middlebury. By 1908, six freight and express stages were running. Ray Stiles operated a stage between Woodbury and the Southbury station for many years, finally replacing his team with a motor vehicle converted from an old Chevrolet truck. An important Colonial route was the New Haven to Albany Stage, whose 15th milestone is opposite the Woodbury Soldiers Monument. It is said to have been laid out by Benjamin Franklin in 1750. (SHS.)

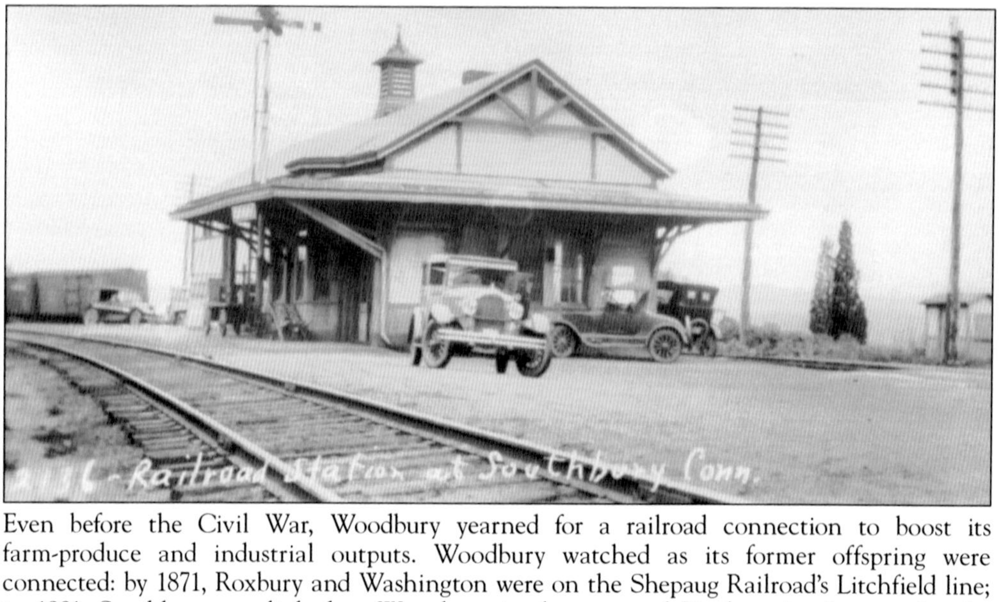

Even before the Civil War, Woodbury yearned for a railroad connection to boost its farm-produce and industrial outputs. Woodbury watched as its former offspring were connected: by 1871, Roxbury and Washington were on the Shepaug Railroad's Litchfield line; in 1881, Southbury was linked to Waterbury in the east and Danbury in the west by the New England Railroad, at the time a competitor of the New Haven; even Watertown had its own spur line out of Waterbury. This photograph shows the Southbury Station of the former New England Railroad. (TL.)

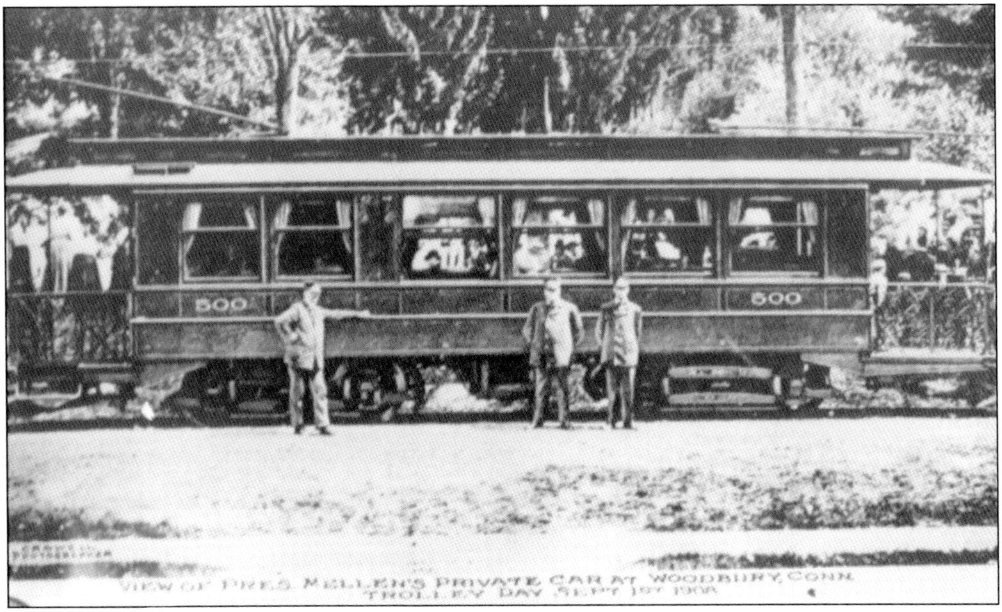

Rail relief came to Woodbury from the Connecticut Company, a subsidiary of the New Haven Railroad. Civil engineer Charles R. Harte laid out a trolley line from Lake Quassapaug, down rugged Sherman Hill, and up Main Street to the old Woodbury Town Hall. The new line was opened on Tuesday, September 1, 1908, an occasion for oratory and other expressions of civic pride. This photograph shows car No. 500 in Woodbury on that day. Later views of car No. 500 appear on pages 81 and 82. (CRH.)

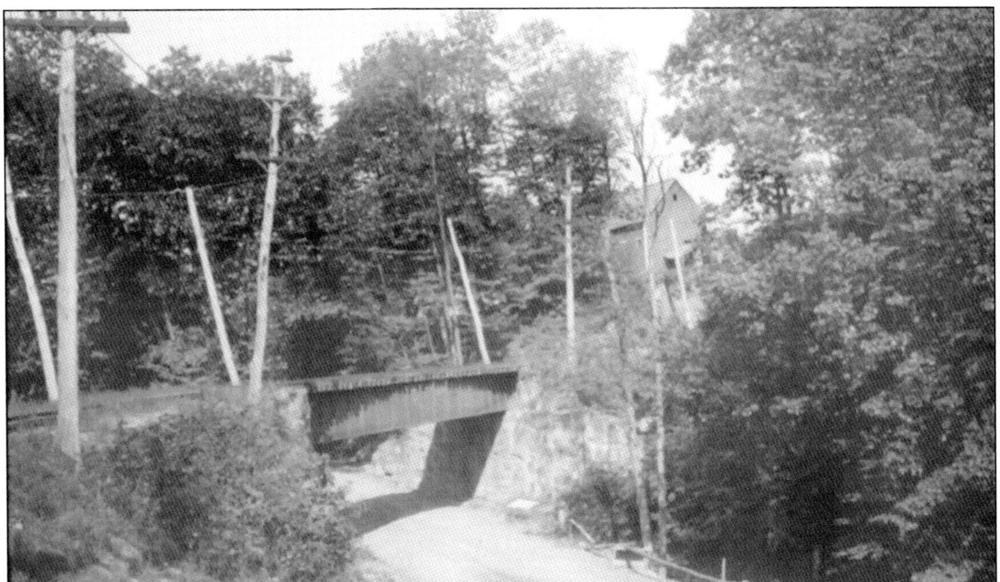

Leaving Quassapaug, the trolley would race down the steep Stevens Cut and then across this trestle between Woodbury and Middlebury. The photograph was taken on September 20, 1913. Note the offset poles. (CRH.)

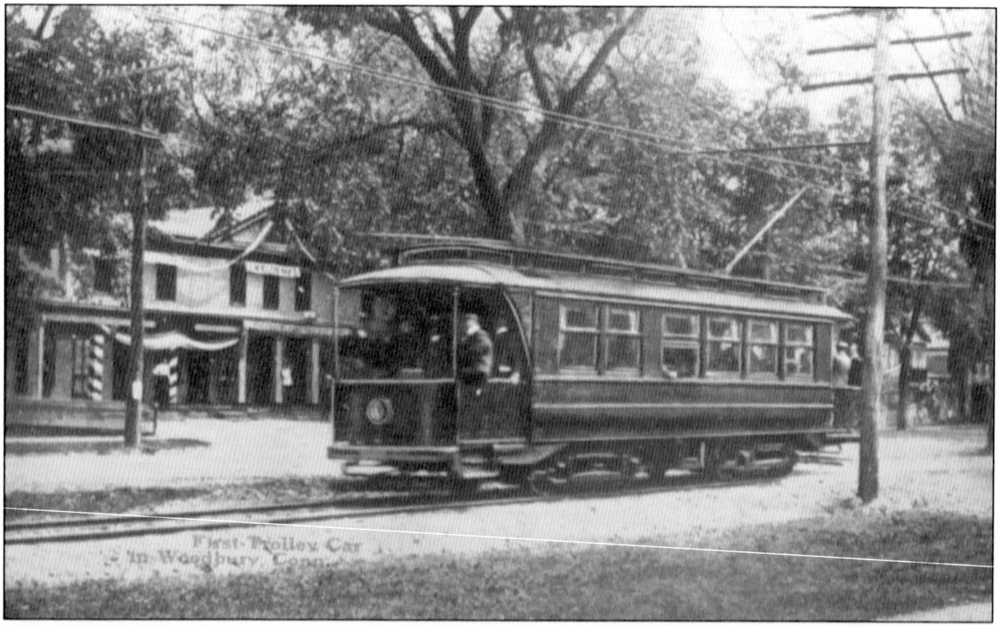

The welcome banner hanging on the front of the Lewis Building greets this trolley arriving from Waterbury. (TL.)

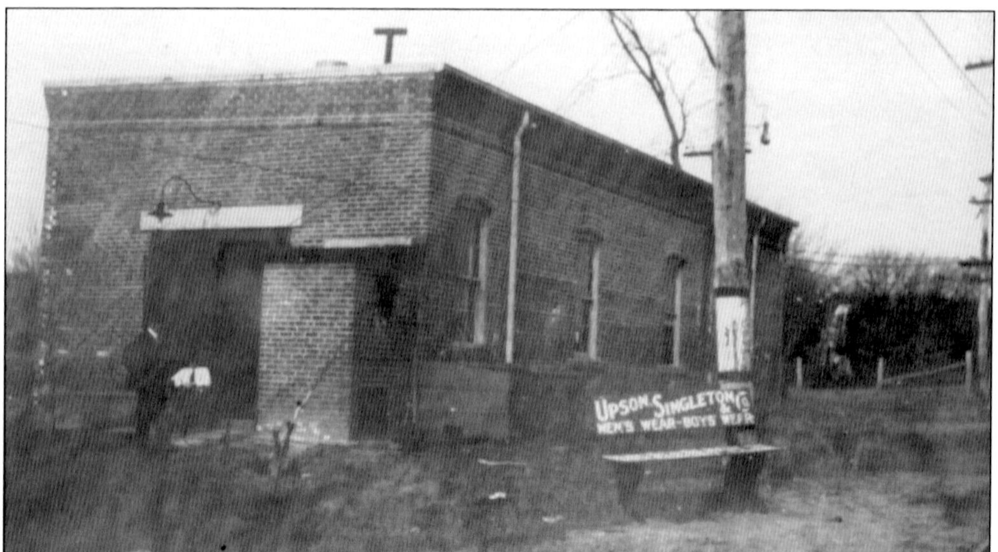

The trolley powerhouse was atop Sherman Hill. Note the Waterbury clothier's advertisement on the waiting bench: "Upson, Singleton & Company, Men's Wear – Boys' Wear." (FWC.)

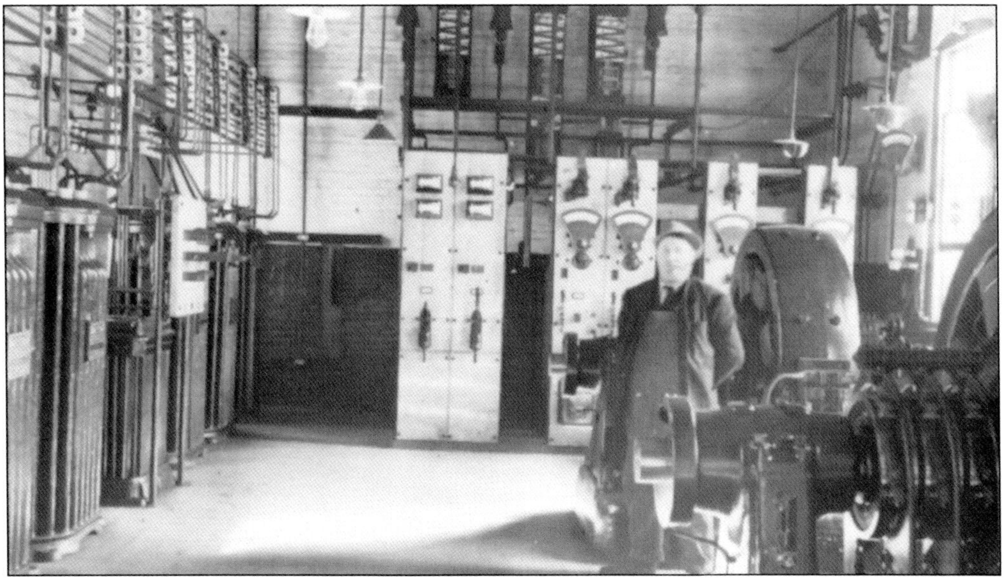

Within the powerhouse, rotary converters furnished the 600 volts of direct current necessary to get the cars up Sherman Hill. Mr. Tuttle, whose farm was nearby, stands by the switchboard. The powerhouse was located at the corner of Route 6 and Tuttle Road. After it was abandoned in 1930, highway department equipment was stored there. The building was demolished in the late 1900s. (FWC.)

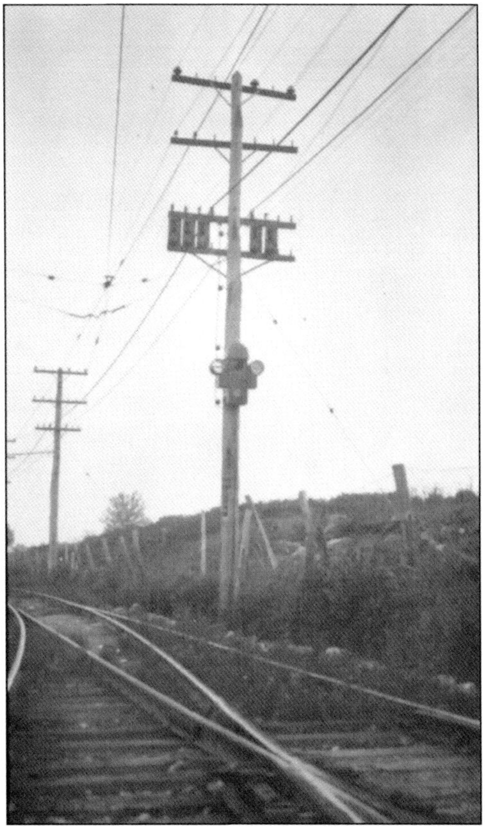

Trolleys were supported by an expensive infrastructure of roadbed, rails, overhead wires, and signals. This photograph of the siding at Quassapaug Station was taken on June 15, 1923, looking east. (CRH.)

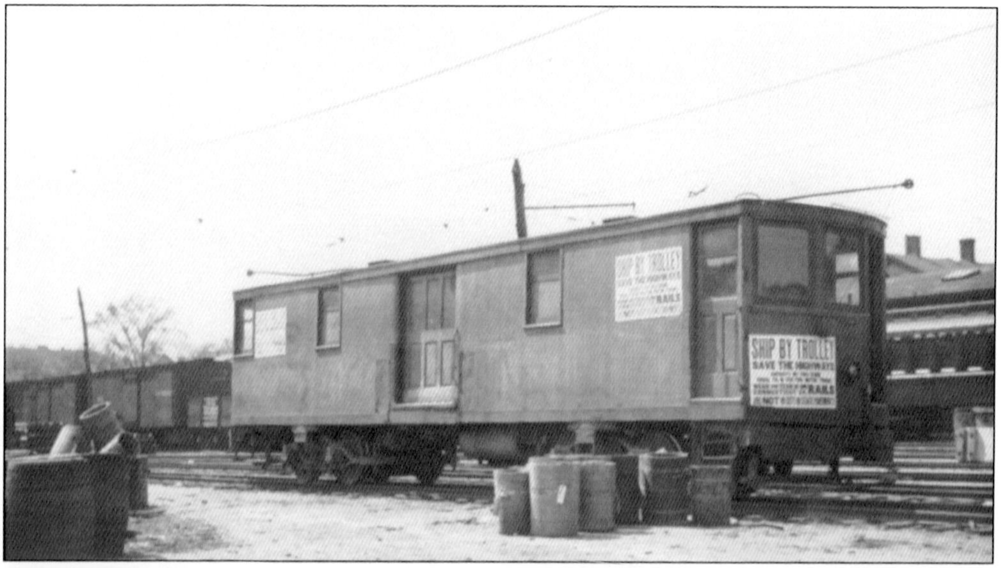

Trolley express cars, such as this one photographed on June 15, 1920, carried packages and food—eggs, milk, and other local produce—over the Connecticut Company's statewide trackage. The sign on the car advises "Ship by trolley. Save the highways. Capacity of this car equal to four 5-ton motortrucks. Wear and tear is on Connecticut Company rails and not on city or state pavements." (CRH.)

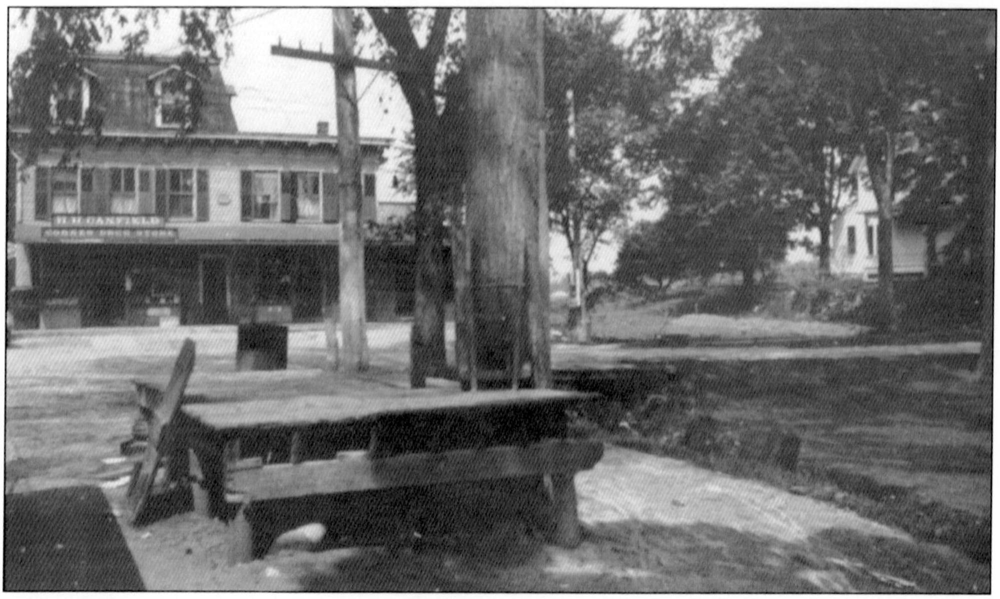

The trolley express loading platform, shown in this photograph taken on July 13, 1921, was located across from the H.H. Canfield Corner Drug Store, in North Woodbury. It lingered as a relic long after the last trolley car had left in 1930. Plans for line extensions to Hotchkissville and even Watertown were proposed, but they never materialized. The increase in motor traffic after World War I diminished the trolley's transportation monopoly. (CRH.)

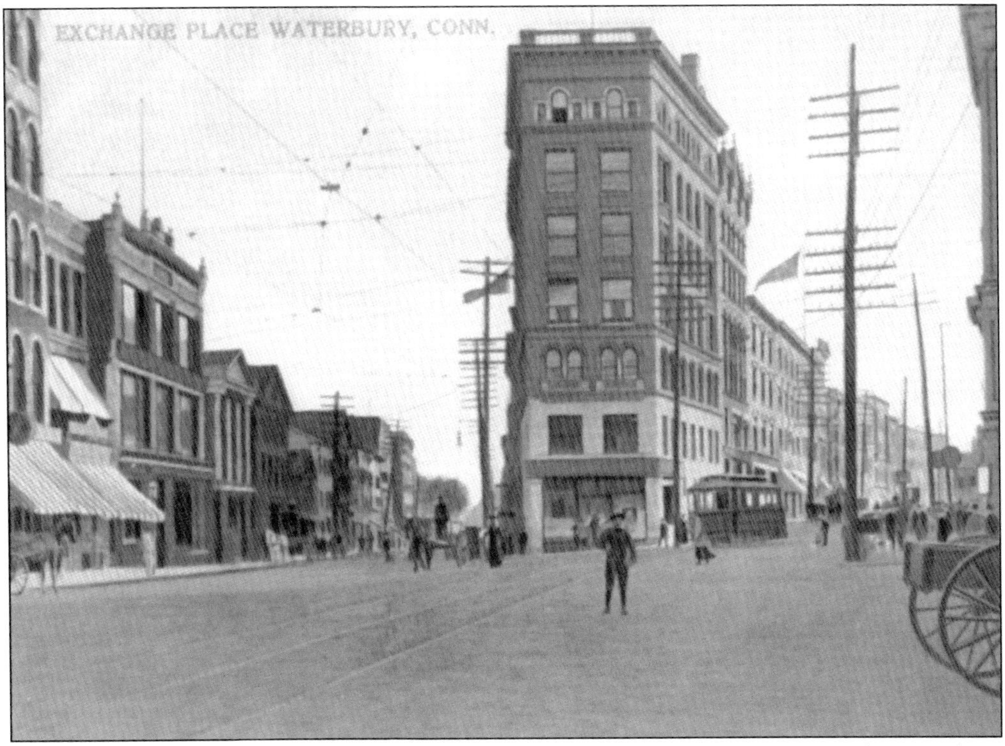

Shoppers and students could regularly travel into Waterbury. Here, at Exchange Place, they could continue on to Cheshire, Meriden, Watertown, Thomaston, Naugatuck, and even New Haven. Along with having the required fare, it helped to have patience, endurance, and good connections. (FWC.)

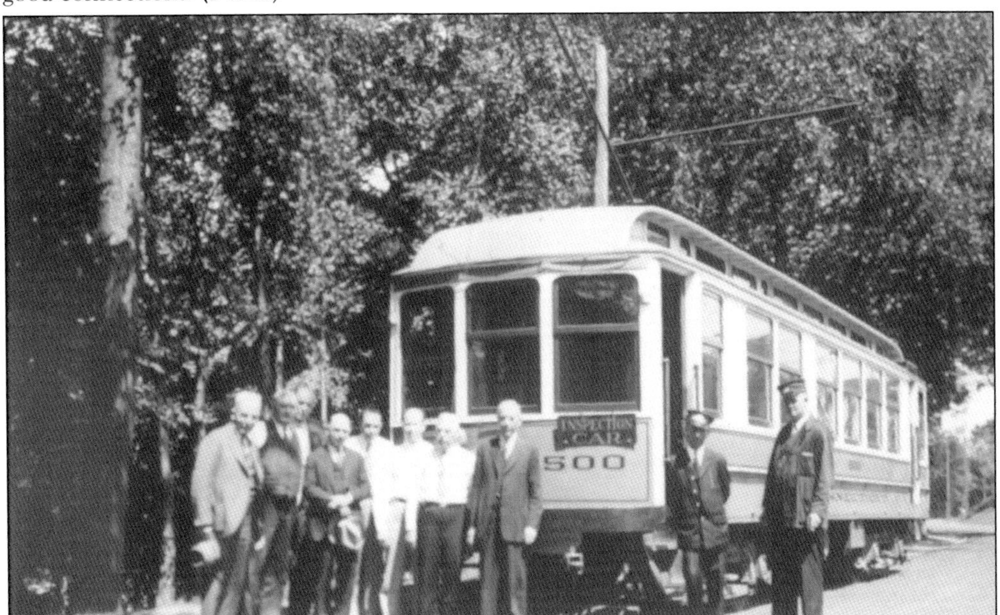

Special car No. 500 was used when Public Utility Commission inspections were made annually. Car 500 lives on at the Shore Line Trolley Museum in Branford. (C-H.)

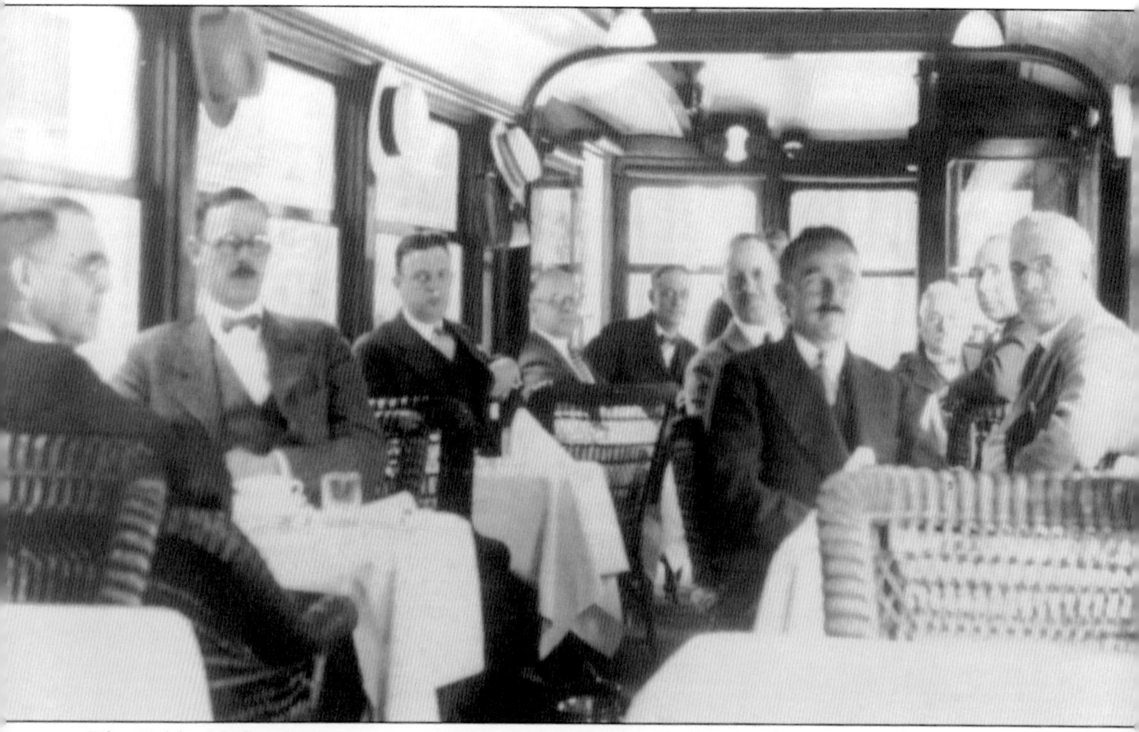

The Public Utility Commission inspectors' travel was eased by wicker seats with plush cushions, a galley, and a lavatory. This photograph shows the inspectors in car No. 500 on a trip to North Woodbury. (FWC.)

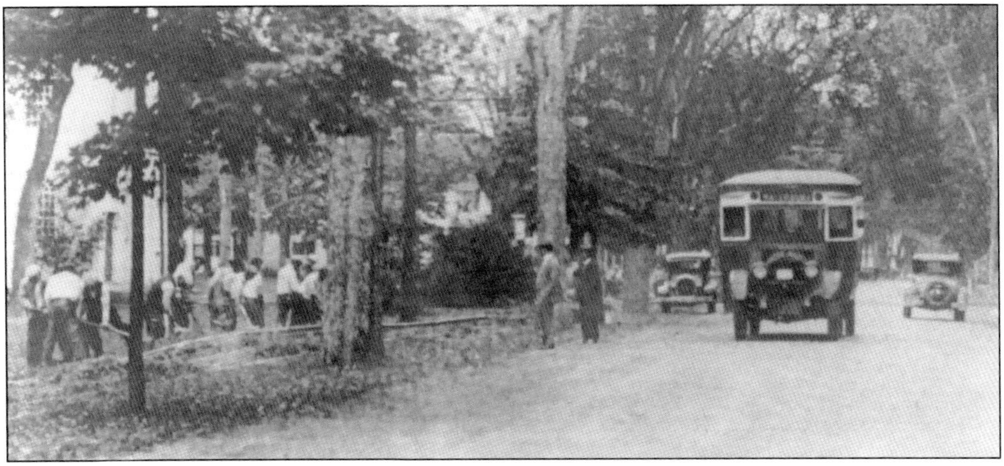

Trolleys were replaced by buses in 1930; the roadbed is now mostly a paved recreational path, save for the eroded grade on Sherman Hill. This photograph shows workmen tearing up the tracks in front of St. Paul's Church on Main Street. A Waterbury-bound bus, which replaced the trolley, has just passed a Ford Model A Roadster. (C-H.)

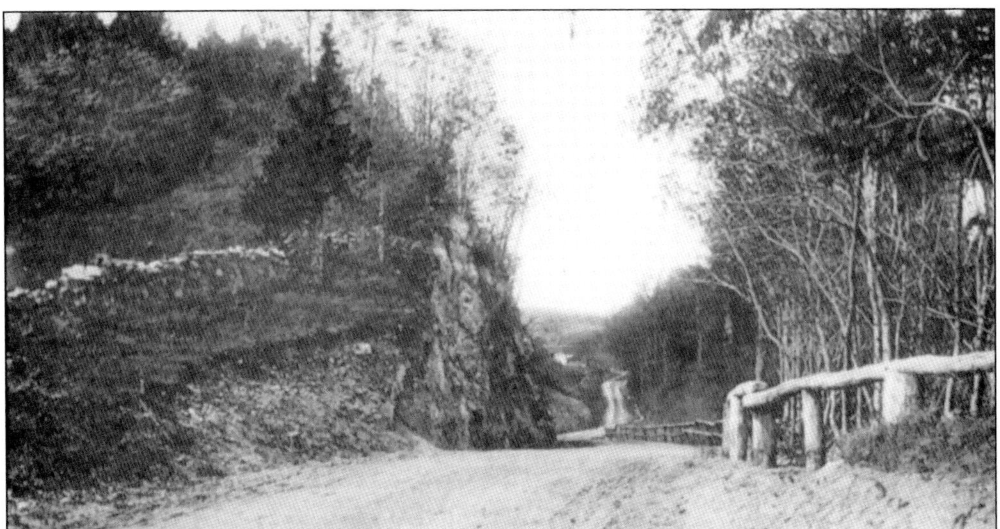

This view of the road to Watertown at the Dugway shows the need for improved streets and bridges faced by the towns around Woodbury in the early 1900s. (FWC.)

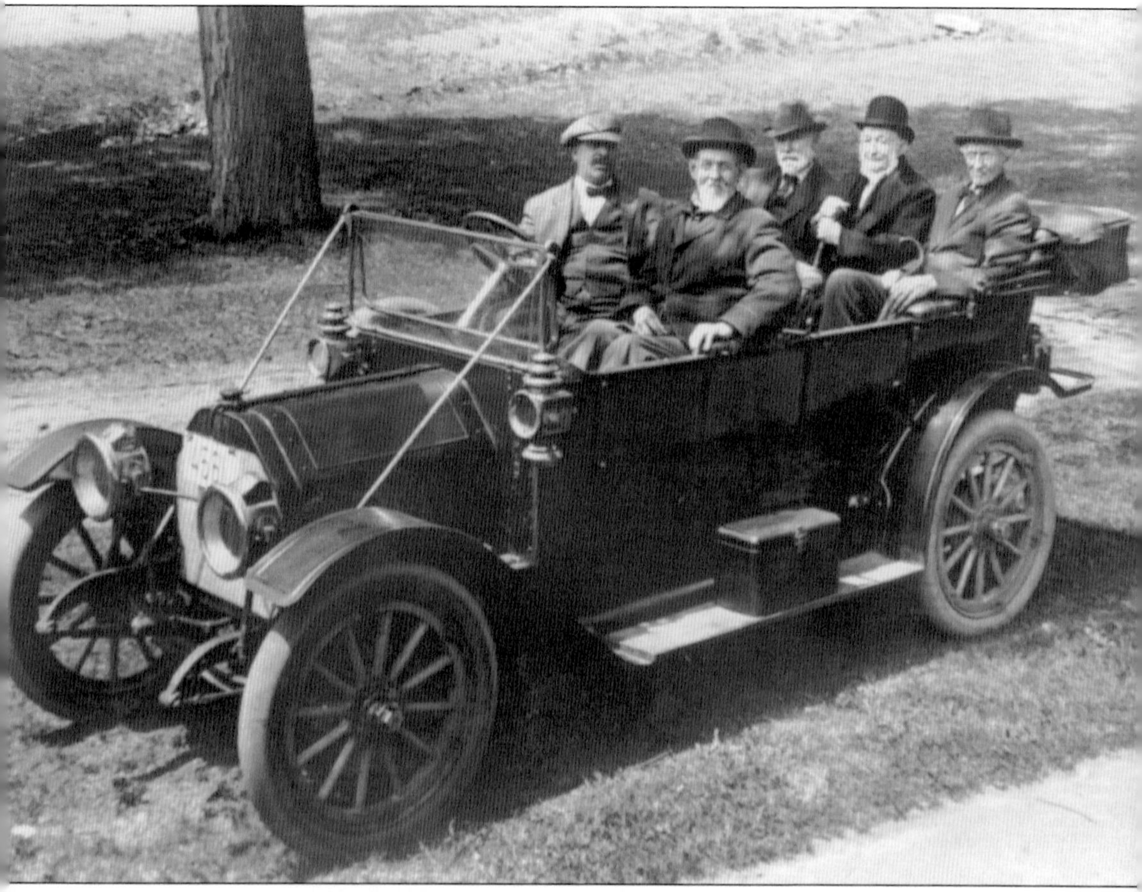

"Grandpa" Saxton and fellow motorists are ready for a spin. The first known owner of a horseless carriage in Woodbury was Wilbur Lindsey. (C-H.)

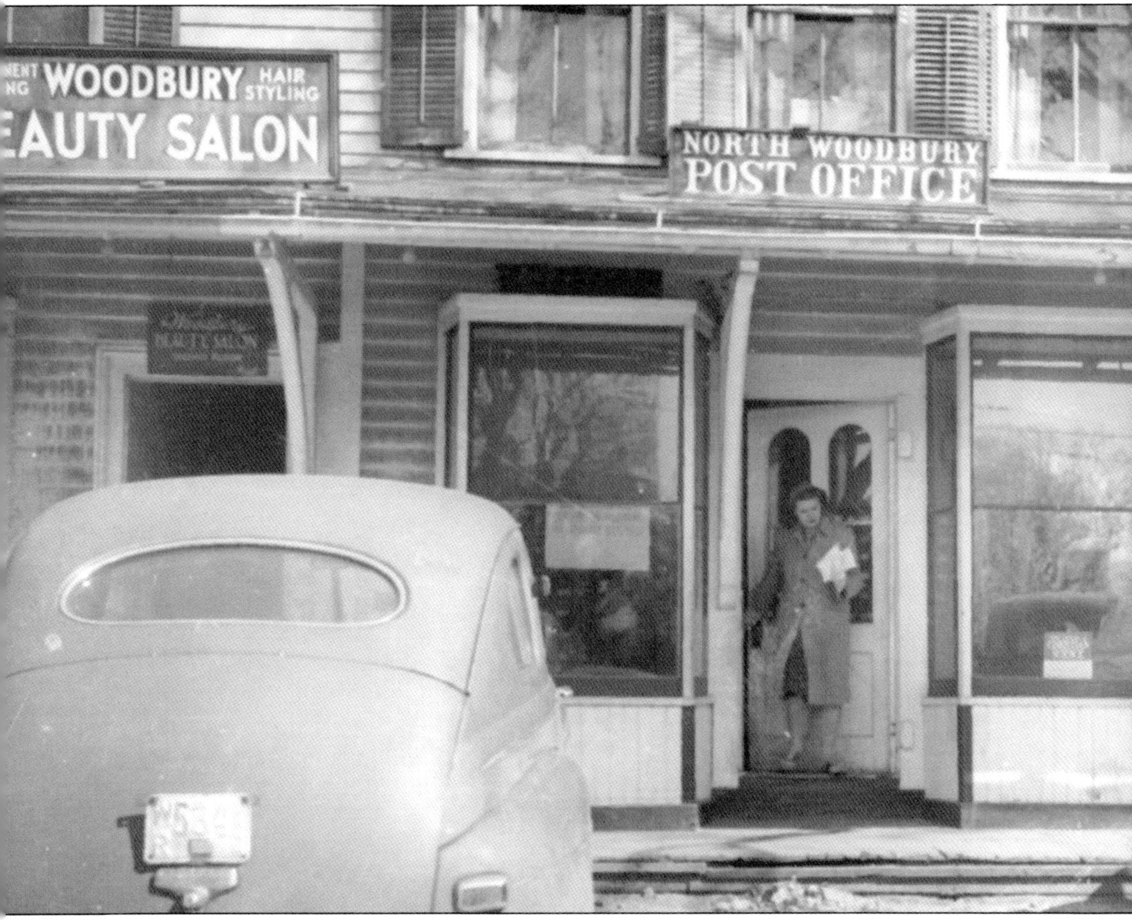

By the 1940s, automobiles carried the mail, either for the rural free delivery (RFD) postman or for patrons going to the post office at Canfield Corner. (C-H.)

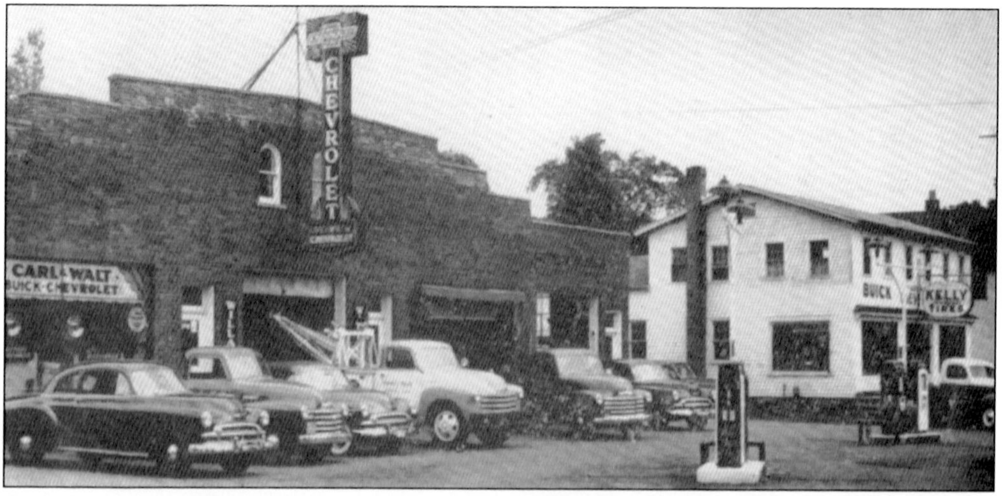

Carl & Walt's garage on Main Street was established in 1927. When this photograph was taken, c. 1949, Carl & Walt Inc. was a Chervrolet-Buick dealer operated by Carl Anderson and Walt Griswold. The first filling station and garage in Woodbury was opened by Fred St. Pierre. (ETT.)

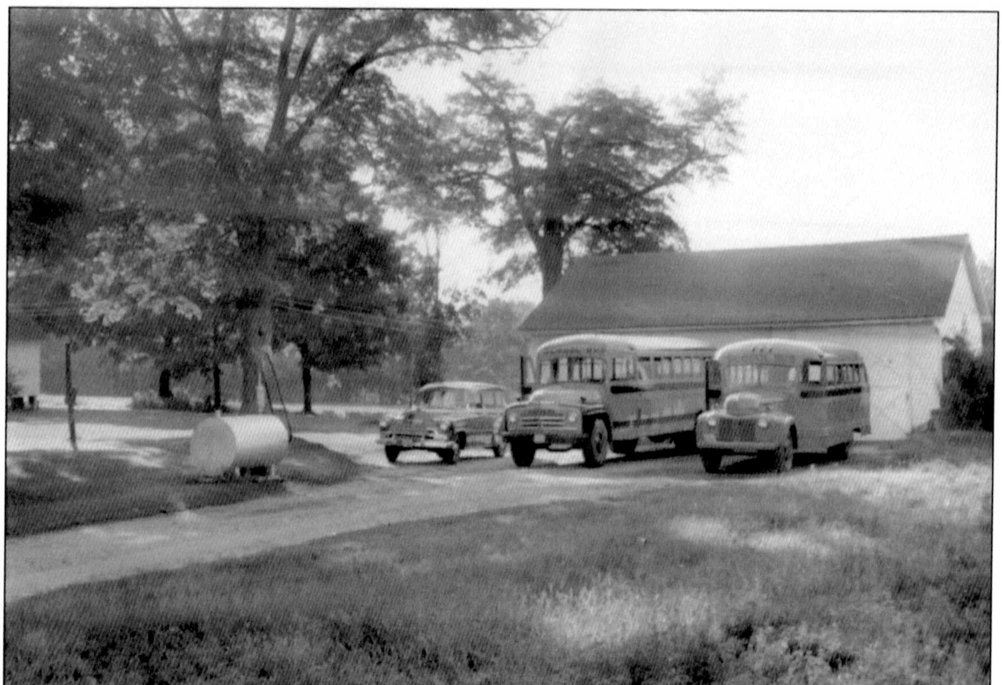

With centralized schools, student transportation became an increasing logistic and budgetary problem for the towns. These are some of Southbury's school buses. (SHS.)

Six

At Ease

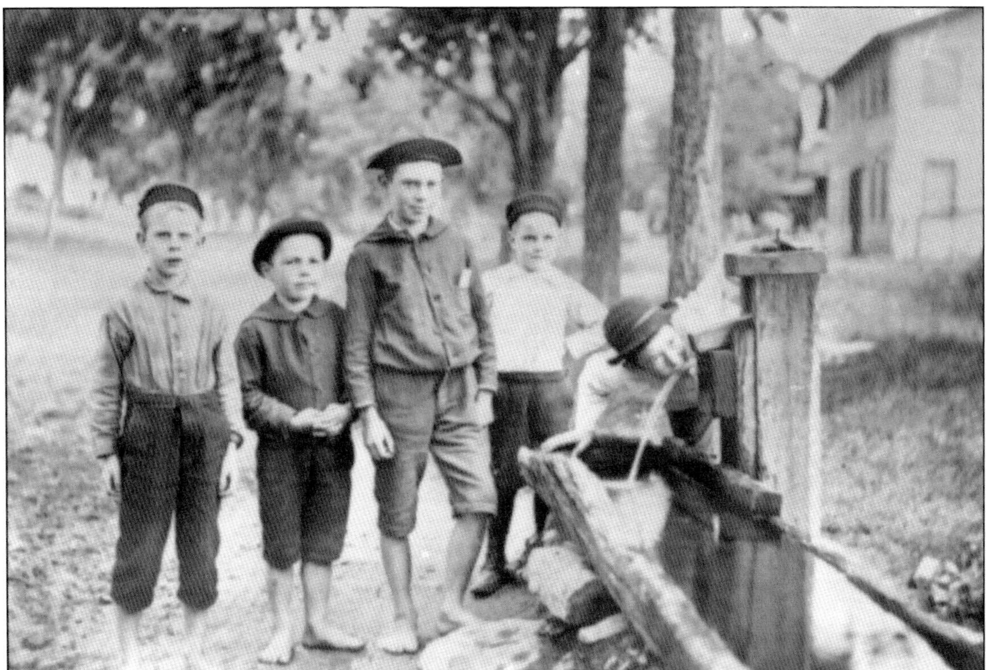

Time stands still on a hot summer's day in 1895. For these five Woodbury boys, what could be finer than a refreshing drink of cold springwater, filling the Gordon Tannery trough on upper Main Street? The photographer is unknown; the boys have been tentatively identified as Dave Barlow, Winfred Dawson, George Scott, and the Comber brothers. (C-H.)

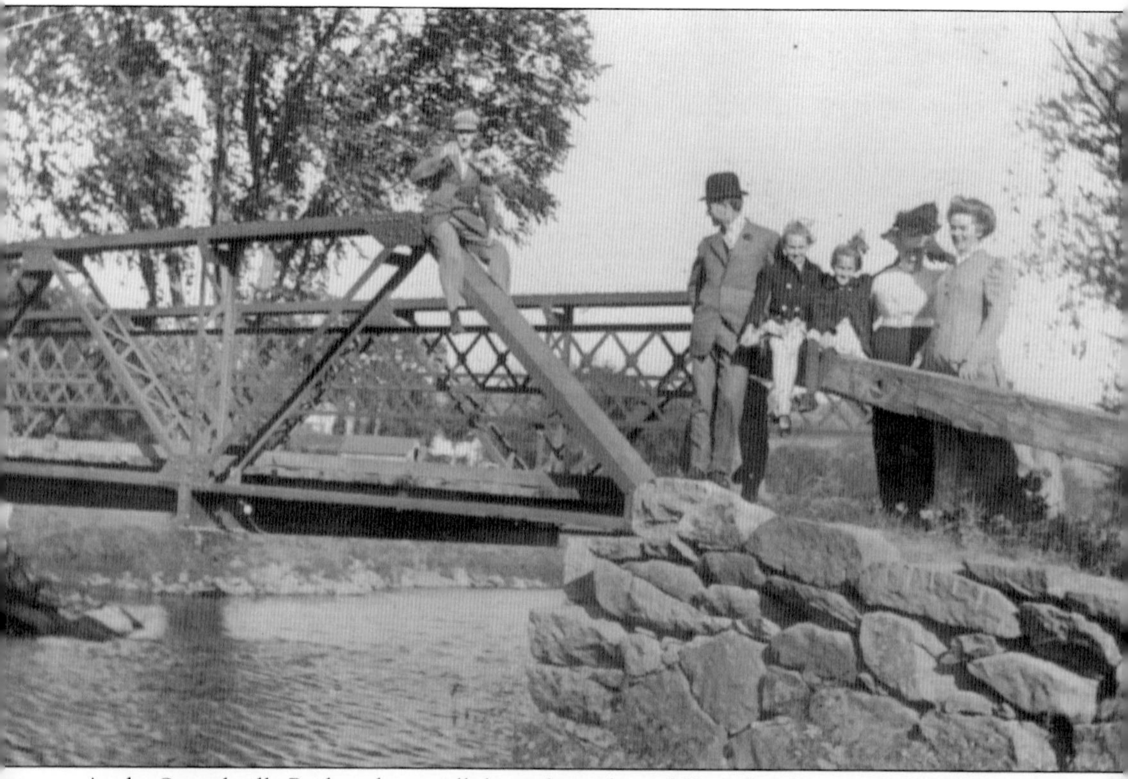

At the Scratchville Bridge, these well-dressed people could be a family just out for a walk to see how the Nonnewaug River is running. (C-H.)

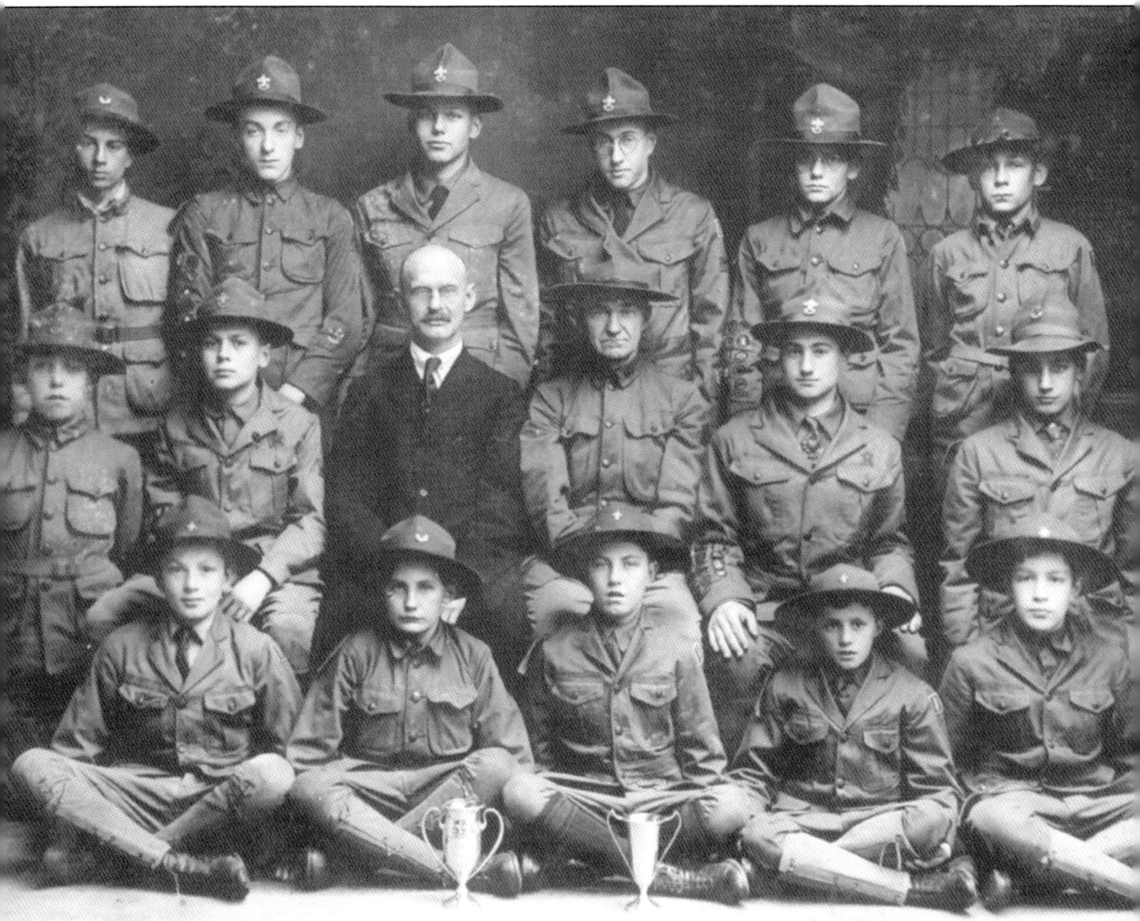

These Boy Scouts, shown in 1921 with various awards, were part of a long Scouting tradition in the Woodbury area. They are identified, from left to right, as follows: (front row) Jack German, Walter Dixon, Sherwood Dawson, George Coad, and Henry Dormitzer; (middle row) Herbert Fowler, Stedman Hitchcock, Mr. Bryant, martin Martus, Oscar Warner, and Karl Warner; (back row) Clifford Evitts, Dr. Rufus Munsell, James Tomlinson, Frank P. Strong, Curtis Hitchcock, and Earle Munson. This photograph was taken in the Betts Studio. (ETT.)

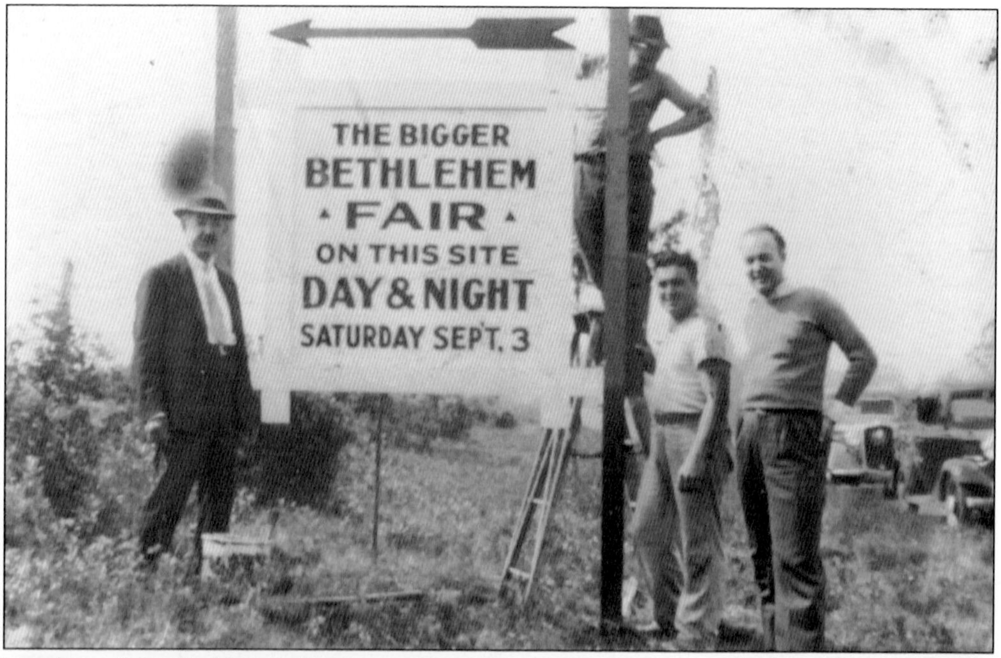

Members of the Bethlehem Fair Committee pose at the entrance to the Saturday, September 3, 1946 fair. The sign announces that the fair will be bigger than ever and will be held "day & night." By 1870, Woodbury's growth was such that the town could afford to have a regular fairgrounds. The location was in a floodplain by the Pomperaug River. The main feature was a racecourse, where local and imported horses were put through their paces. Though a much smaller town, Bethlehem in 1921 first organized its fair, which is still going strong. Since 1972, Roxbury has held regular Old Time Roxbury Days, with action displays of tractor and farm equipment. (BHS.)

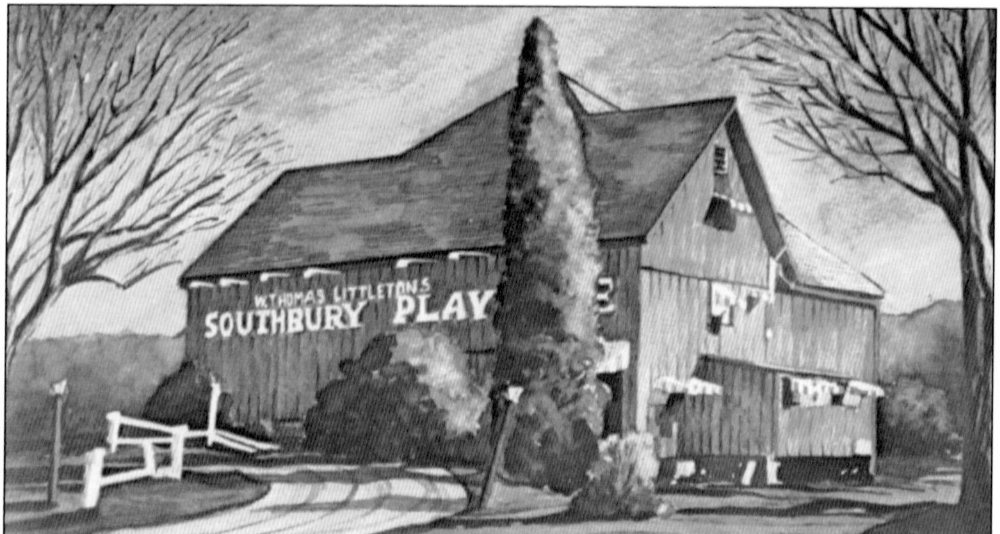

In Southbury at the junction of Routes 6, 67, and Interstate 84 is Jack Quinn's Playhouse, also known as W. Thomas Littleton's Southbury Playhouse. For decades, the playhouse featured both summer stock and new productions. (TL.)

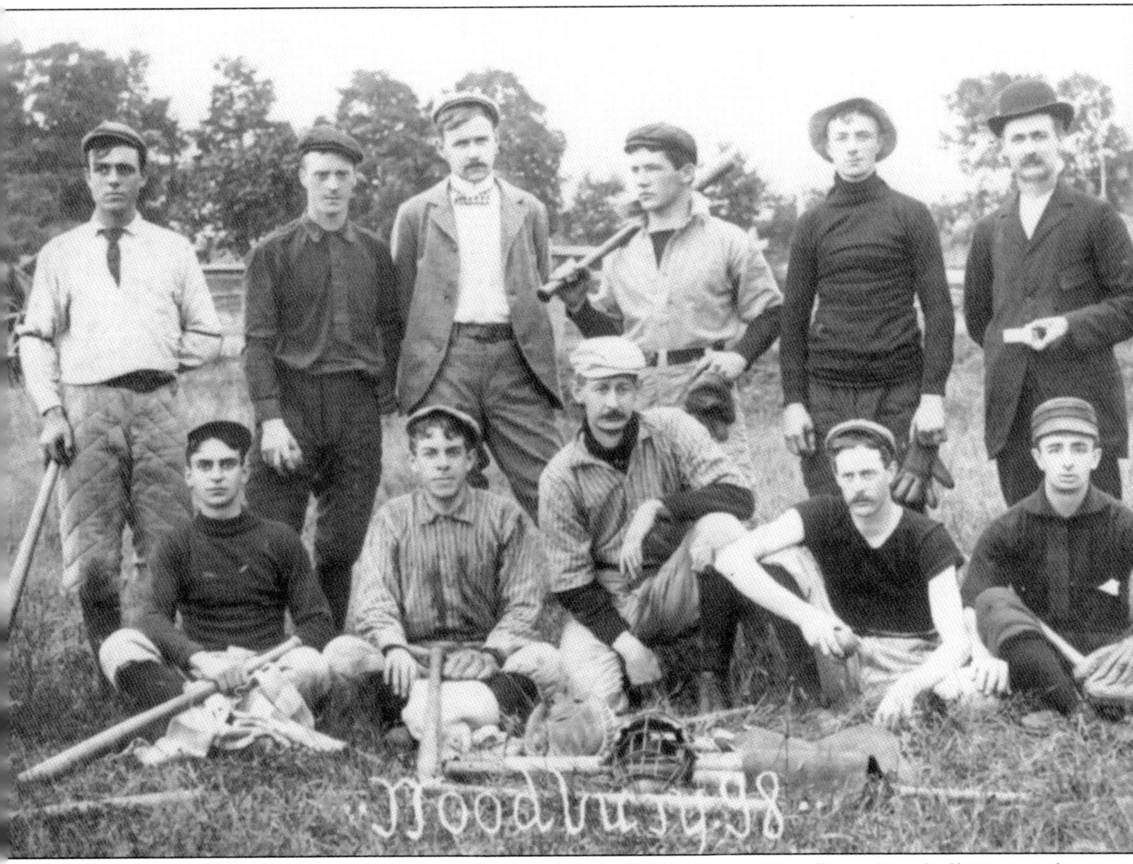

Local baseball teams sprang up after the Civil War. This is the Woodbury Baseball Team of 1898. (C-H.)

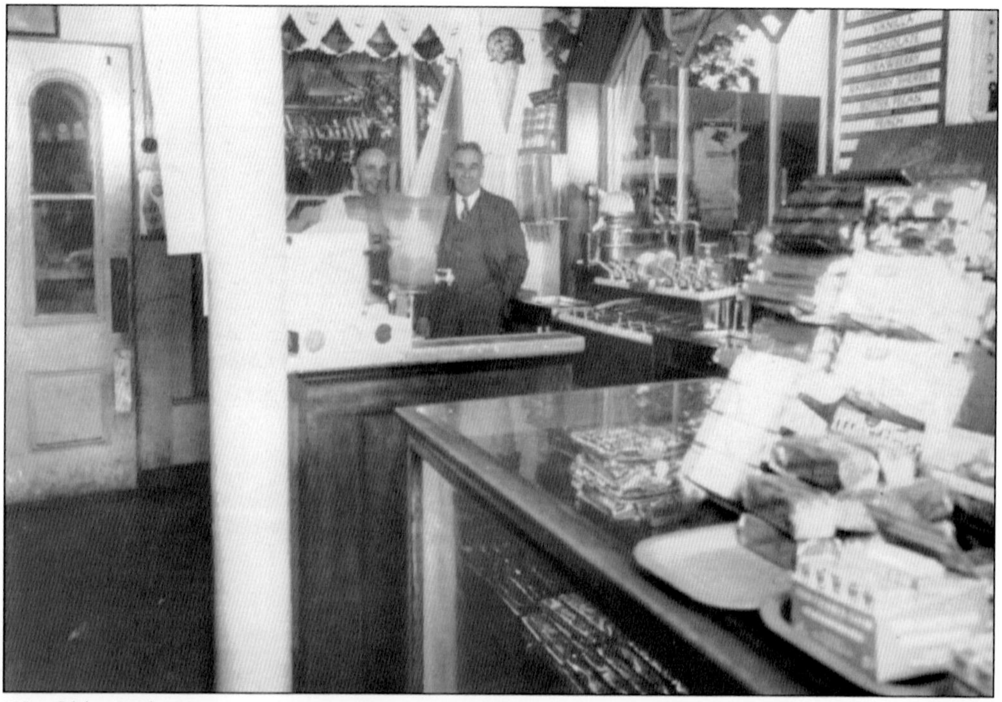

"Ye Olde Soda Fountain" was always a popular town location in summer. This one was in Woodbury. (C-H.)

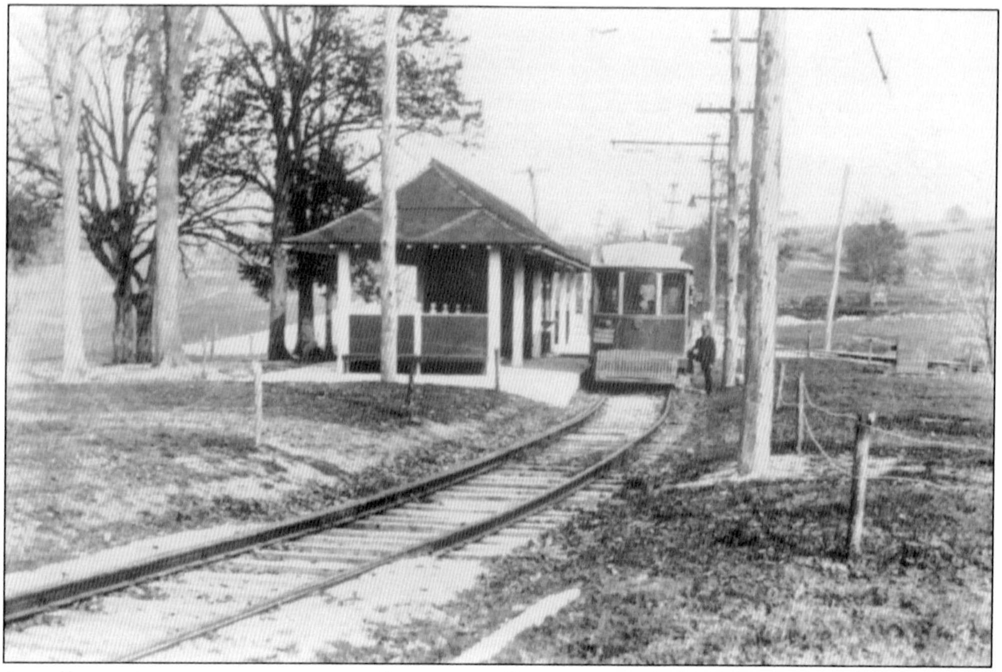

A trolley and a motorman pause at Quassapaug Station c. 1925. (C-H.)

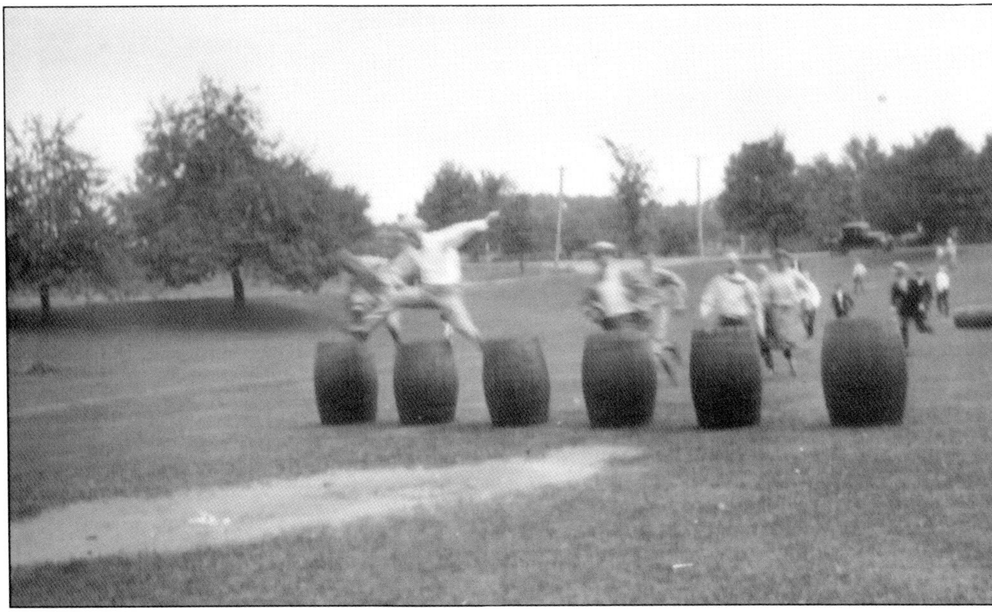

Waterbury trolley employees compete in an obstacle race at Lake Quassapaug during a Connecticut Company outing on August 16, 1923. (CRH.)

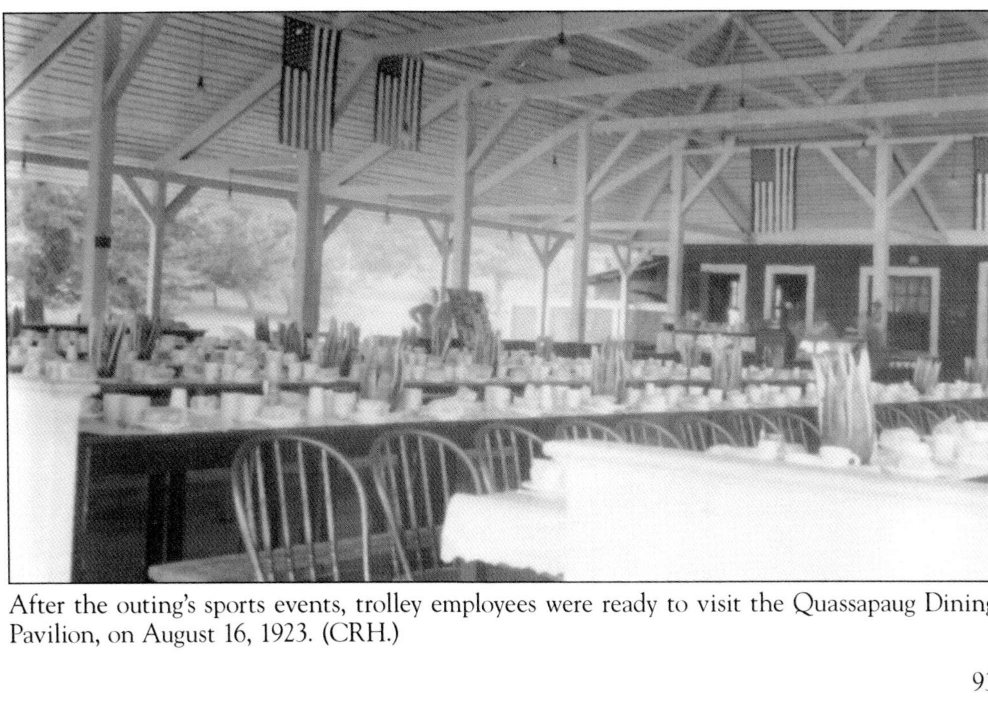

After the outing's sports events, trolley employees were ready to visit the Quassapaug Dining Pavilion, on August 16, 1923. (CRH.)

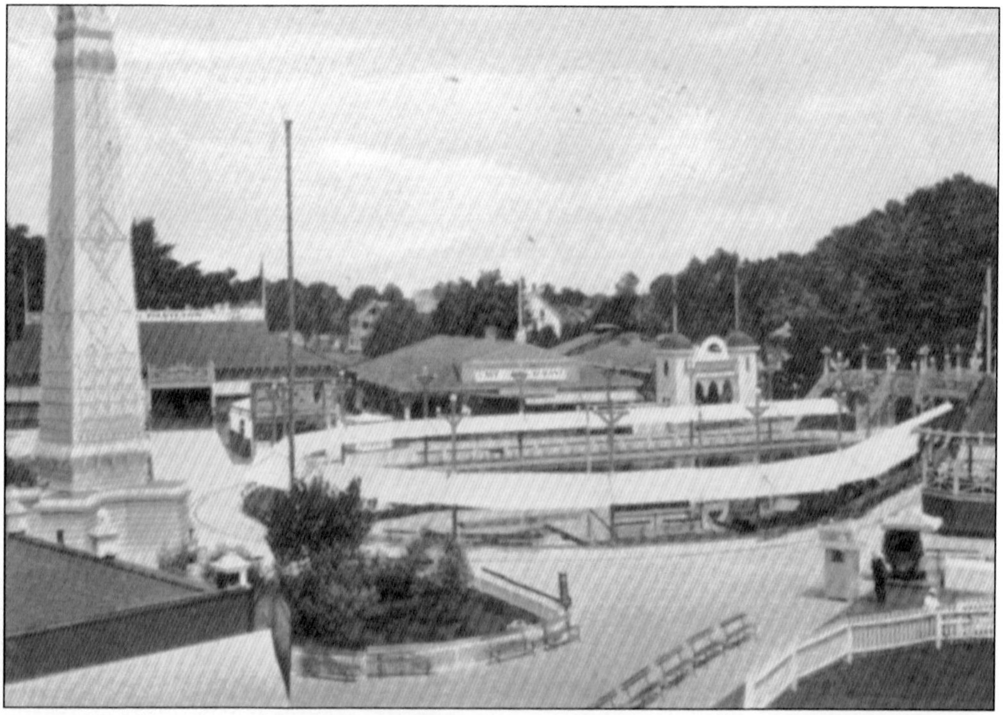

Seasoned trolley riders could go via Waterbury to New Haven, where the Connecticut Company maintained its own White City within the overall Savin Rock amusement complex. This view was taken *c.* 1907. (FWC.)

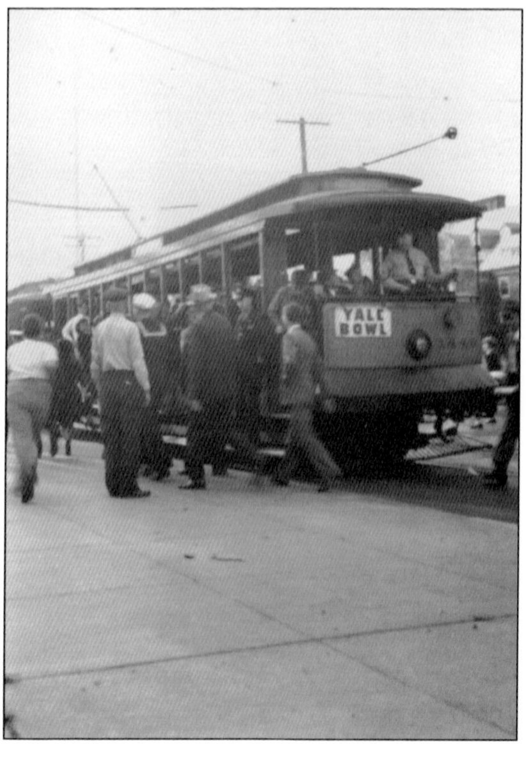

Even an afternoon at Yale Bowl was possible, if one started out early enough in the day. Taken on October 7 1944, this photograph shows a group of patrons boarding car No. 1448 after the game. (CRH.)

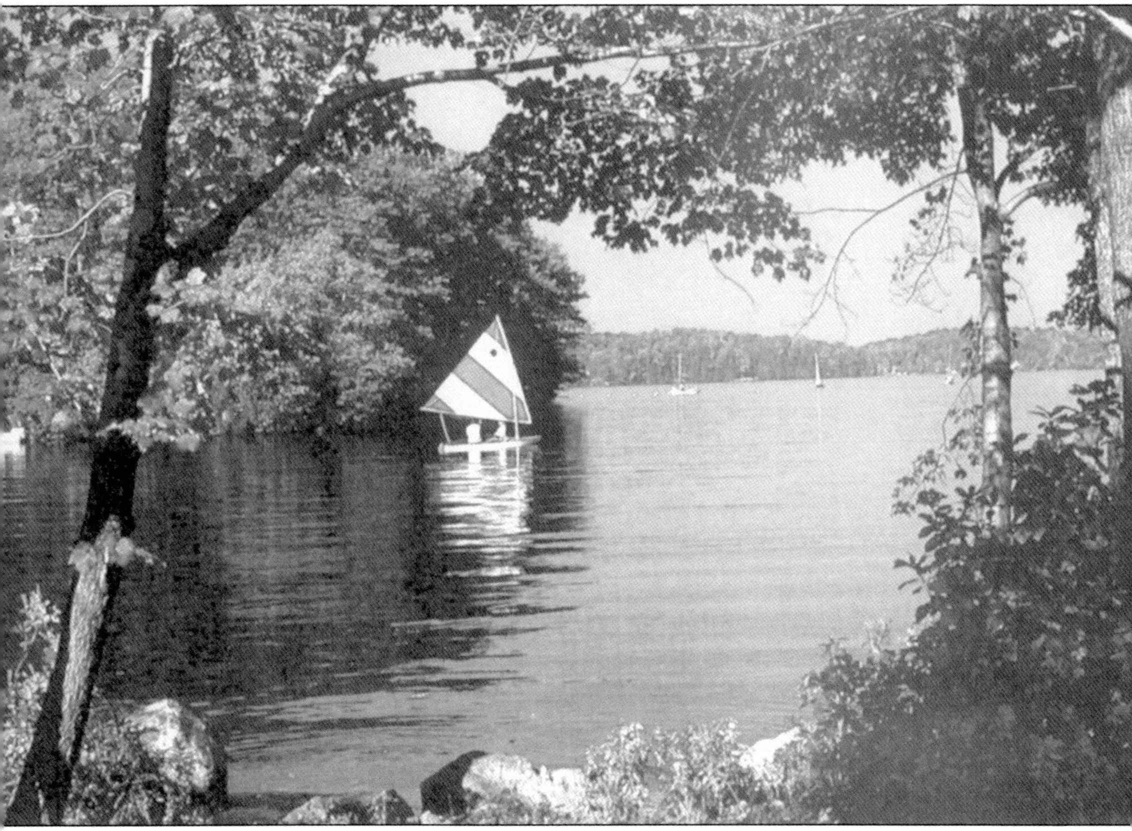

This photograph taken on an early fall day shows a Waterbury-made Sun Fish sailing near the Quassapaug Yacht Club. (FWC.)

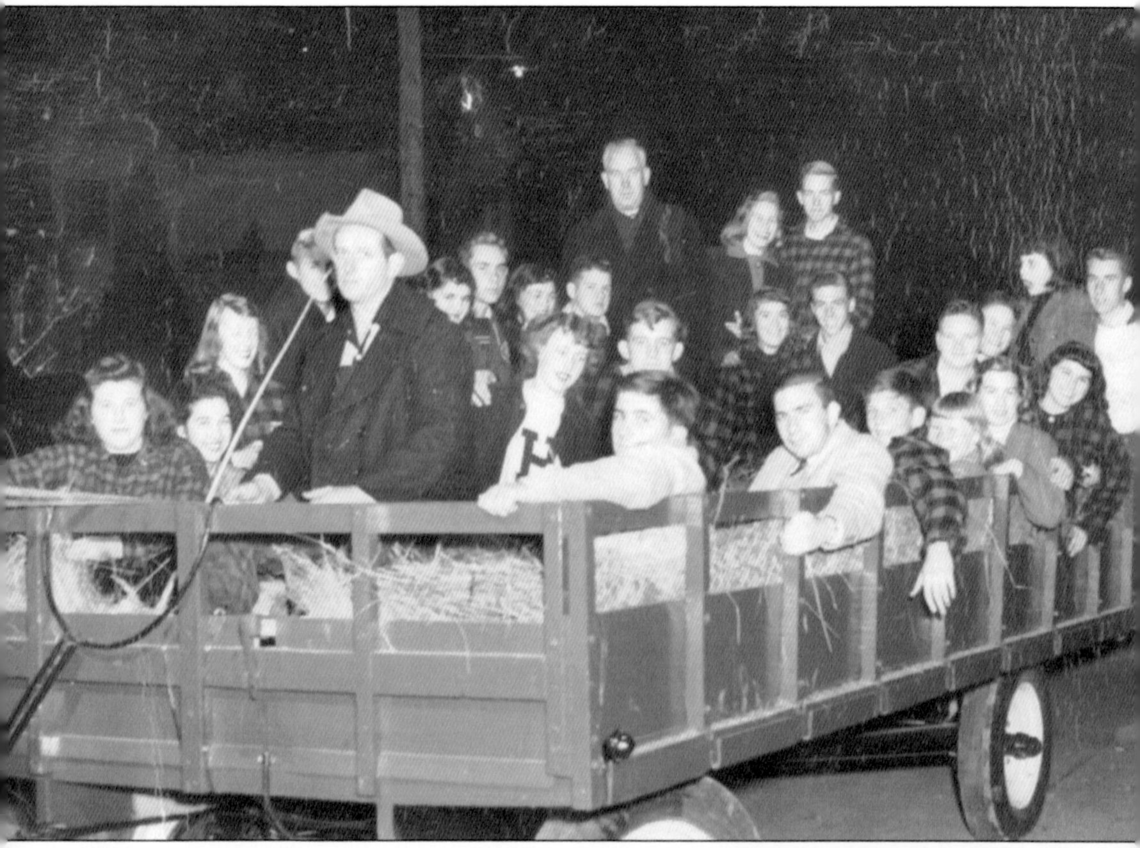

What could be more fun than an October hay ride in 1947? Enjoying themselves are the following members of the Woodbury High School sophomore class: Emily Metcalf, Anne Bower, Kay Kanerzel, Bill Brandt, Betty Rhoades, M. Bunny Lautenschlager, Larry Brownell, Ray Opperman, Jackie Fawcett, Timmy Dawson, Danny Candido, teacher Mr. Israel, Bill "Red" Clark, Nancy Mitchell, Shirley Saylers, Velma Deschino, Bob Chase, driver H. King, Olive Guy, Don Meyers, Esther Terrell, Dick Manville, principal Mr. Coombs, Betty Nordstrom, Bobby Beardsley, and Claire Fleming. (ETT.)

Seven

Meeting the Test

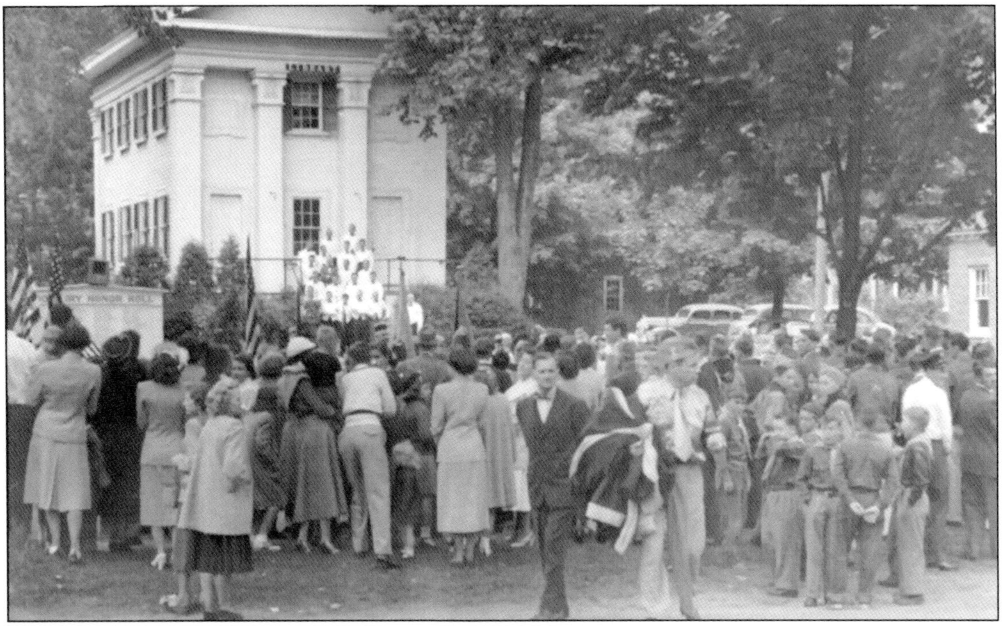

Indian raids were not a major concern for the area's early settlers, though alarm over King Philip's War in 1675 sent most hurrying back south to the relative safety of Stratford until mid-1678. The French and Indian War had some Woodbury area participants. Up to 1,000 men served in the Revolution; also, large amounts of supplies, including thousands of shoes, were sent off to Gen. George Washington's army. In the Civil War, 142 men marched off to preserve the Union, and 46 of them perished in combat or from disease; their names went on Woodbury's War Memorial. More than 100 area men served in World War I and nearly 200 in World War II. Korea and Vietnam have since added to the names on the town honor roll. During this Memorial Day ceremony in Woodbury, the men's chorus performs on the steps of the old town hall. (C-H.)

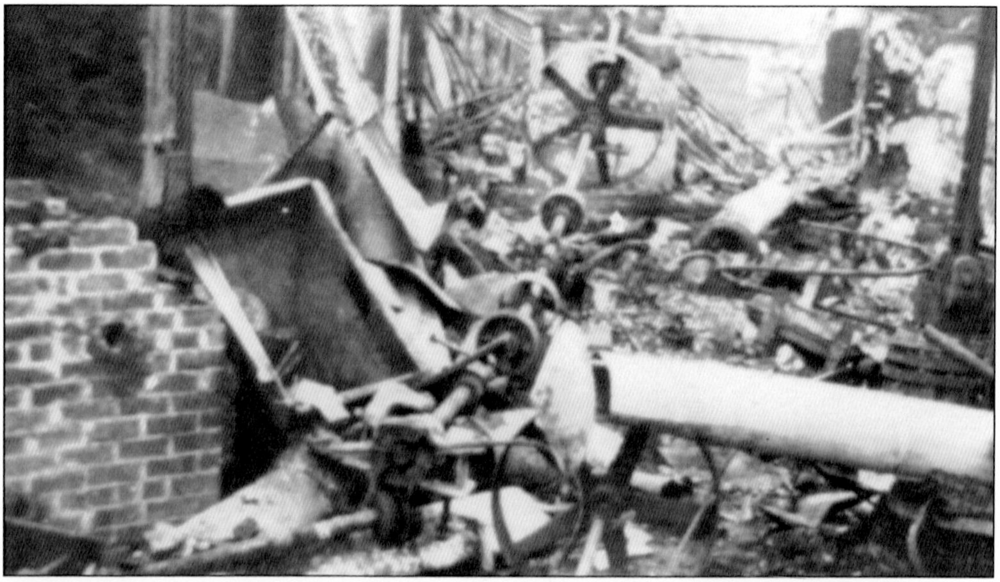

These are the ruins of the Knife Factory, which burned in a 1914 fire of suspicious origin. Improved fire protection for Woodbury began in 1894, with the laying of a 6-inch water main down Main Street and the subsequent organization of the Orenaug and Hotchkissville Fire Districts. The *Barnes Directory of 1896* listed these districts as each having a hose cart, foreman, and assistant foreman. The directory included instructions for reporting a fire: "Alarm boxes will be found on the outside of each of the four churches. Any citizen discovering a building on fire will repair to the nearest church, break the glass in front of the box and give ten quick strokes upon the bell. After a brief pause, ten more are to be given. If the fire is below the Town Hall, a succession of single strokes, with short pauses, will indicate the locality; if above, two strokes. The glass in the doors of the Hose Cart Houses may be broken, and a key, to unlock the door, will be found suspended on a hook, two inches to the left of the opening." (C-H.)

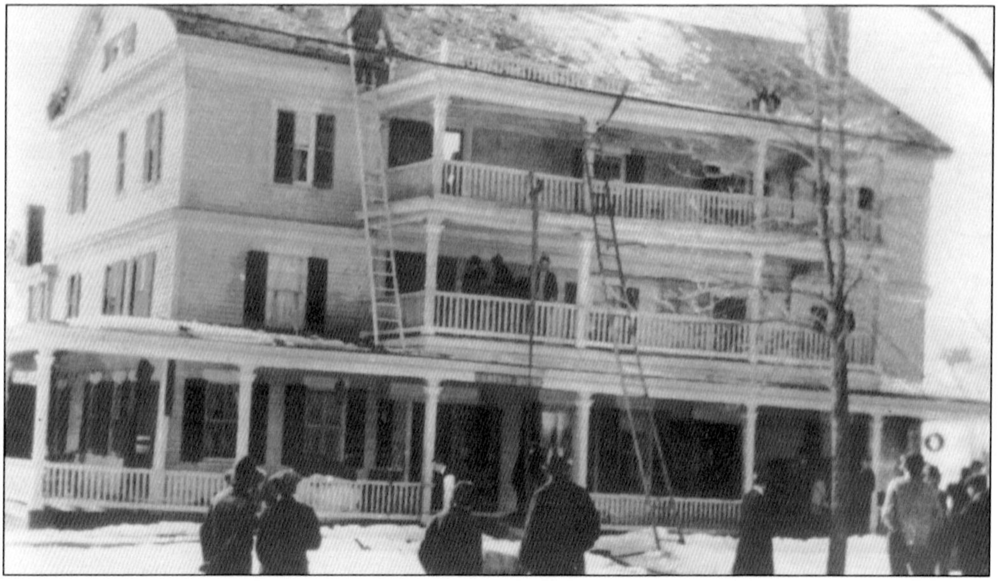

Early in 1916, the Curtis House sustained serious damage from a roof fire. The frigid January weather hampered firefighters' efforts to save the prominent structure. (C-H.)

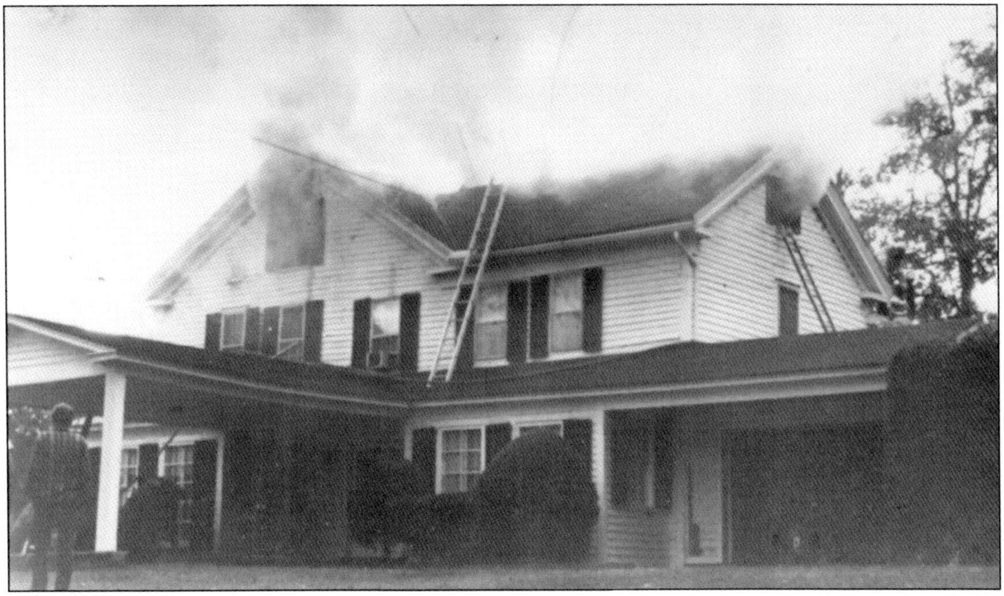

This photograph shows the fire that struck the Munson Funeral Home. In 1929, the Woodbury Fire Department was formed by combining the Orenaug and Hotchkissville Companies. A new Seagrave pumper was put into use and remained active for more than 30 years. Its engine was so loud that, when driven full speed down Main Street by Fred St. Pierre, its siren was not only inaudible but also "totally superfluous." (C-H.)

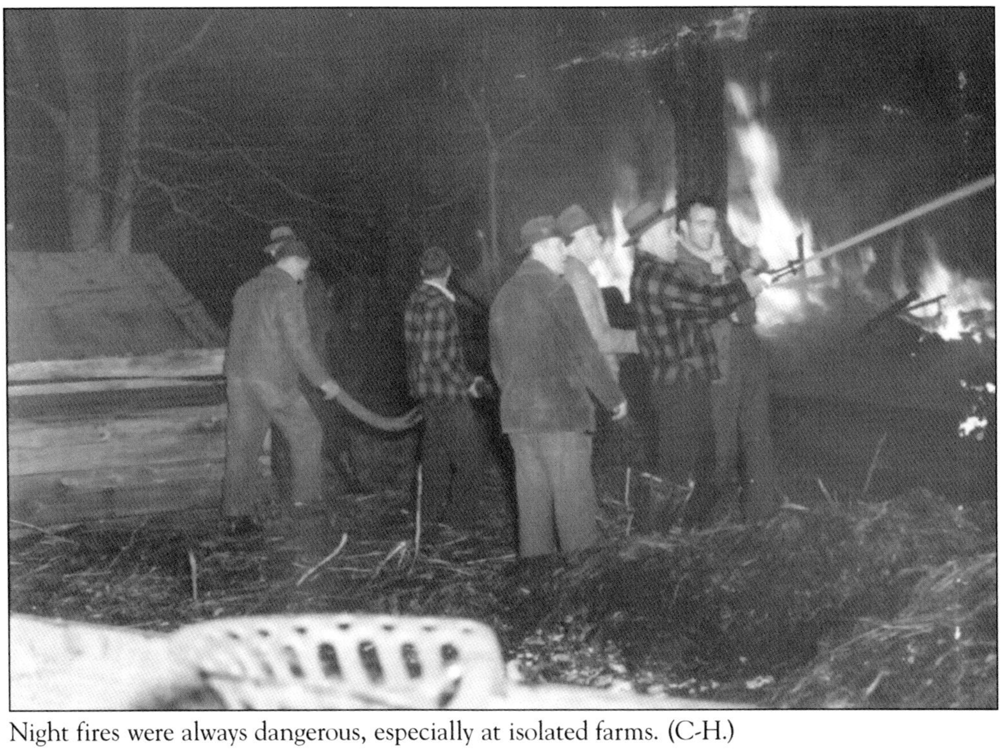

Night fires were always dangerous, especially at isolated farms. (C-H.)

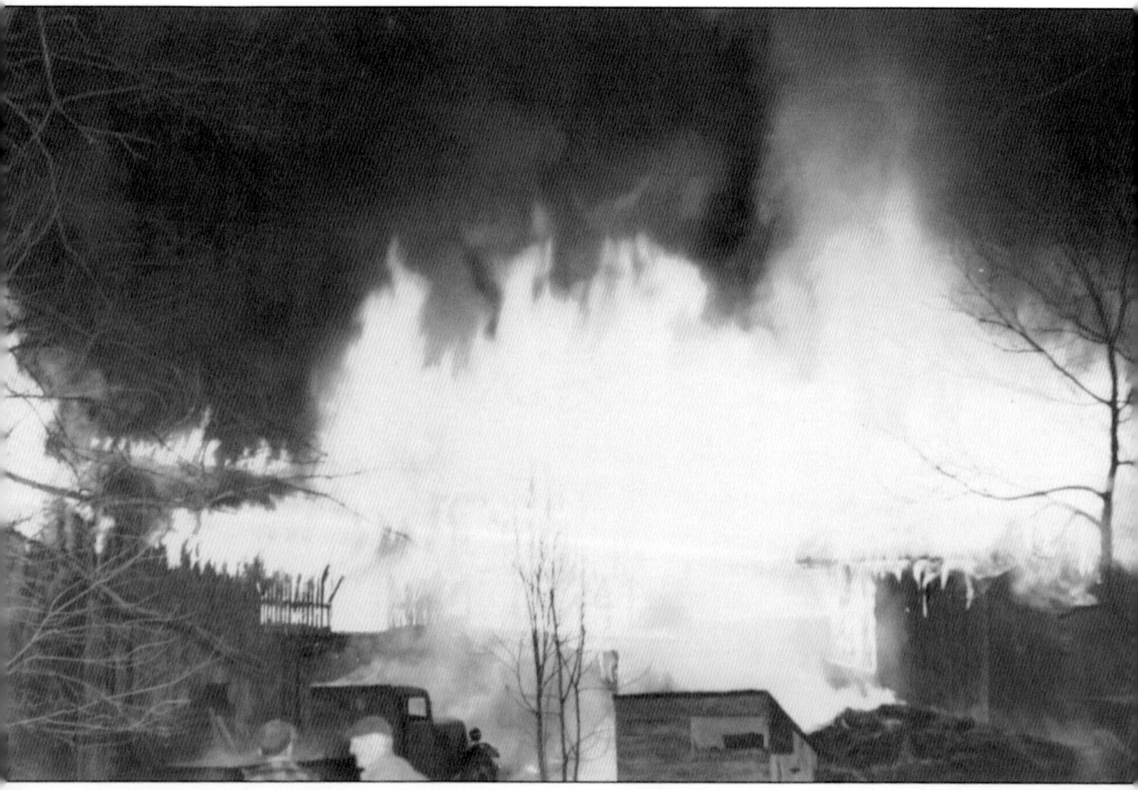

This blaze consumed Fowler's barn in March 1948. (C-H.)

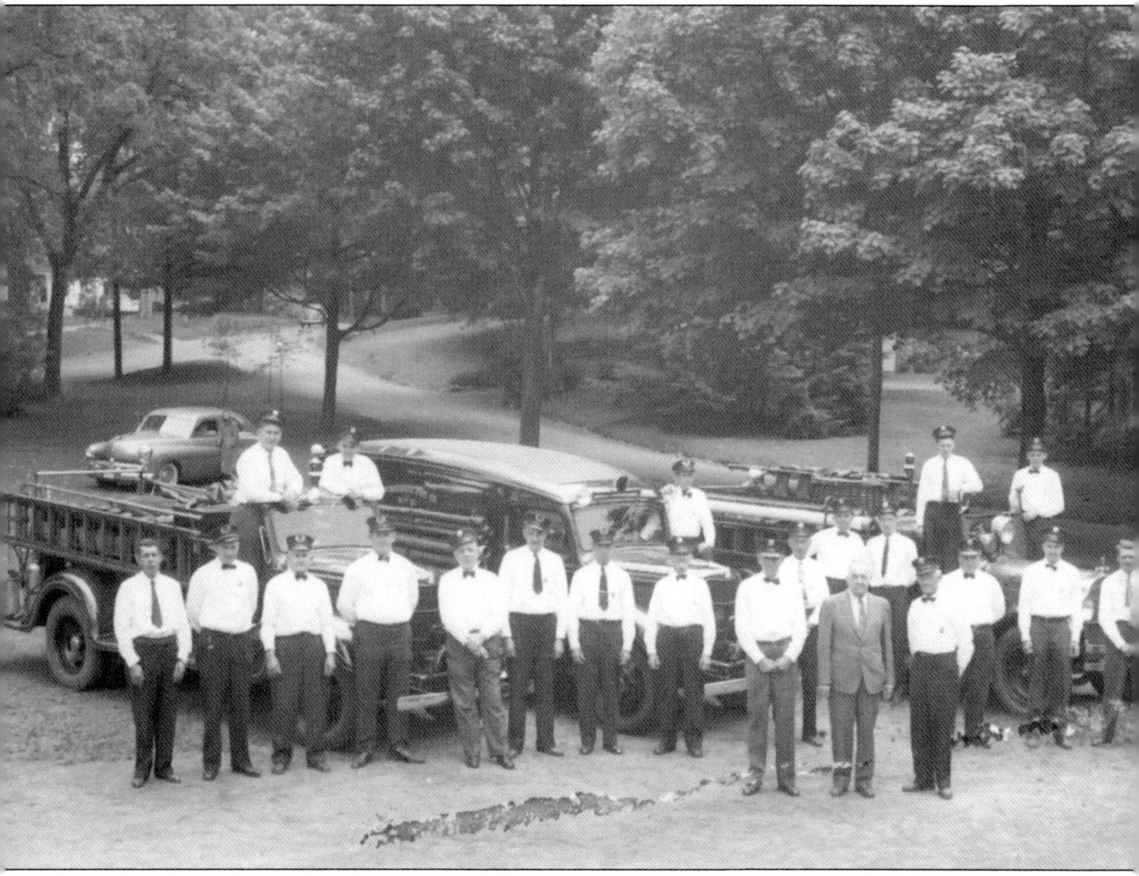

This photograph shows the Woodbury Volunteer Fire Department in May 1949. (C-H.)

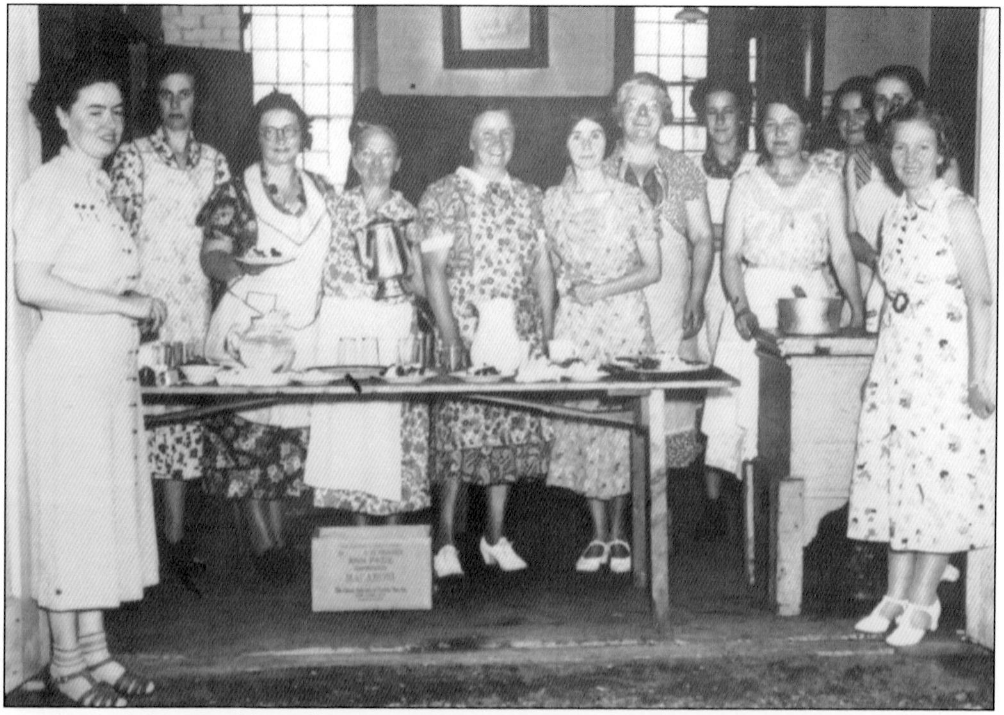

Members of the Hotchkissville Fire Company Auxiliary prepare a meal. Notice the carton under the table, which at one time held 24 8-ounce packages of "Ann Page Improved Macaroni," made by the Great Atlantic and Pacific Tea Company. (C-H.)

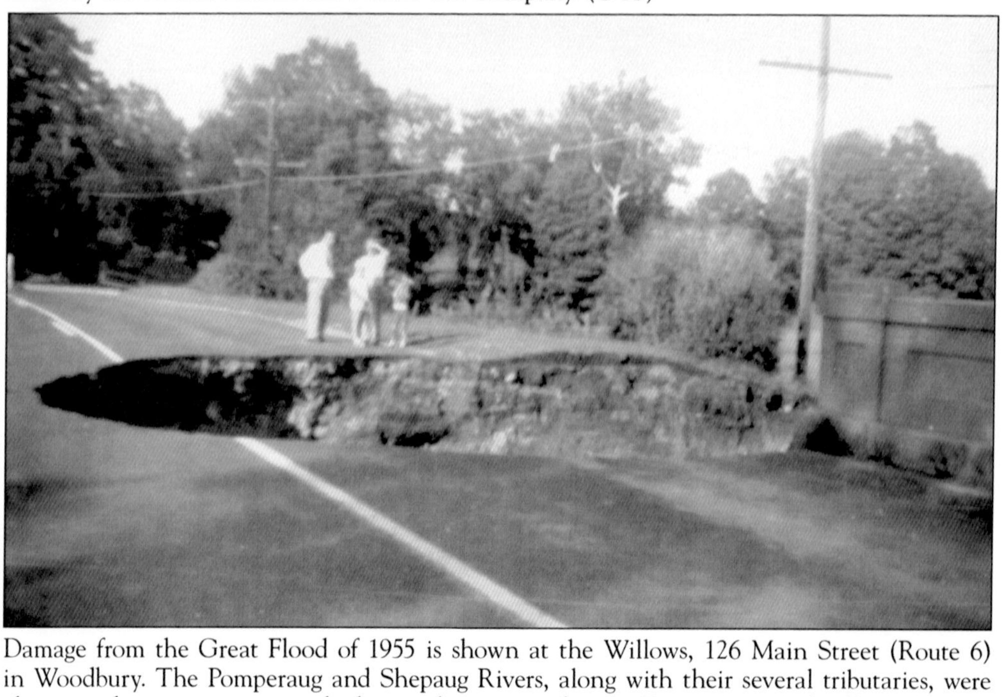

Damage from the Great Flood of 1955 is shown at the Willows, 126 Main Street (Route 6) in Woodbury. The Pomperaug and Shepaug Rivers, along with their several tributaries, were always ready to rise precipitously during above-normal rains. From spring melt-off to torrential summer downpours, damage to property and sometimes life and limb could occur. (C-H.)

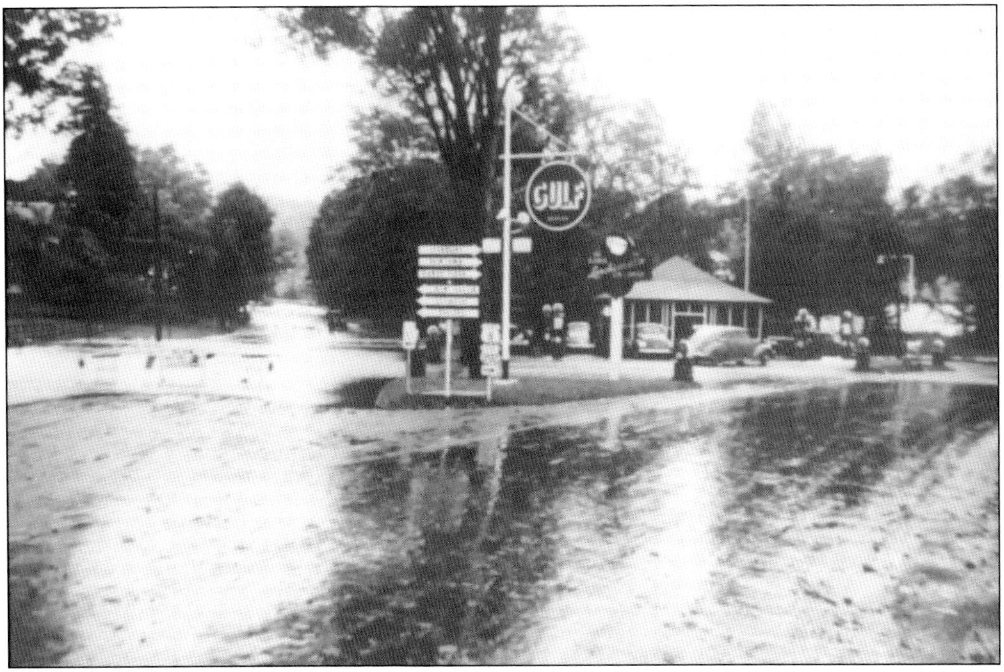

This is the Triangle in Southbury during the 1955 flood. The floodwaters caused vast destruction down both river valleys and resulted in a providentially successful test of the just-completed Shepaug Dam and the overnight filling of Lake Lilinoah. (SHS.)

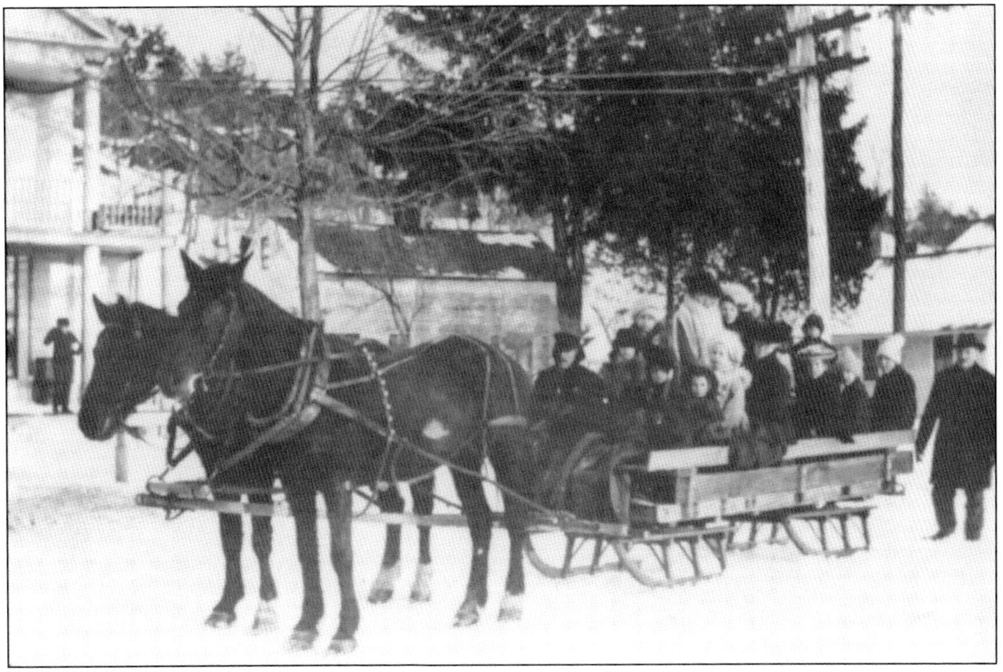

The "Gospel Sleigh" is shown after a snowstorm in Hotchkissville. Among those pictured are Bernice Lewis, Ethel Dunworth, Ruth Fairchild, Milton Karmon, Frank Ford, Edson Cowles, Harriet Hilton, Elizabeth Butkis, Elsie Rabbet, and Alma Frazier. Services were held in the Good Templars Hall in Hotchkissville. (C-H.)

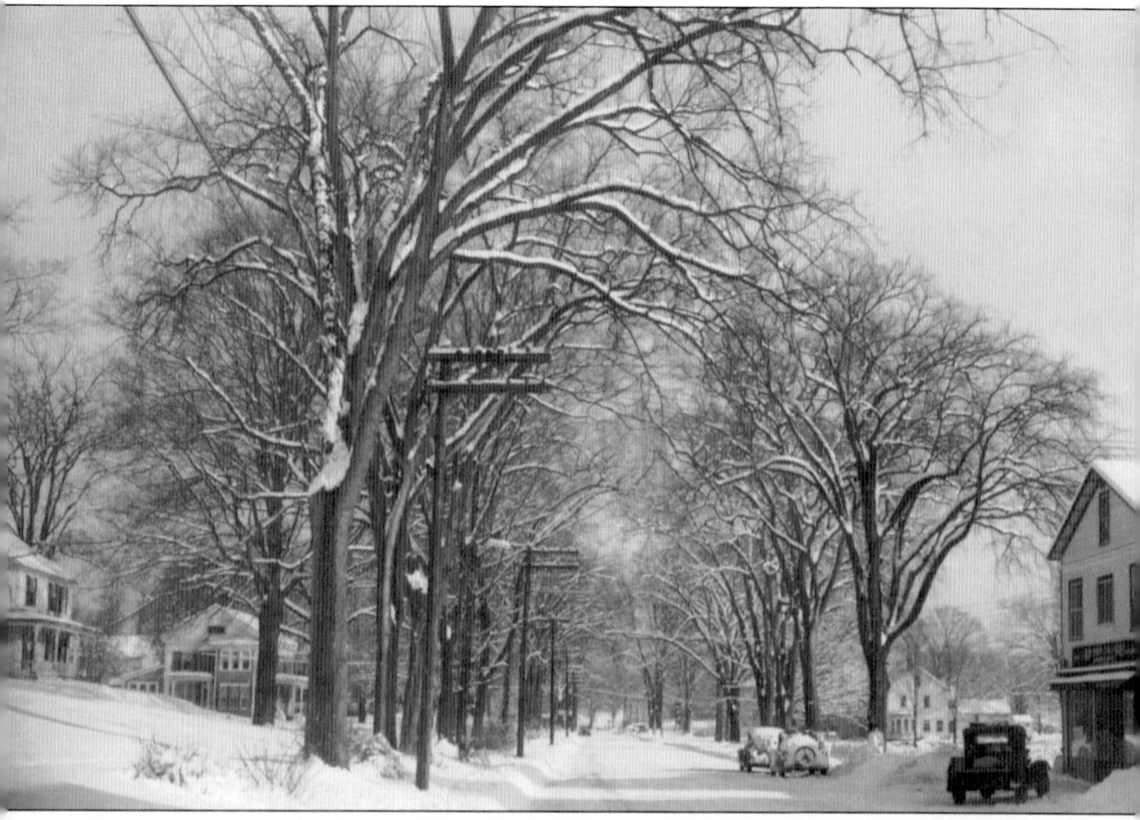

Snowstorms, even the famous Blizzard of 1888, were but seasonal events to a largely rural population. "Wheeling" became "sleighing," and even bulky grain and wood essentials were moved by ox-powered sleds. Canny Yankee farmers and even some townsfolk made their own convertibles out of basic wagon bodies with provision for either wheels or runners. (C-H.)

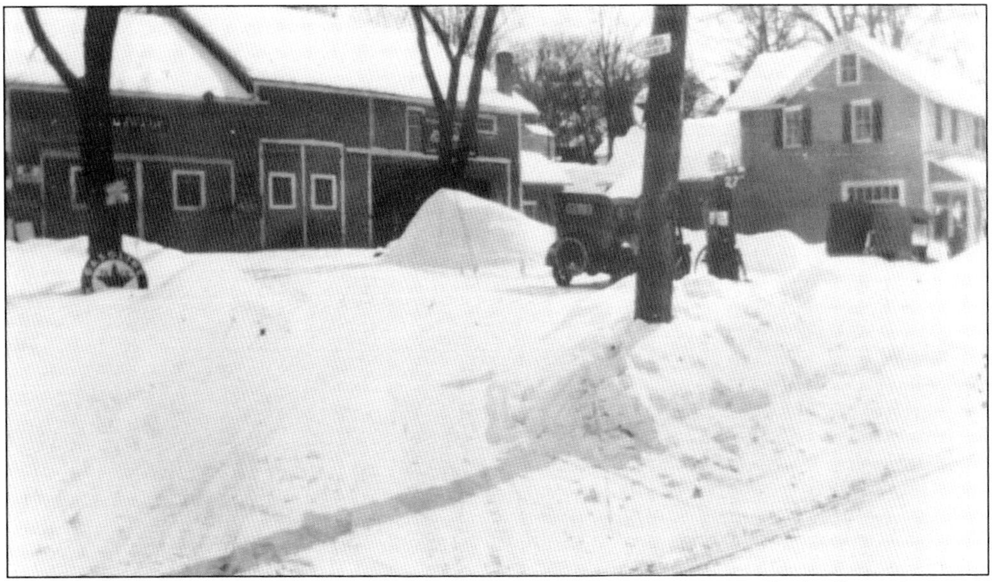

The automobile age required new techniques for transportation. Instead of rolling the snow smooth for sleighs and sledges, it now had to be removed and sanded for the passage of motorized wheels. This winter scene shows the Beardsley Garage on the left and Martin's store on the right. (C-H.)

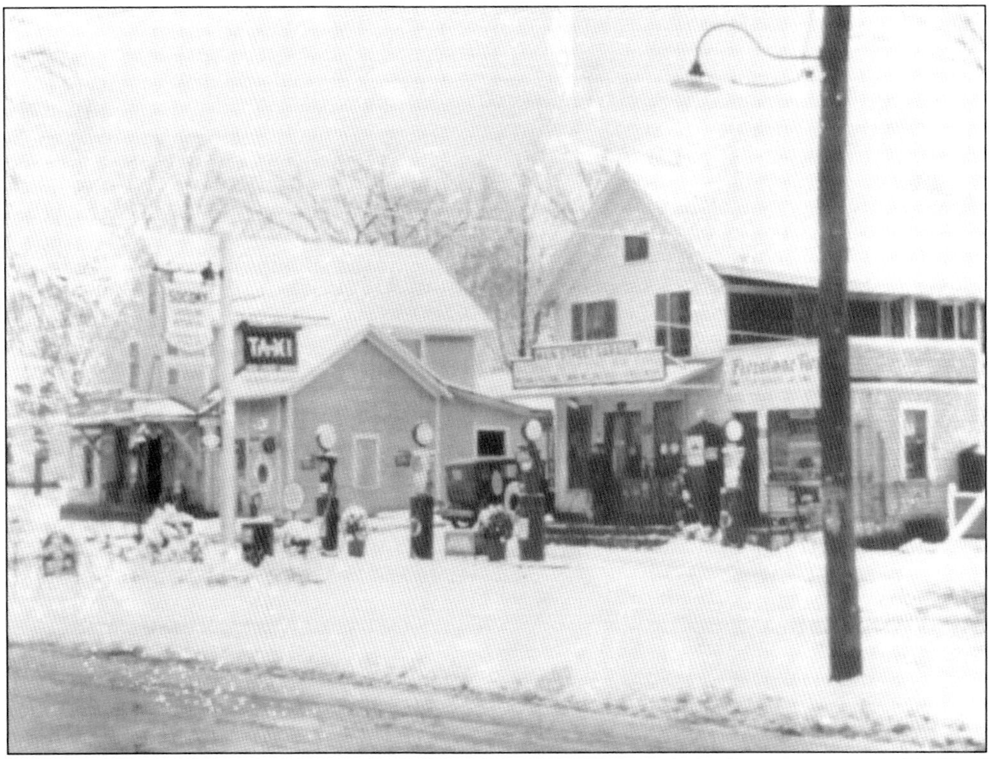

The Markham Garage on Main Street weathers another winter—the winter of 1928. Fred Markham started this garage before Carl & Walt ran it. Over the years, other owners of the building included Charles Mallett, C.L. Adams, and Czar Winton. (C-H.)

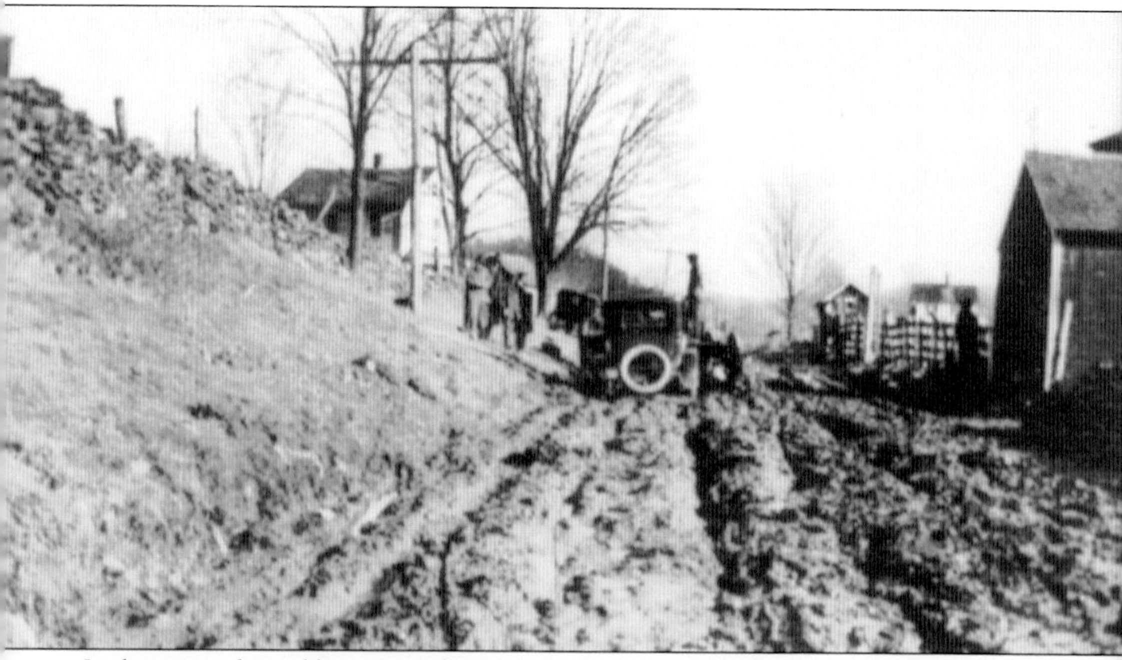

In the spring, the problem was mud. This is the Anderson Farm during the mud season of 1914. In later years, the property was used as an auction barn. (C-H.)

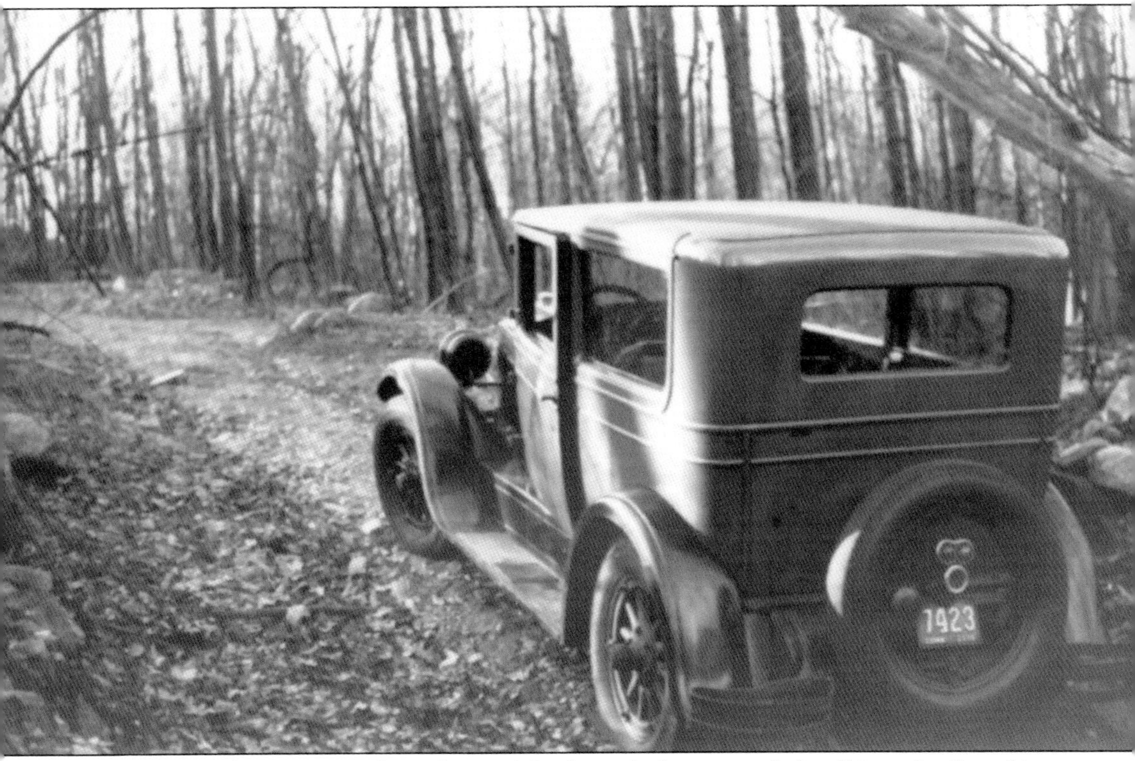

Spring thaws culminating in the infamous March mud often extended well into April, making life difficult for farmer and commuting worker alike. This car has become stuck on a dirt road in April 1935. (CRH.)

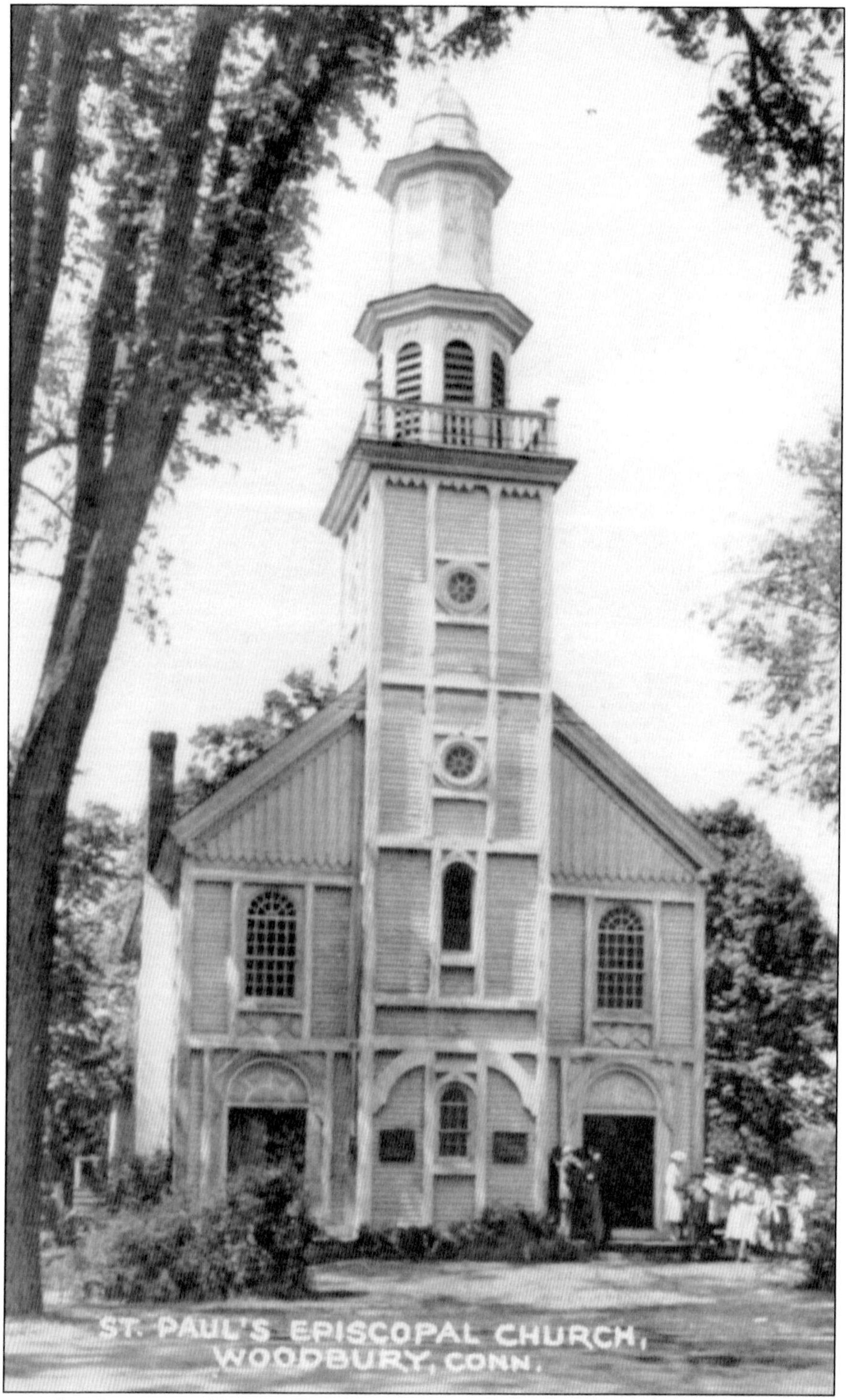

A taverner by the name of Lucius Foot came to a violent end in the horse sheds behind St. Paul's Church on March 4, 1856. Edward Bradley was accused and put on trial three times, and on each occasion he was saved from hanging by a hung jury. (FWC.)

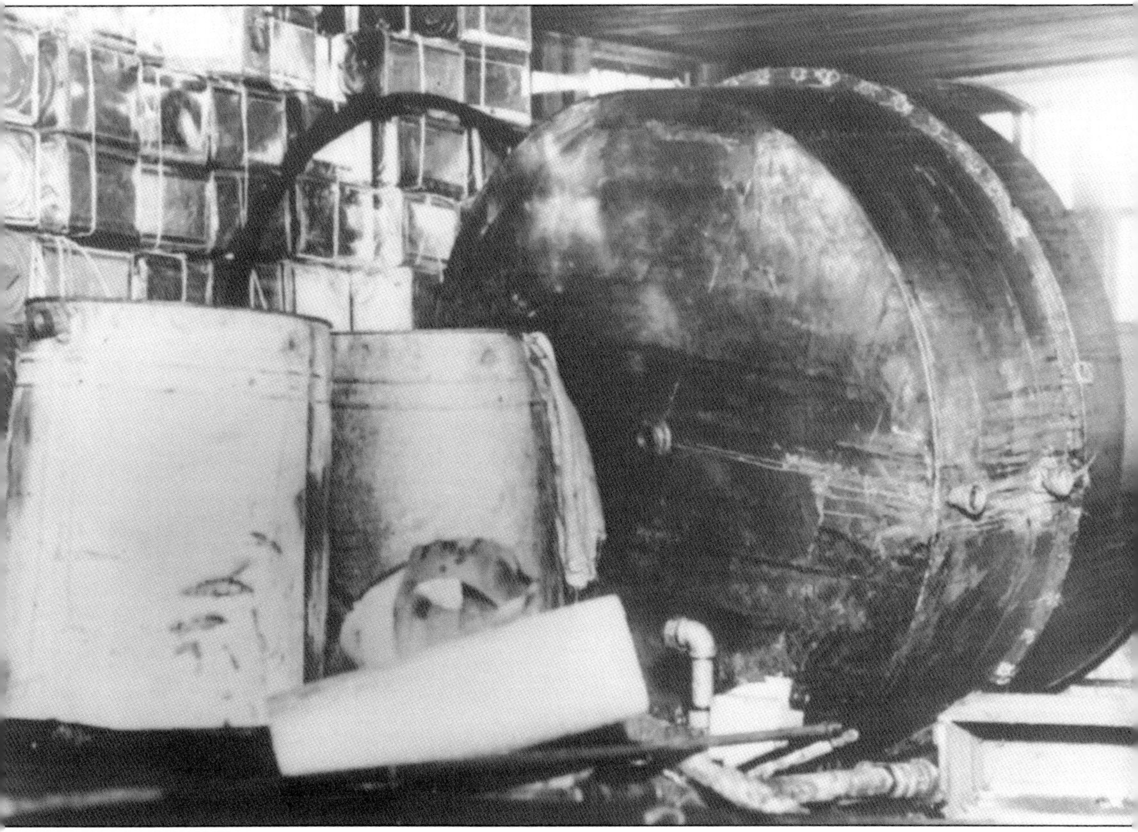

Despite police raids on rural stills, such as this one at the corner of Routes 6 and 61, Prohibition was a national failure and led to the rise of organized crime. (C-H.)

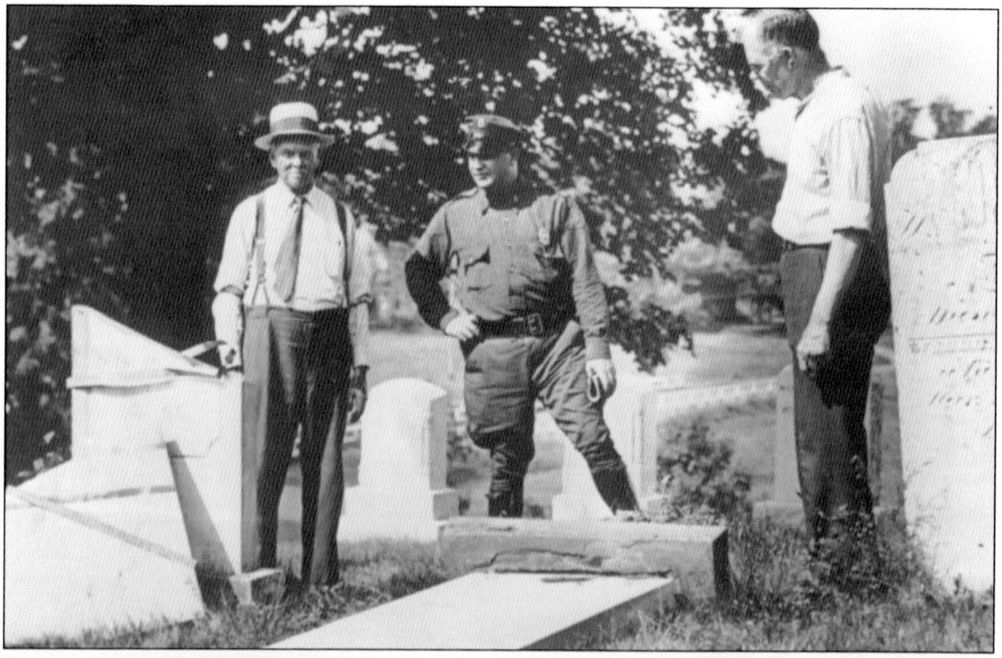

Cemetery vandalism, unfortunately, is not a modern invention. This desecration, involving some of Woodbury's oldest stones, occurred in 1933. (C-H.)

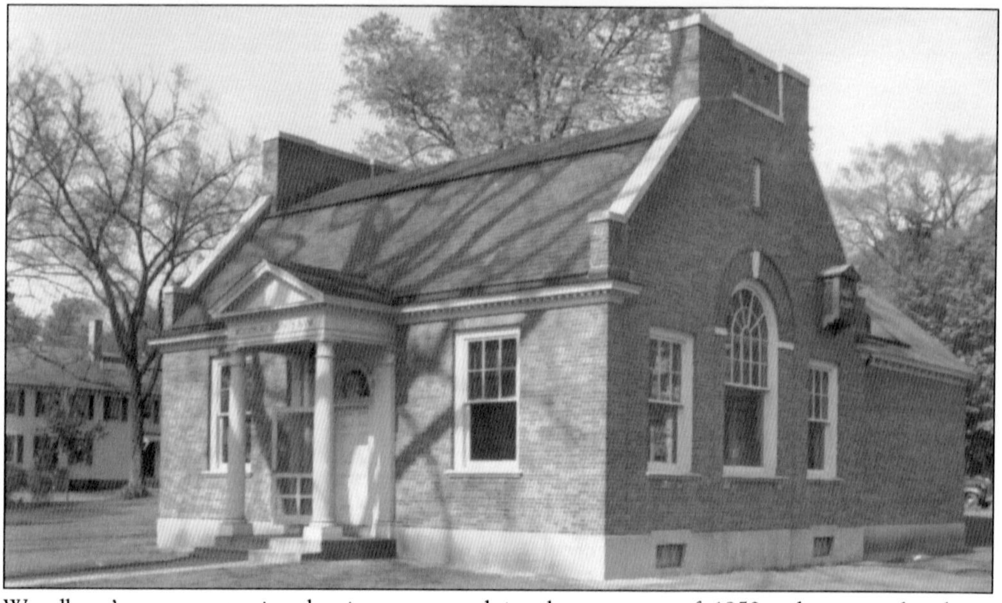

Woodbury's most sensational crime occurred in the summer of 1950, when two brothers, already on parole from Sing Sing Prison, robbed the Woodbury Savings Bank. After an intensive manhunt and bullet-punctuated car chase, the pair were nabbed near the Housatonic River in Southbury. Curiously enough, a public service movie short had recently been filmed, using the same bank as the crime scene. The plot had a pair of robbers fleeing on motorcycles, only to be halted by a state police roadblock at Zoar Bridge. If the brothers-in-crime had been so inspired to hit the Woodbury Bank, they should have also considered the film's ending! (C-H.)

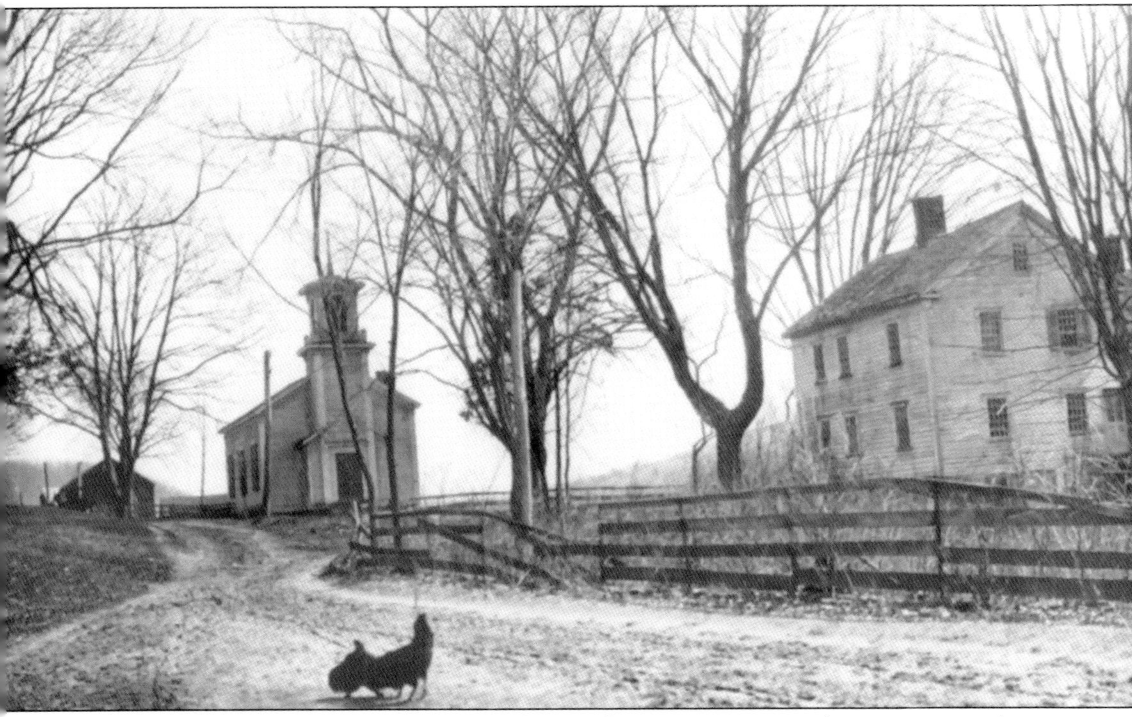

When hard times hit, population declined. Woodbury's greatest population rise was during Colonial times. Between the 1756 census and the Revolution, the number of inhabitants essentially doubled, going from 2,911 to 5,313 in 1774, making Woodbury seventh in size for Connecticut towns. By the Civil War, however, the population had declined to just over 2,000 and to barely 1,800 in 1890, as old farms were abandoned and local industry waned. By 1920, the nadir was reached, with a mere 1,700 residents recorded. Not until the 1970 census was the 1774 figure again exceeded, with 5,869 inhabitants listed. The ghost town in the photograph is Southville in March 1913. When Charles Harte visited that year, the town had already been abandoned, doomed by the rising waters of Lake Zoar. What was left of the population, a couple of chickens, turned out to greet him. (CRH.)

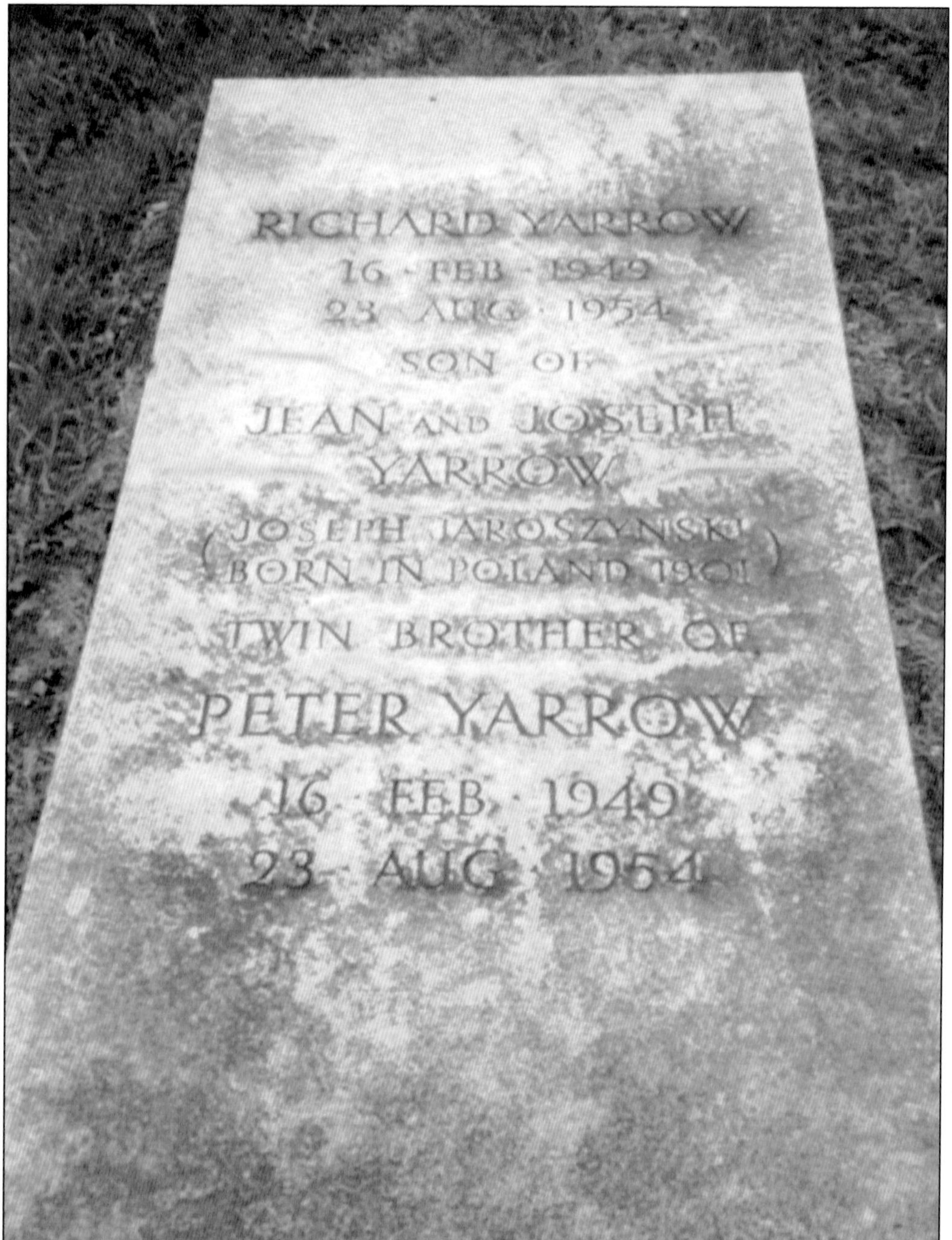

An air disaster claimed the lives of a Woodbury family in late August 1954. Joseph and Regina Yarrow and five-year-old twins Richard and Peter Yarrow were on their way to visit relatives in Europe when tragedy struck. Their KLM plane out of New York was nearing Amsterdam when it plunged into the North Sea. Only Richard Yarrow's body was recovered, and he now reposes alone in the Old North Cemetery. (FWC.)

Eight

At Rest

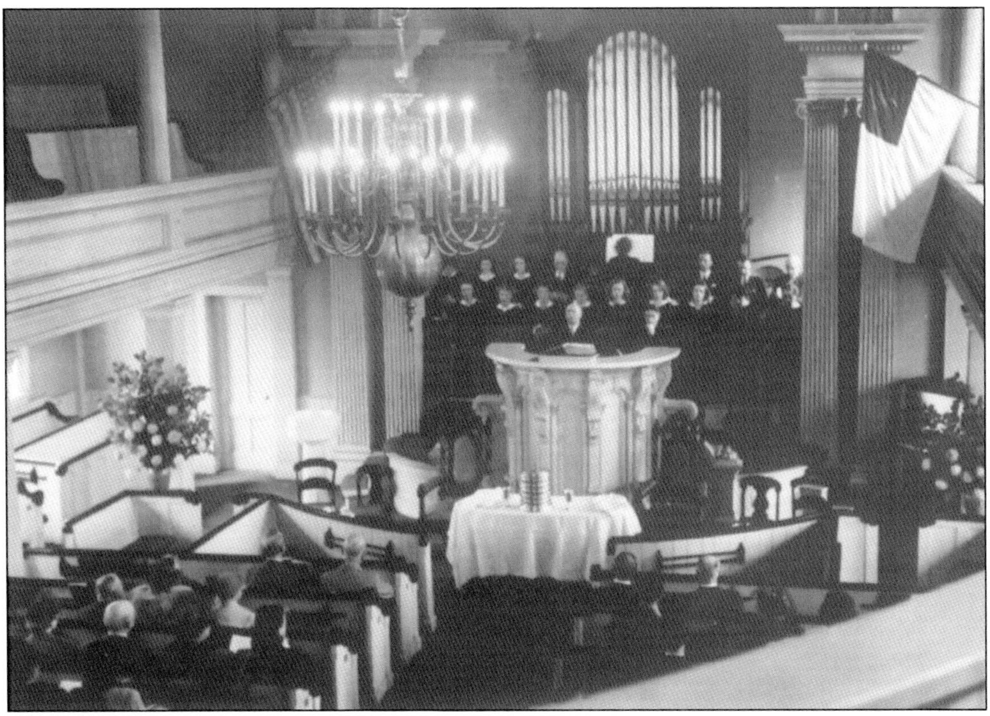

Shown is a Communion service at the First Congregational Church of Woodbury. The photograph was taken on July 17, 1954. (ETT.)

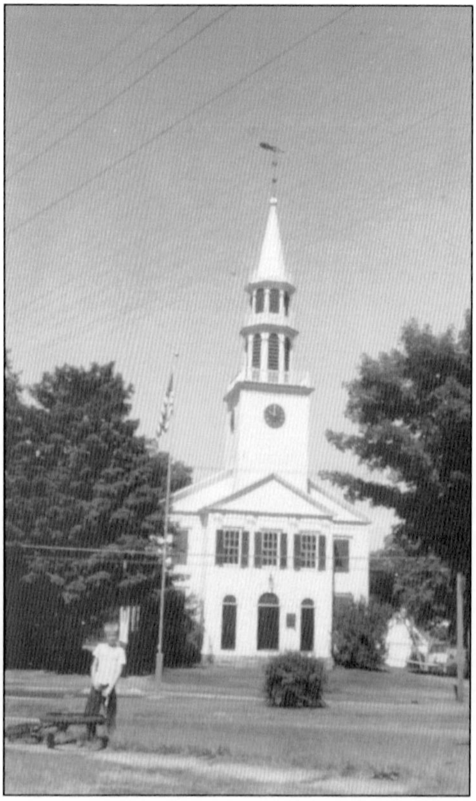

Having been founded for ecclesiastic reasons, Woodbury and its offspring parishes were Congregational bastions of theocracy; only church members were allowed to vote in civil matters. Taxes were levied on all residents for the support of the local minister. Soon, however, divergent internal views and the arrival of outsiders with different religions brought about pragmatic adjustments. Newcomers with skills and sound work ethics were most apt to be tolerated. (CRH.)

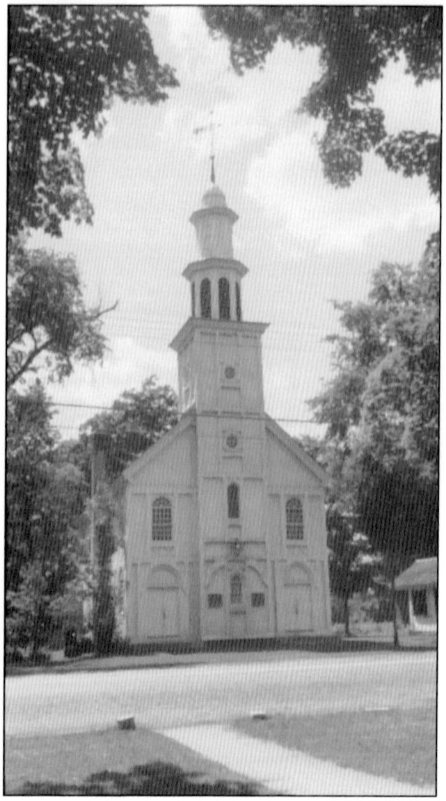

This photograph shows St. Paul's Church in the early 1900s. (C-H.)

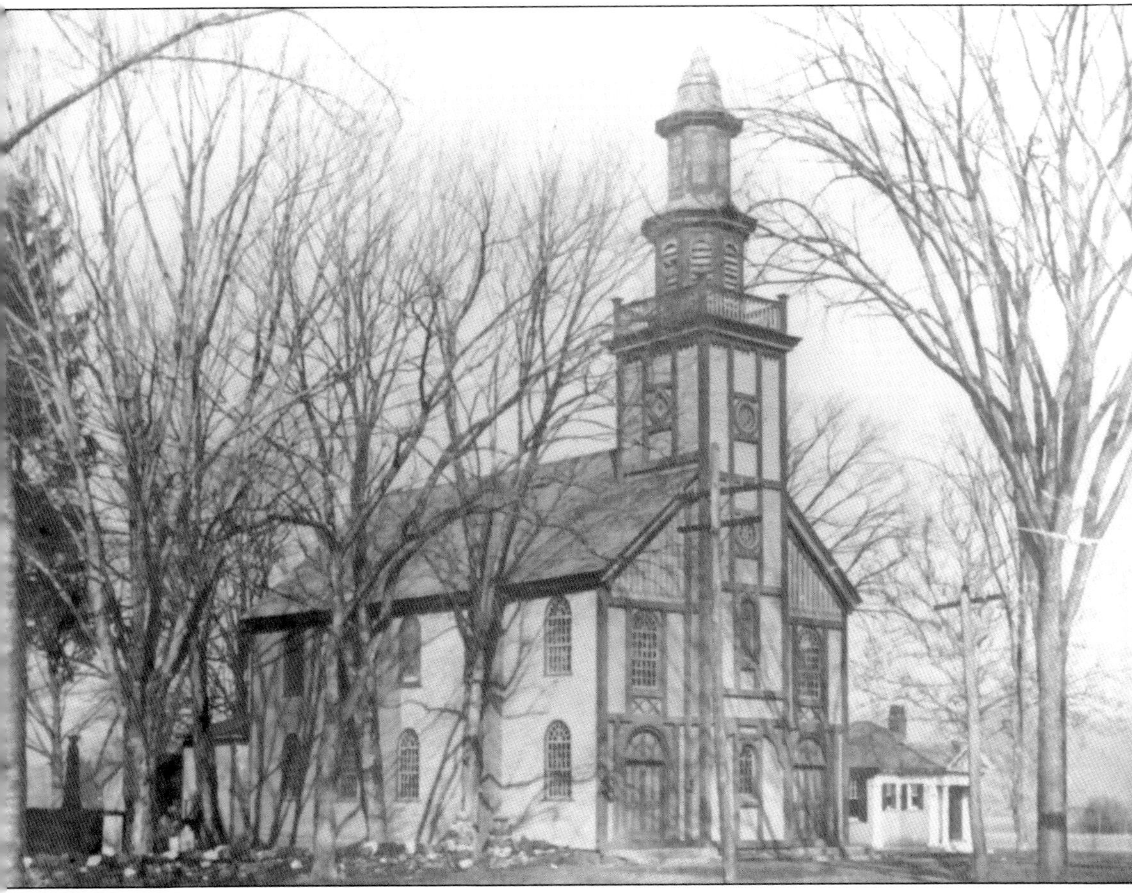

St. Paul's Church of Woodbury, an Anglican Episcopal Church representing England's state religion, was early on the scene, being backed as it was by the Crown, itself. St. Paul's parish was established in Woodbury in 1740. The present church is a continuation of the simple structure of 1785. This photograph was taken on July 17, 1954. (CRH.)

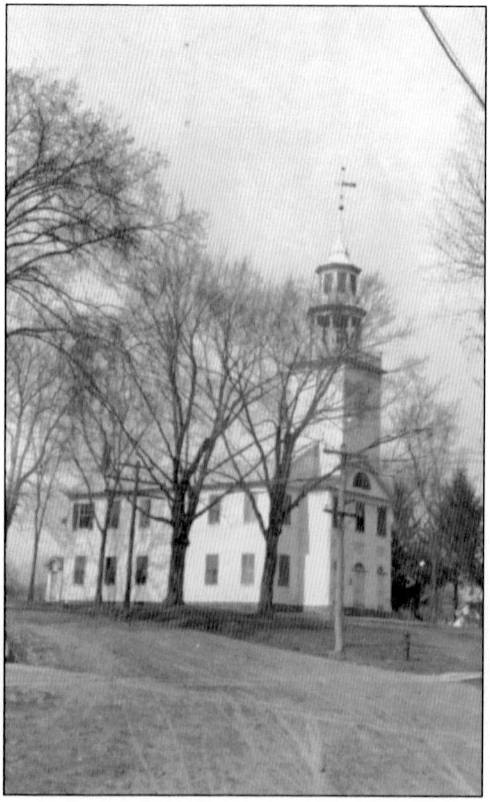

A 20-year movement within the Ecclesiastical Society led to the founding of the North Congregational Church in 1818. This photograph of that church was taken on April 7, 1908. (CRH.)

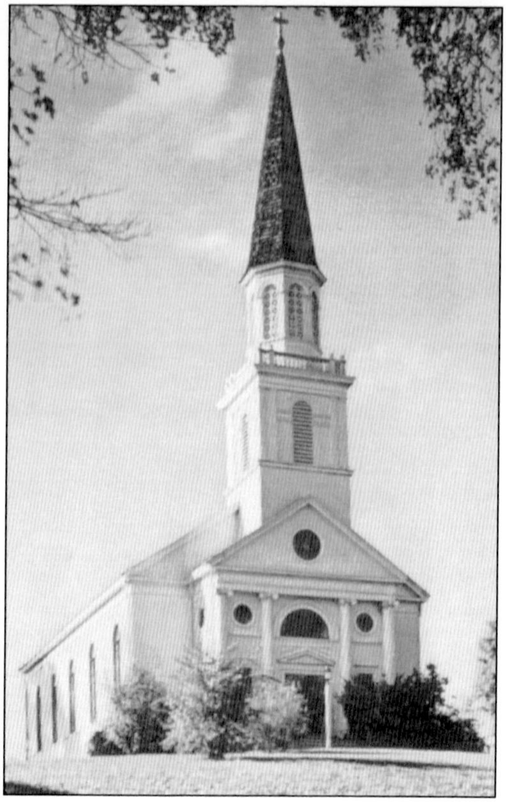

St. Teresa's Catholic Church of Woodbury is shown in this winter scene. (C-H.)

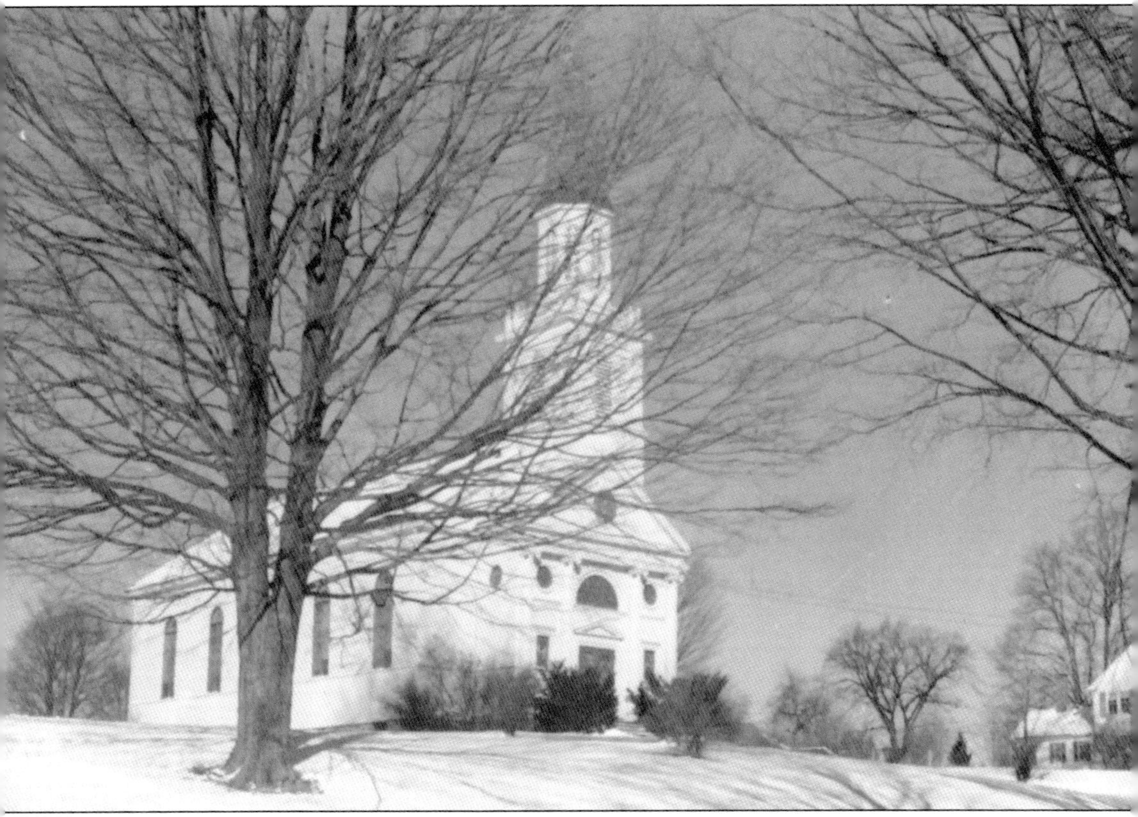

St. Teresa's Church started as a mission of St. John's Roman Catholic Church of Watertown. St. Teresa's was dedicated on September 4, 1904. (C-H.)

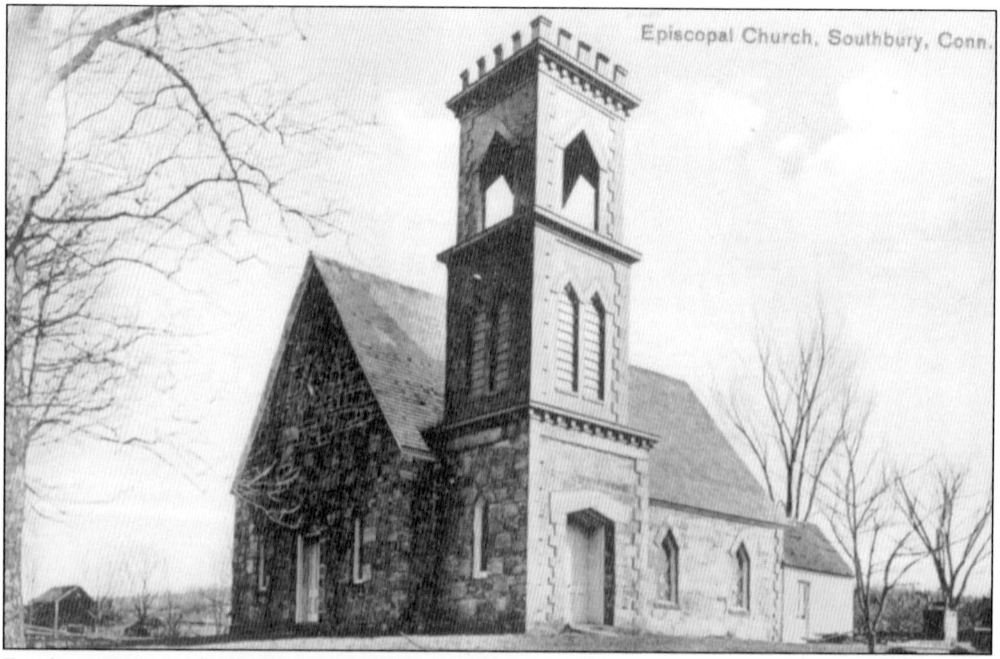

Epiphany Episcopal Church in Southbury was built at the time of the Civil War. (TL.)

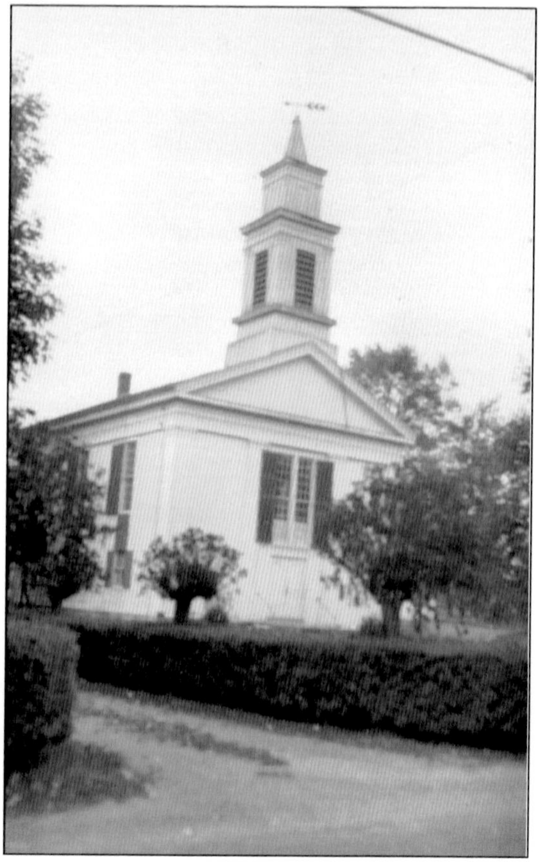

The Southbury Methodist Church, photographed on October 9, 1954, was later merged into the Congregational church. (CRH.)

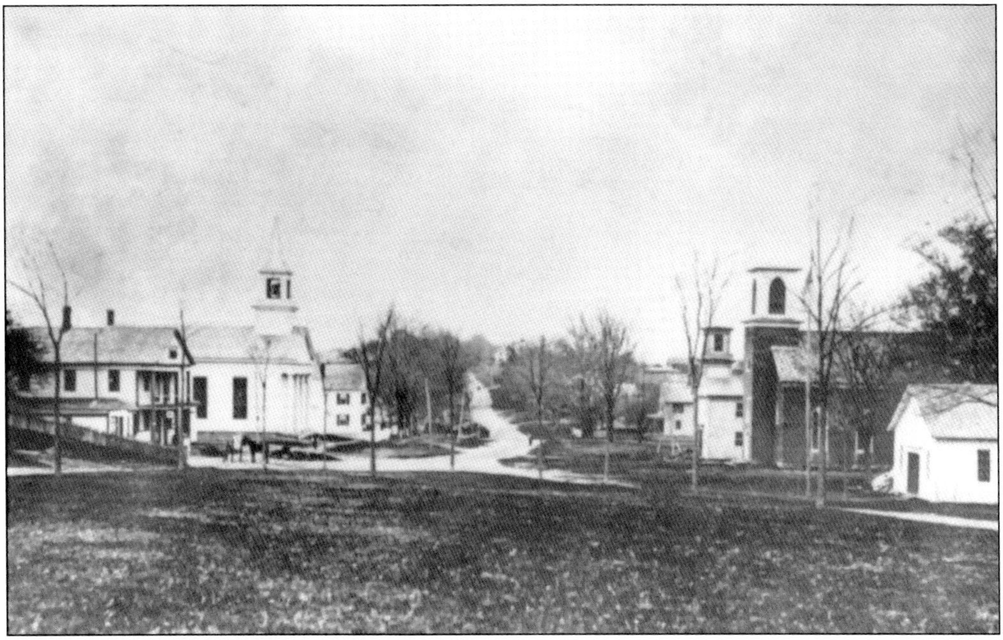

Bethlehem became a separate Ecclesiastical Society *c.* 1740 and was incorporated in 1787. This view shows the town center with its churches. The Federated (Congregational) Church was built in 1836. Christ (Episcopal) Church was constructed of locally made brick in the early 1830s. The Methodist church was erected 1860. In 1947, the Regina Laudis Abbey was established about a mile southwest of town by Rev. Mother Benedict Duss; the abbey has since grown in size and reputation. (BHS.)

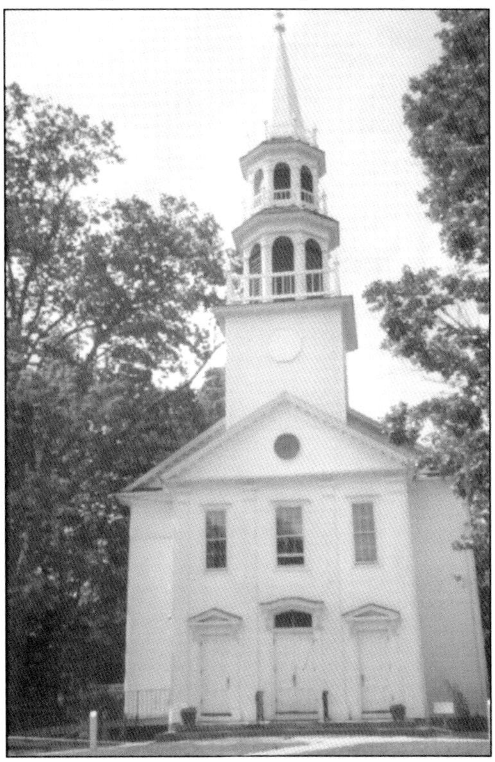

The South Britain Congregational Church was built in 1825. (FWC.)

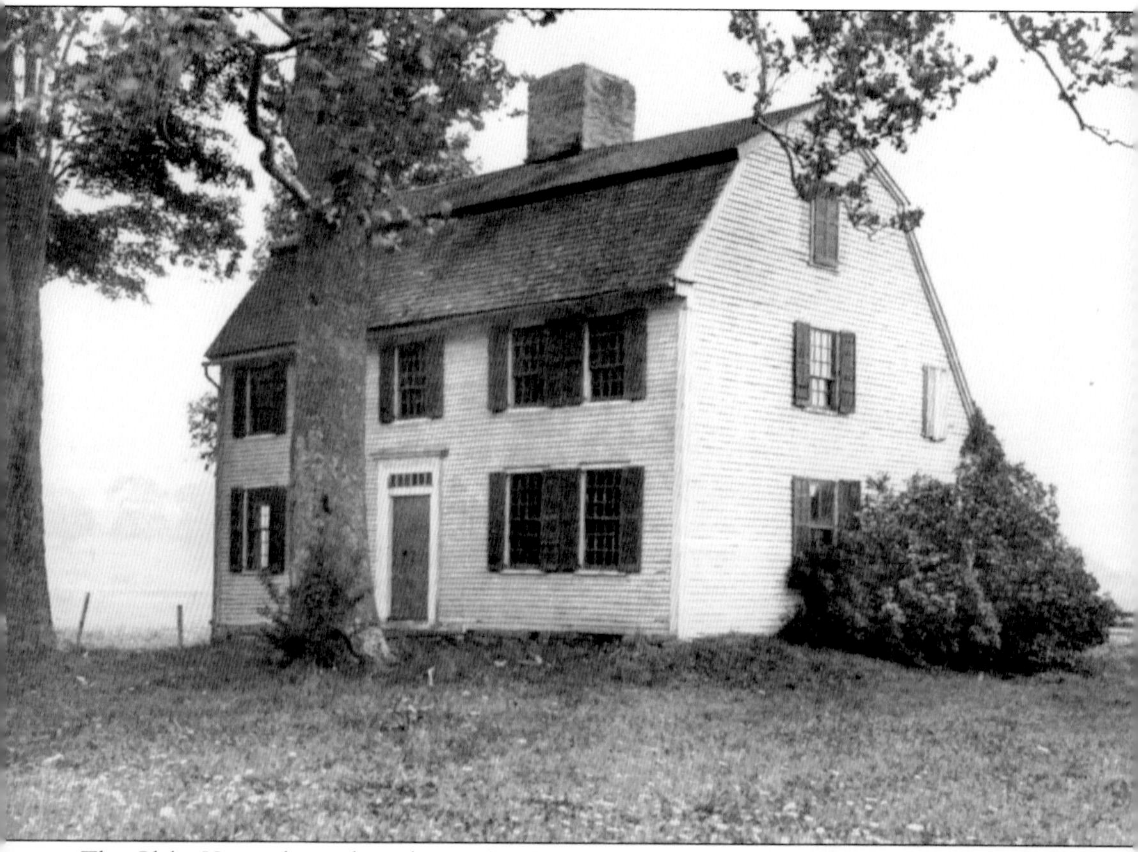

The Glebe House, located on the south side of Hollow Road, is Woodbury's historical, if not architectural, gem. A typical saltbox house, it has a large central fireplace and chimney, with gambrel roof and lean-to. It was built *c.* 1750 and was later enlarged. This photograph shows the Glebe House as it appeared *c.* 1914. The name comes, not from any personage, but from an old English term for a plot of land or farm whose products supported the local minister. It was the parsonage for Episcopal church minister the Reverend John Rutgers Marshall, who had studied under Rev. Joseph Bellamy in Bethlehem and later came under the influence of Stratford's Rev. Samuel Johnson. Marshall settled in Woodbury as a missionary in 1771, just when relations between Great Britain and her restive colonies were becoming strained. During the Revolution he was under suspicion of being a Loyalist and was confined at times to his home lot by the authorities. In March 1783, after the preliminary Treaty of Peace was signed, a secret meeting was held in the Glebe House, attended by 10 out of 14 of Connecticut's Episcopal clergy. Samuel Seabury from New London was chosen to become first bishop of the new Episcopal Church of the United States. Traveling to England to be ordained, Seabury found the Anglican clergy unwilling to perform the rite for political reasons. He finally headed north and was consecrated bishop on November 14, 1784, in Aberdeen by the Episcopal Church of Scotland. (WP.)

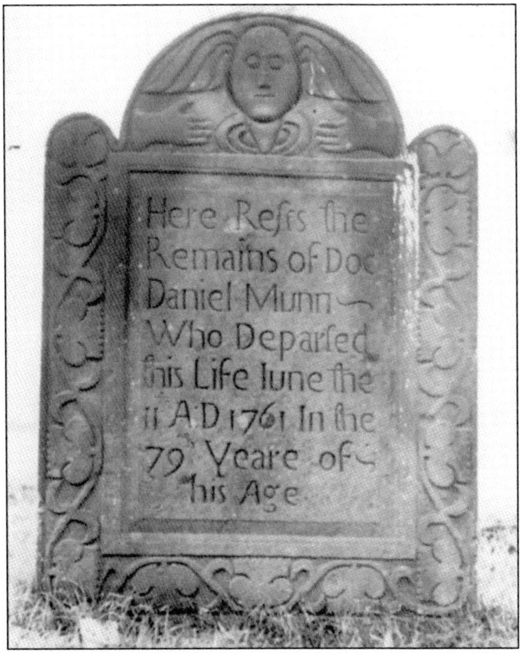

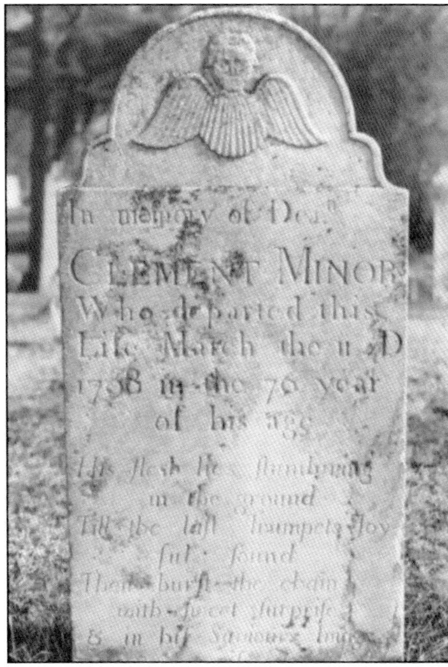

When Charles Harte reached Woodbury in his survey for the trolley line, he took time to visit the old South Cemetery. On February 18, 1908, he photographed a few ancient stones. Almost 30 years later, in November 1937, he returned and took more photographs with the same venerable folding Kodak camera. The gravestone at the left, bearing the traditional winged head, is that of Deacon Daniel Munn, who died on June 11, 1761, at the age of 79. On the right, the stone with a torso head and wings belongs to Deacon Clement Minor, who died on March 11, 1798, at the age of 76. (CRH.)

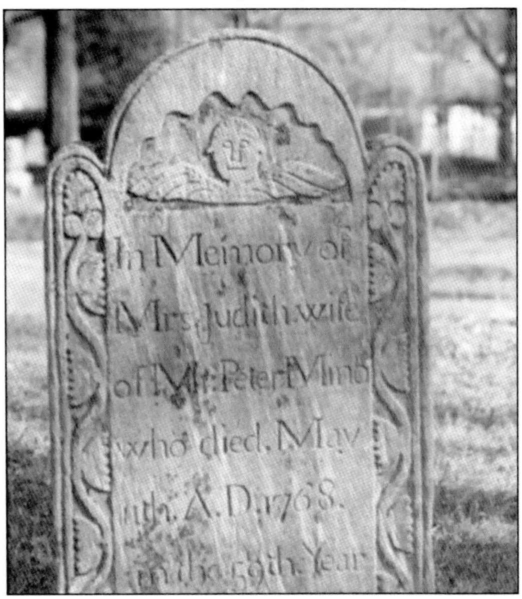

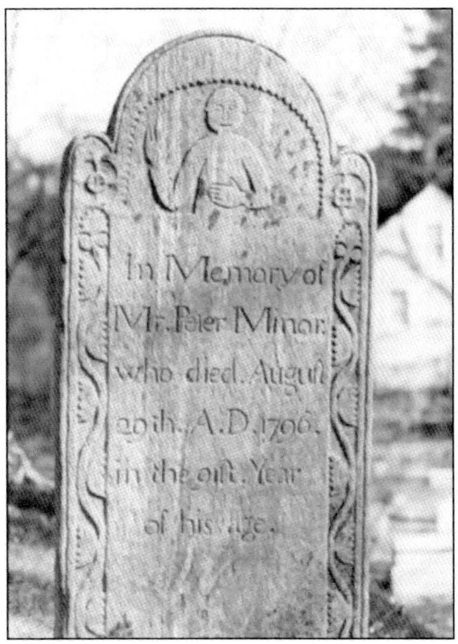

The gravestone on the left, bearing a winged head, is that of Judith Minor, who died on May 11, 1768, at the age of 59. On the right, with an unusual effigy design, is the gravestone of her husband, Peter Minor, who died on August 29, 1796, at the of 91. (CRH.)

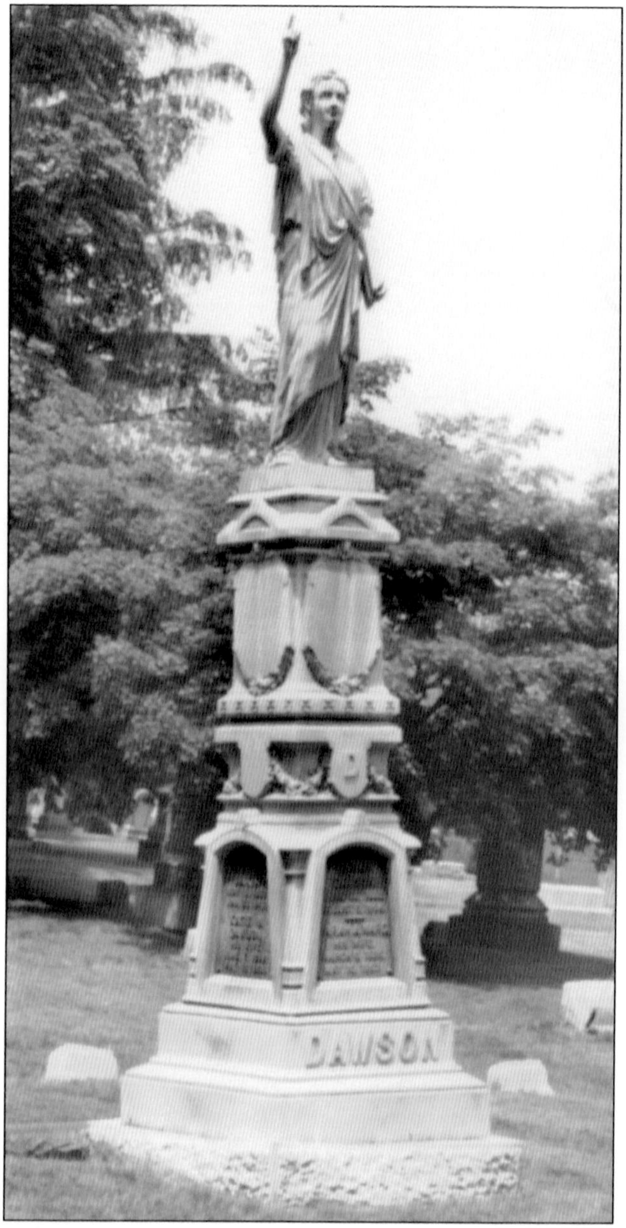

The tilting angel is one of five interesting monuments made of cast zinc that stand in Woodbury's North Cemetery. These white bronzes were made by the Monument Bronze Company of Bridgeport, mainly between 1880 and 1920. They can be recognized by a bluish-gray surface and their often elaborate Victorian decorations. Their embellishments include symbols such as urns, anchors, floral crosses, crowns, chains, severed roses, and Masonic devices. The tilting Dawson-Ward monument, by the west side of Washington Avenue, is the most prominent and the most imperiled. Its south base is now crumbling from its own weight, causing the figure of Hope atop its base to list alarmingly. Hopefully, some human "angel" will come to the rescue before a tragic and permanent "fall from grace" occurs. (FWC.)

Nine

THE PASSING PARADE

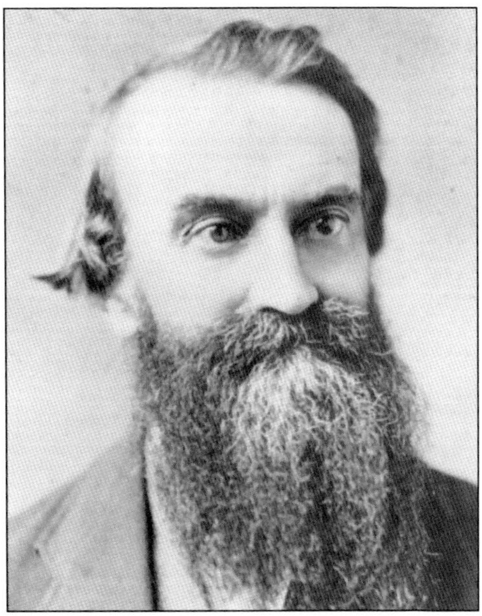
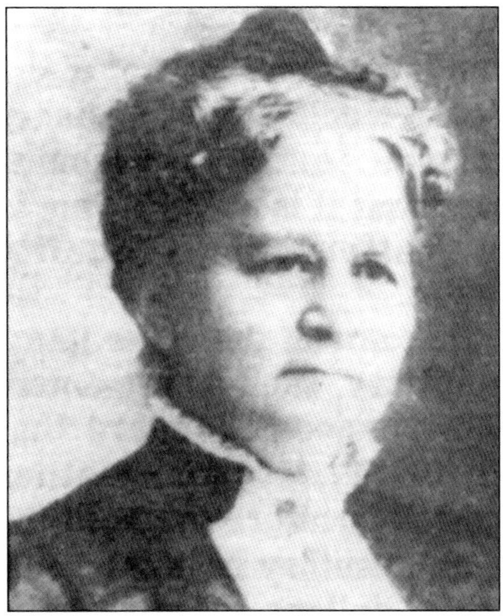

Two strong Yankee faces look down through the years. They are those of William A. Strong and Mrs. N.M. Strong. The *Barnes Directory of 1896* shows Strong and other old Yankee names still in predominance. Leading the January 1896 local census of almost 2,000 residents is Atwood, with 26 entries. Next are Allen and Judson, with 21 each. Others include Smith 17, Curtiss 16, Terrell 13, Minor 12, Cowles 9, and Galpin 8. Agriculture was the area's primary occupation, with 146 listed farmers. A majority of others gave their occupation as laborer, indicating a general connection with farming. On the industrial side, 77 listed connections with the American Shear and Knife Company in the Hotchkissville section. The latter ranged from Edward Cowles, president, and Julius Cowles, secretary-treasurer, down to numerous cutlers, grinders, finishers and shear makers. (C-H.)

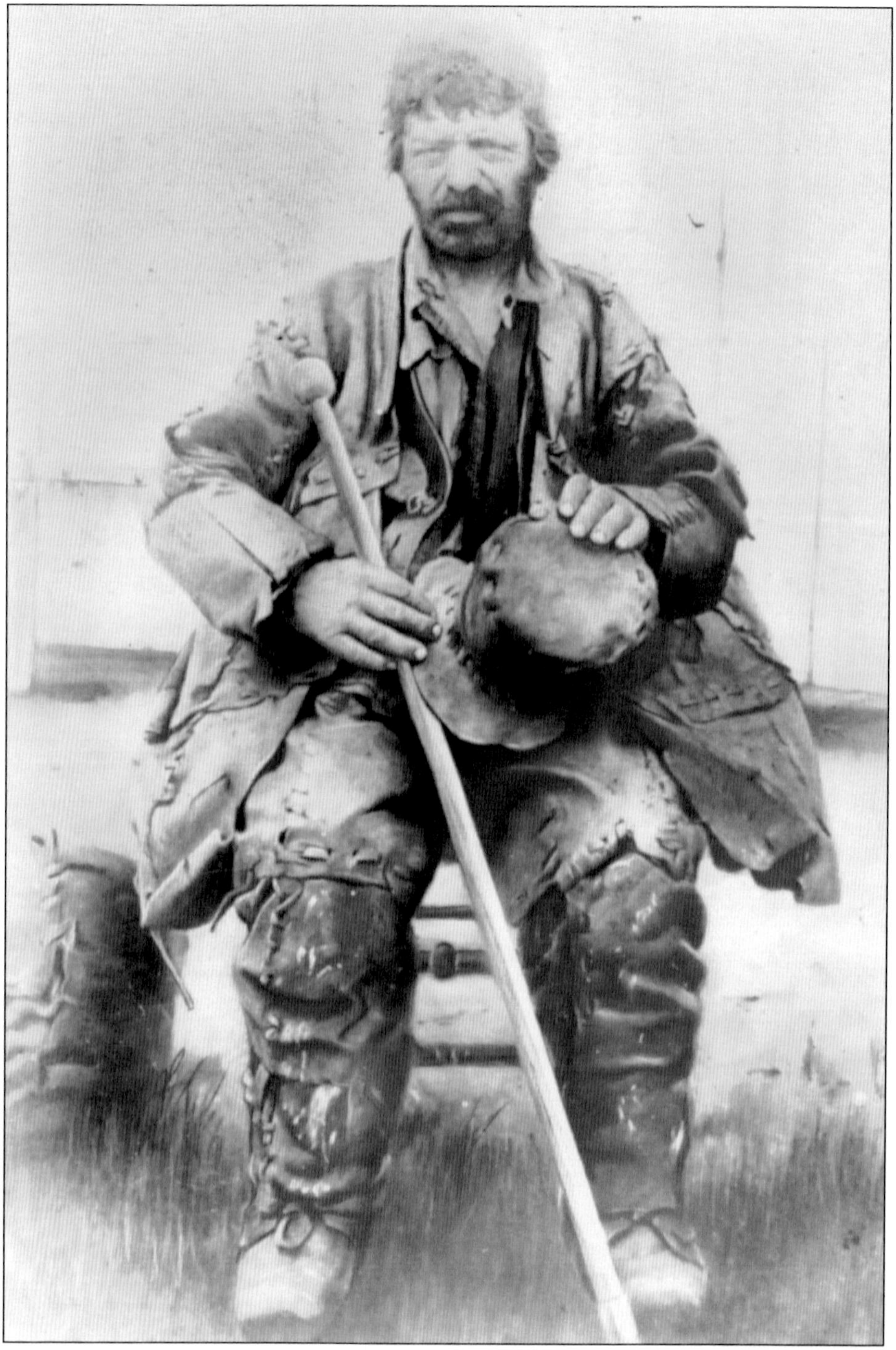

The "Old Leather Man" was a roving recluse, who followed a circular route through parts of Connecticut and New York, year in and year out. Considered to have been the victim of a lost love affair, he wore heavy, hand-fashioned leather garments in all seasons. He had a regular series of friendly farms and shelters where he took refuge. He was found dead in a cave near Pawling, New York, after the infamous Blizzard of 1888. (C-H.)

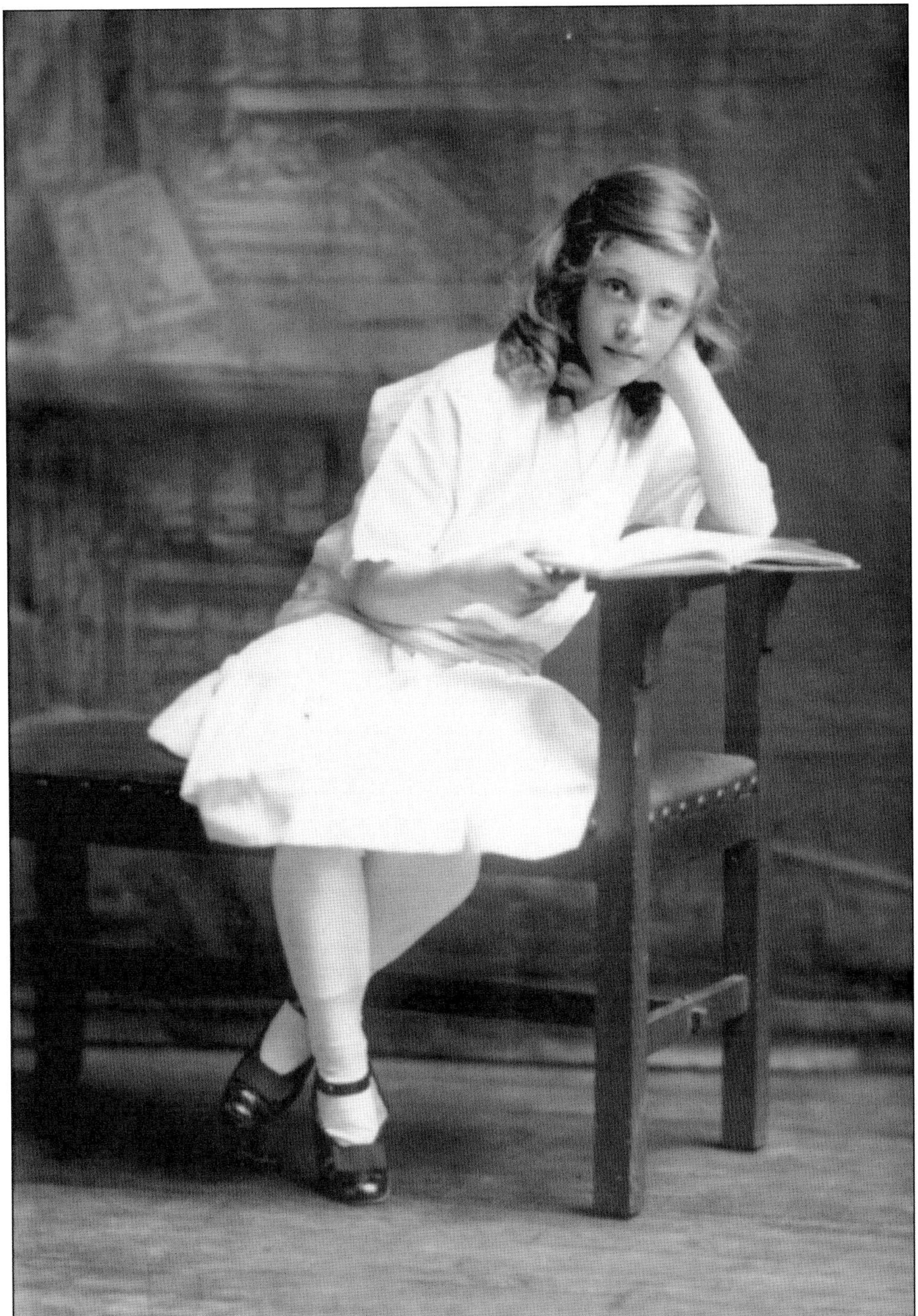

The author's cousin Louise Cooke was aged 12 when this photograph was taken c. 1915. She lived on the west side of Main Street North in Woodbury. As an adult she shared ownership of Mercy Boyd's Bookstore in Waterbury for many years. (FWC.)

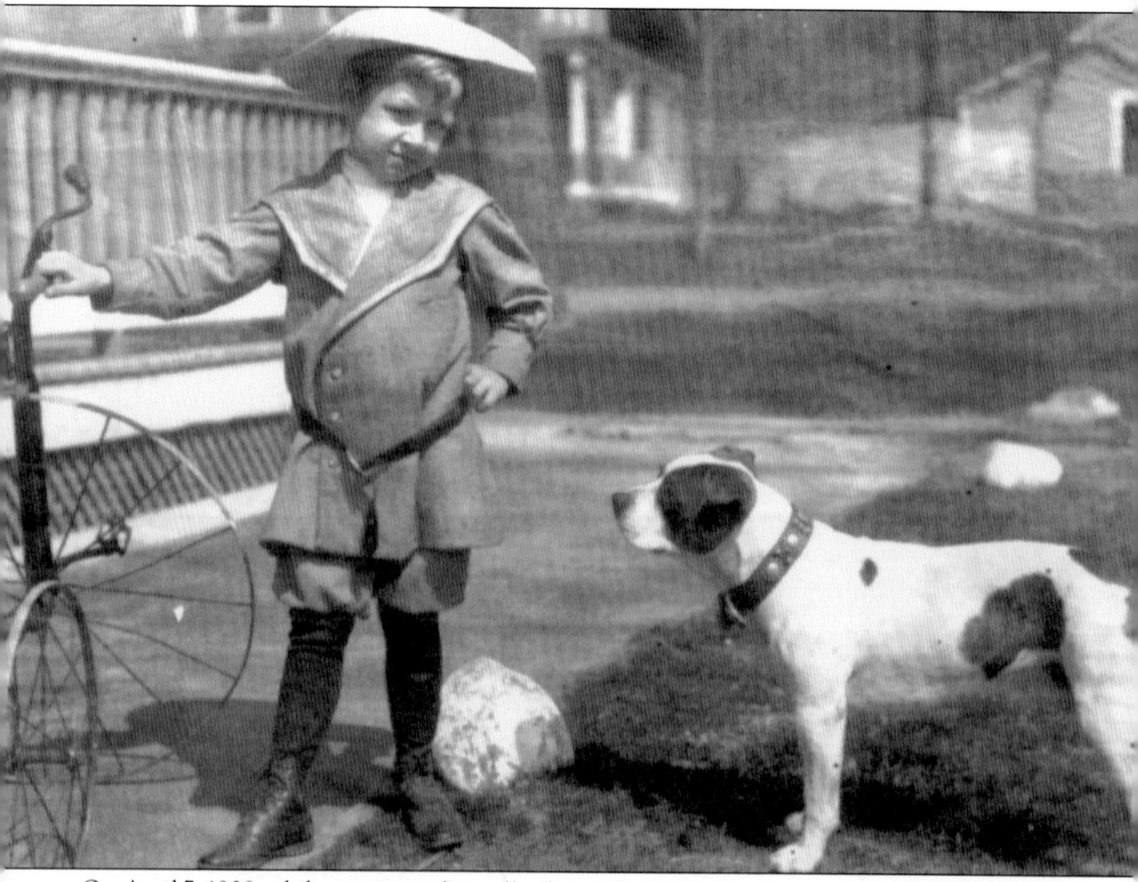

On April 7, 1908, while surveying the trolley line, Charles R. Harte paused from his engineering duties to photograph six-year-old Charlie Daniels with Pete, the Tomlinson dog, in a classic "Buster Brown and Tige" pose of impish innocence. (CRH.)

A.E. Knox, shown in this *c.* 1917 image, was the longtime publisher of the *Woodbury Reporter.* (TL.)

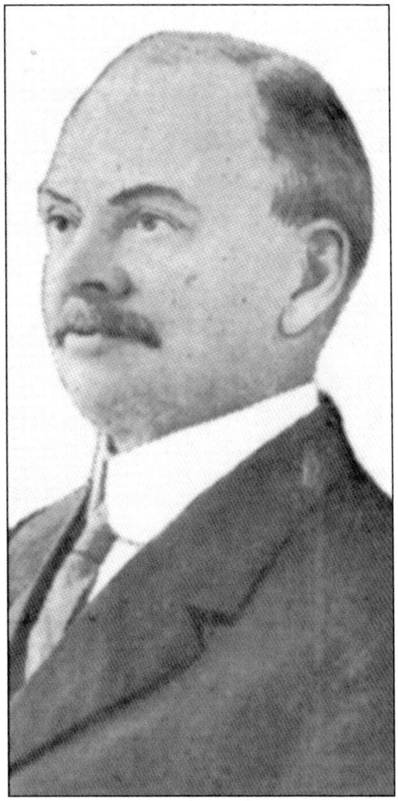

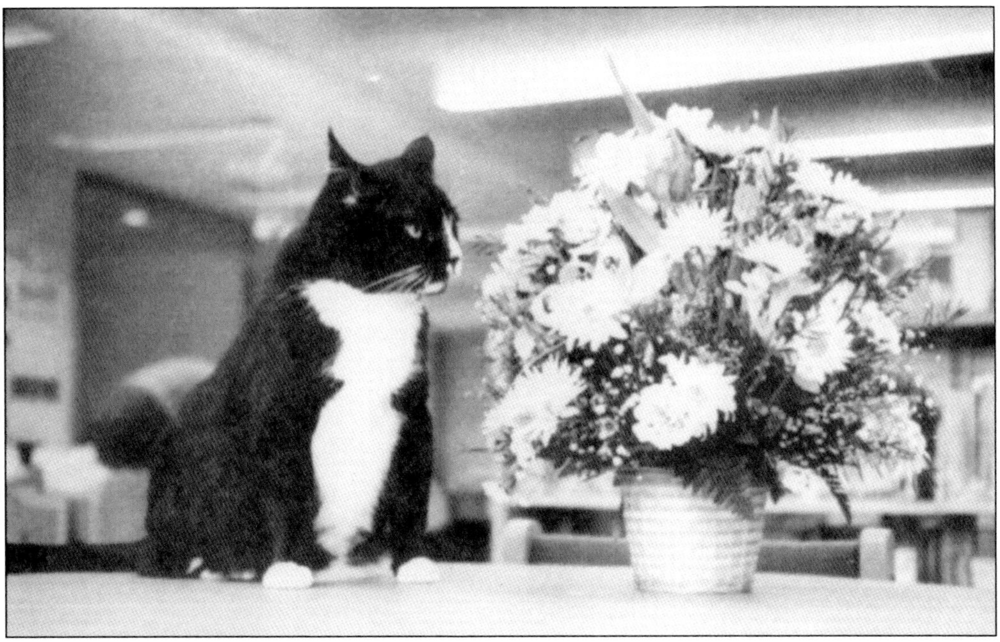

Last is Fred, the library cat. In spite of her name, she was a female feline, whose nine lives were well spent in a literary environment––occasionally enlivened, it is said, by a bit of light "mouse-keeping." (TL.)

EPILOGUE: A SENSE OF PLACE

(Adapted from This Woodbury of Ours, *by Bud Morgan,* 1999 Lions Club Town Guide*)*

Woodbury has existed as long as its grass and trees, dirt and stone, rain and rivers. Of course, it did not know that it was Woodbury until the mid-17th century, when it was so named by the early settlers. They came the hard way, toiling up trails and rivers from Stratford, from whence they had departed because of differing religious opinions with their neighbors.

They sought freedom to practice worship according to their own ideas, but the realities of life demanded that this be exercised in a place where the land was rich, the waters plentiful, and the natives reasonably friendly. When they discovered these attributes in the lovely, fertile Shepaug River Valley, they knew they need seek no further.

Having reached amicable arrangements with the local tribe, they set about building homes and a meetinghouse and raising crops. Of utmost importance, however, was the creating of a community of residents who both recognized and respected the need for cooperation in protecting their mutual interests.

As the early needs for sheer survival centered upon agriculture were met, the potential of the Pomperaug River and its many tributaries for water-powered gristmills and sawmills was recognized. With the arrival of the 18th century, this resource was increasingly used. Indeed, by the early 1800s, Woodbury's own Industrial Revolution was producing a host of manufactured products, including textiles and cutlery.

After the Civil War, the growth of large factory complexes, such as the brass factories in Waterbury, plus a lack of rail transportation brought a decline in both area industry and population. The nadir was seen in the census of 1920, with only 1,700 souls recorded. It took 50 years for the Revolutionary War head count of 5,300 to again be reached, with 8,130 counted in 1990.

Now that the 21st century has arrived, we find that Woodbury has achieved its largest population, approaching 10,000. Easy access to Interstate 84, without irritating proximity to it, combined with the prevailing general affluence, which affords many the pleasures and advantages of country living at its best, have contributed to the transformation of this once agricultural, once industrial community into one of the more highly-regarded bedroom towns in Connecticut.

Who knows what the future holds for Woodbury. We can only hope that the town and its citizens continue to reflect the positive attributes that have served them so well thus far.